NEW YORK REVIEW BOOKS
CLASSICS

PICTURE

LILLIAN ROSS (1918–2017) was born Lillian Rosovsky in Syracuse, New York. Raised in Brooklyn, she published her first piece of journalism, an article about a new library, in her junior high school newspaper. After graduating from Hunter College in 1939, Ross wrote for the leftist New York tabloid *PM* until she was hired by *The New Yorker* in 1945. She filed dispatches for the Talk of the Town section until her first major article, a 1949 profile of a matador from Brooklyn; she would go on to write more than five hundred pieces for the magazine. In 1966, she adopted a son, Erik, from Norway. Ross edited three collections of Talk of the Town feuilleton and published a dozen books, including one work of fiction, *Vertical and Horizontal* (1963); several anthologies of her journalism; and a memoir, *Here But Not Here: A Love Story* (1998), about her long relationship with William Shawn, the editor of *The New Yorker*. In 1974, she was awarded a Guggenheim Fellowship. Her last piece for *The New Yorker* was a 2012 memoir of her friend J. D. Salinger.

ANJELICA HUSTON is an actor, director, and writer. The daughter of John Huston, she has appeared in more than fifty films, including *Prizzi's Honor* (1985), for which she won an Academy Award for Best Supporting Actress. She has written two volumes of memoir, *A Story Lately Told: Coming of Age in Ireland, London, and New York* (2013) and *Watch Me* (2014).

Lillian Ross on the set of The Red Badge of Courage. *Photograph by Silvia Reinhardt.*

PICTURE

LILLIAN ROSS

Foreword by
ANJELICA HUSTON

NEW YORK REVIEW BOOKS

New York

THIS IS A NEW YORK REVIEW BOOK
PUBLISHED BY THE NEW YORK REVIEW OF BOOKS
435 Hudson Street, New York, NY 10014
www.nyrb.com

Library of Congress Cataloging-in-Publication Data
Names: Ross, Lillian, 1918–2017, author.
Title: Picture / by Lillian Ross.
Description: New York : New York Review Books, [2019] | Series: New York
  Review Books Classics
Identifiers: LCCN 2018024728| ISBN 9781681373157 (alk. paper) | ISBN
  9781681373164 (epub)
Subjects: LCSH: Red badge of courage (Motion picture)
Classification: LCC PN1997.R383 R6 2019 | DDC 791.43/72—dc23
LC record available at https://lccn.loc.gov/2018024728

ISBN 978-1-68137-315-7
Available as an electronic book; ISBN 978-1-68137-316-4

Printed in the United States of America on acid-free paper.
10 9 8 7 6 5 4 3 2 1

CONTENTS

FOREWORD

DURING his lifetime and after his death, much has been written about my father, John Huston. The stories have abounded, often from first-hand witnesses, working partners, ex-wives, girlfriends, rivals, fellow-journeymen, and strangers. He has transcended biography on occasion and even been presented in the form of a novel. Among other things, he has been described as a hedonist, a womanizer, a man's man, a sports-man, a gambler, a practical joker, a drinker, and an adventurer. On many occasions, he has been compared to Ernest Hemingway, which I think does neither of them a great service. What seems to me the great disappointment of these somewhat superficial, often spurious compari-sons, is that, somewhere in all the adjectives and descriptions, an essen-tial point is lost. My father was all these things and more. He was an artist. It was my father as an artist that fascinated Lillian Ross. She never sought to write gossip or to go beyond a particular line that she drew for herself in his personal life.

In May of 1986, my father asked Lillian to accept the Brandeis Uni-versity Creative Arts Award in New York City on his behalf, as he was recovering from eye surgery. She told the Creative Arts presenters:

> Throughout his life, he has looked intently at, and continues to look at, the art, in all its forms, of other artists, from the earliest time to the present. He looks at art in the happiest of ways: with his entire being and without intellectualization. And whenever possible, in the case of living artists, he transmits to its creators, with his own Hustonian enthusiasm, his utter joy and astonish-ment at what he sees.

Much the same can be said of Lillian herself. They shared a bound-less interest in life.

I remember flying to New York with my father in 1986. He was very ill at the time, permanently connected to an oxygen tank in order to stay alive. Journeys of this kind were always touch-and-go and the con-sequences life-threatening. I was worried. We arrived in New York late at night. My father was pale and exhausted. The next morning, I was awakened from a deep sleep by the telephone. It was 8 A.M. "Lillian and I are off to the museums. Want to come?"

I hadn't been born yet when Lillian came out to California to write *Picture*, her account of my father's making of *The Red Badge of Courage*. After the publication of *Picture*, her friendship with my mother and father not only continued but flourished, until my mother's death in 1968 and my father's in 1987. I grew up hearing about Lillian and meet-ing her from time to time. My parents loved and respected her, and trusted her. She was, they would say, different from other reporters.

A key to that difference is, I think, revealed in her statements about her principles in the introduction to her book *Reporting*. She writes:

> As soon as another human being permits you to write about him, he is opening his life to you and you must be constantly aware that you have a responsibility in regard to that person. Even if that person encourages you to be careless about how you use your intimate knowledge of him or if he is indiscreet about himself or actually eager to invade his own privacy, it is up to you to use your own judgement in deciding what to write. Just because someone "said it" is no reason for you to use it in your writing. Your obliga-tion to the people you write about does not end once your piece is in print. Anyone who trusts you enough to talk about himself to you is giving you a form of friendship. You are not "doing him a favor" by writing about him, even if he happens to be in a profes-sion or business in which publicity of any kind is valued. If you

spend weeks or months with someone, not only taking his time and energy but entering into his life, you naturally become his friend. A friend is not to be used and abandoned; the friendship established in writing about someone usually continues to grow after what has been written is published.

Lillian's writing is the proof of what she says. She maintains her own integrity and she respects the integrity of her subject. She never stoops to gossip or speculation. Her powers of observation are immense.

In the country recently, my husband, Robert Graham, and I were reading *Picture* aloud to each other. We were laughing and having a lot of fun when suddenly I realized that reading this book was like being in the same room with my father again.

I thank Lillian for her marvelous and timeless documentary—and for this portrait of my father, with all his changing profiles, as observed by one who shared his talent for beauty, humor, simplicity, and truth.

—ANJELICA HUSTON

AUTHOR'S INTRODUCTION

IT'S GREAT fun for me to have *Picture*'s age—half a century—celebrated. In the summer of 1950, when John Huston invited me to come out to Hollywood to watch him work, movies as we know them had been around for less than half a century. (The seminal film *The Great Train Robbery* was forty-five years old, and the landmark *Potemkin* was only twenty-five.) Yet the basic and high-stepping patterns and mores of the moviemaking industry had already settled in, and they seem to have persisted to this day.

I went west to see Huston make his movie *The Red Badge of Courage*, which was based on Stephen Crane's famous Civil War novel. Huston, a unique, magnetic, many-faceted director, gave me special, generous, and open access to himself and the project, and that is what made it possible for me to tell this story.

It turned out, long after *Picture* was published, that the making of this film had been a key issue in the struggle for control of the studio. The entire movie industry at that moment in its history was being shaken up by the emerging monster, television, and the studio powers in New York used this issue, among others, as a way of wrestling control from L. B. Mayer in order to face the threat.

During World War II, Huston had been a major in the Pictorial Service of the Army Signal Corps and had directed now famous documentaries, including *San Pietro*, a film about a group of American soldiers assigned to capture a town in Italy, and *Let There Be Light*, a film about psychologically damaged veterans. The first feature movie he directed was *The Maltese Falcon*. In 1948 he directed *The Treasure of the Sierra Madre*, for which he won two Oscars—Best Direction and Best Screenplay—and for which his father, Walter, won the Best Supporting Actor Oscar.

Later that year, I went to Hollywood to do a story for *The New Yorker* about the congressional investigation of what was called, by the investigators, "un-American activities" in the movie industry. Despite the pressure of the investigation, Huston, a man of unfailing spirit and lighthearted high jinks, was brave, outspoken, independent, and funny. Conversation with him was like fresh air. He voiced courageous views about all the nonsensical fear and paranoia going on around him, and he showed, with his particularly sardonic and wry diplomacy and humor, his impatience with the cowardly and silly behavior of some of his peers. While I was there, he was directing *Key Largo* with Humphrey Bogart, Lauren Bacall, and Edward G. Robinson, among others. I had a good time visiting Huston on his set and meeting an assortment of people in the business. In the story I wrote, titled "Come In, Lassie!" I told about meeting John Huston for the first time, at lunch one day with cast members of *Key Largo* at the Lakeside Golf Club, a favorite buffet eating place among stars on the nearby Warner lot:

> The actors were in a gay mood. They had just finished rehearsing a scene (one of the new economies at Warner is to have a week of rehearsals before starting to film a picture) in which Humphrey Bogart is taunted by Robinson, a gangster representing evil, for his cowardice, but is comforted by the gangster's moll, who tells Bogart, "Never mind. It's better to be a live coward than a dead hero." Bogart had not yet reached the point in the movie where a guy learns he must fight against evil.
>
> Huston was feeling particularly good, because he had just won a battle with the studio to keep some lines in the film from President Franklin Delano Roosevelt's message to the Seventy-seventh

Congress on January 6, 1942: "But we of the United Nations are not making all this sacrifice of human effort and human lives to return to the kind of world we had after the last world war."

"The big shots wanted Bogie to say this in his own words," Huston explained, "but I insisted that Roosevelt's words were better."

Bogart nodded. "Roosevelt was a good politician," he said. "He could handle those babies in Washington, but they're too smart for guys like me. Hell, I'm no politician. That's what I meant when I said our Washington trip was a mistake."

"Bogie has succeeded in not being a politician," said Huston, who went to Washington with him [to protest the investigation]. "Bogie owns a fifty-four-foot yawl. When you own a fifty-four-foot yawl, you've got to provide for her upkeep."

"The Great Chief died and everybody's guts died with him," Robinson said, looking stern.

"How would you like to see *your* picture on the front page of the Communist paper of Italy?" asked Bogart.

"Nyah," Robinson said, sneering.

"The *Daily Worker* runs Bogie's picture and right away he's a dangerous Communist," said Miss Bacall, who is, as everybody must know, Bogart's wife. "What will happen if the American Legion and the Legion of Decency boycott all his pictures?"

"It's just that my picture in the *Daily Worker* offends me, Baby," said Bogart.

"Nyah," said Robinson.

"Let's eat," said Huston.

After the story was published in the magazine, Huston wrote to Harold Ross, the editor, and congratulated him on running it. Huston and I then began an unusual friendship that lasted until his death in 1987. Often when he was planning to come to New York, he would alert me, and we would meet. Hanging out with him was always high-spirited fun; it invariably felt as though I were part of one of his dramatic, intriguing movie scenes.

When I entered a restaurant with him—"21" for example—life inside seemed to stop, with the action fixed on this tall, gracious, conquering figure arriving, with his characteristically slow, loping walk, to bestow the royal favor of his presence equally on the grateful owner, the grateful maître d', and the grateful waiters, all of whom lent themselves enthusiastically to his performance. I accompanied him to Tony's—the restaurant owned by Tony Soma, father of Ricki, the beautiful young dancer Huston married and with whom he had a son and daughter, Tony and Anjelica. Soma, a Yoga devotee, might be found in a corner standing on his head, and Huston would insist forcefully on not disturbing this ritual. He would then bend down, contorting himself into a position that afforded consultation with the upside-down Tony, in a deeply conspiratorial manner, about what we would drink and eat. The New York dinners that Huston valued above all others, however, were those he was led to blindfolded, late at night, in mysterious Sicilian restaurants lacking a conventional address. He was sworn to secrecy and hosted personally, Huston claimed, by the most powerful anonymous Mafia lords in the criminal universe. "Their food," he would report in his strictly confidential whisper, "is . . . by all means . . . in*comp*arable!"

On his visits, I would also accompany him to museums, one of his favorites being the Hispanic. "They've got half a dozen El Grecos in there!" he would say. "My God, those El Grecos!"

"Three of the greatest Goyas I've ever seen," he would add. "Unbe-*liev*able Goyas. And those two Velazquez . Don't they make you *weep*?"

In 1950, when I decided to take Huston up on his offer to come watch him make *The Red Badge of Courage*, I actually was taking that opportunity to try to escape from my personal entanglement with my editor, William Shawn. He was then the managing editor of *The New Yorker* and was married, with young children. He had told me he was in love with me; I was in love with my work, and I was becoming danger-ously drawn to him. I had intended to stay in Hollywood a few months; I stayed for a year and a half. From the moment of my arrival in Holly-wood, Bill Shawn and I talked on the telephone or wrote to each other regularly. In addition to our personal situation, one of the things we talked about was what I was going to write:

"You see, if the story turns out to be what I think it is, it's really al-most a book, a kind of novel-like book because of the way the characters may develop and the variety of relationships that exist among them," I wrote in one of my letters to Shawn. "I don't see why I shouldn't try to do a fact piece in novel form, or maybe a novel in fact form. It's an excit-ing thing to think about. It's almost as though the subject material calls for that kind of form."

Doing the reporting for what became *Picture* was a heady and excit-ing experience. I didn't miss a single day of the filming. Early every morning, I drove from my hotel in Beverly Hills to Huston's ranch in the San Fernando Valley. Huston encouraged me to stay close to him and his cast and his crew before, during, and after each shot and to join every discussion with his producer, his cameraman, his production manager, and his actors. Gottfried Reinhardt, Huston's witty, imagina-tive, and sophisticated producer, was also enthusiastic about my doing the story, and he generously provided me with every scrap of informa-tion I asked for. Both Reinhardt and Huston also brought me along to their meetings with Dore Schary, MGM's production head, and, at my request, they helped set up my sessions with L.B. Mayer.

Early on, I knew that I would make Huston, Reinhardt, Schary, and Mayer my four leading characters. In their presence, I was always taking notes in my little three-by-five-inch notebooks. I went to their homes and to their parties. I met their families and their friends. I watched movies, listened to music, played tennis, and rode horseback with them. I ate breakfasts, lunches, and dinners with them. They always included me in holiday celebrations and entertaining events with scores of people in the movie industry. It seemed to be the Hollywood way. They joked and laughed a lot, often at themselves. I liked, and still like, these people. I took them on their own terms, and I enjoyed writing about them. Many of them became lifelong friends. I happen to like forthright, up-front crooks and villains, and I gloried in finding some of them in Hollywood.

My story, a long one titled "Production Number 1512," was published in *The New Yorker* in installments over a period of five weeks. The circulation department reported to Bill Shawn that the magazine was selling out on the newsstands almost as soon as it appeared. My colleagues were very generous in their praise, and Joe Mitchell came into my office grinning and laughing and shaking his head and reading lines from my story aloud to me. Praise from my peers has always been the ultimate reward. I couldn't ask for anything better.

When the story was published as a book, Bill Shawn suggested the title *Picture* for it. I dedicated it "To *The New Yorker.*"

For years after *Picture* was published in 1952, I couldn't resist the temptation, every once in a while, to write about Huston for *The New Yorker*. Whatever I did with him always made me laugh, and I hope I made readers laugh, too. In 1965, I went to Rome, where he was directing *The Bible*, in which he had cast himself, with a long white beard, as Noah, wearing a long white robe and leading all the pairs of animals, including elephants, into the Ark.

"Our hippo was the greatest actor in the picture," Mr. Huston told me. "Every time that hippo saw me coming, he broke into the damndest grin you ever saw. The giraffes were the gentlest actors in the Ark. I couldn't ever get past them without their frisking me for something to eat."

Four years later, Huston was in New York, directing *The Kremlin Letter*, for which one scene took place at the Central Park Zoo, in front of cages occupied by two baby gorillas, a black panther, and a lioness. For "luck," as he put it, he cast my son Erik, then three years old, in a non-speaking role, running past the cages. At one point in a story I wrote, I described Huston walking over to the cage of the baby gorillas and greeting them in his usual ultragracious manner:

> "Well. My goodness. Hel-*lo*, babies. How are *you* this morning?"
> The baby gorillas leaped at the bars, as though Huston were a mother gorilla....
> "Those are the babies," Huston said. "Aren't they the dearest, gentlest, most wonderful creatures?"
> "Well, yes," said De Haven [the producer].
> "A friend of mine has eight gorillas as pets," Huston said. "John Aspinall. He runs the Clermont, on Berkeley Square—the biggest gambling house in England.... And John Aspinall is a gentleman, an Oxford man. He lives out in Kent, near Canterbury. He invited me out to meet his gorillas. And I went into the cages with them. And, I tell you, they're the nicest people I've met in a long time." Hustonian laugh. "There was one young lady in the cage," Huston said, lowering his tone. "And she made it clear to me, if I sent her flowers—why, she'd go to the theatre with me."
> "I see," said De Haven.
> "You go for walks with Aspinall's gorillas," Huston said. "He takes the gorillas out for walks, two at a time. Holding each by the hand. I tell you, I'd love to spend the night in the cages with those gorillas, spend the whole *night* with them. To penetrate the *mys*tery of it."

"Forty" was the title of the last "Talk of the Town" story I wrote about Huston, in the issue of October 15, 1984. The number referred to his fortieth movie, *Prizzi's Honor*, which starred his daughter, Anjelica, Kathleen Turner, and Jack Nicholson. Huston—wearing one of the short-sleeved khaki safari-like suits that he designed for himself—

directed, working eighteen-hour days, including some cold, damp nights in various locations in Brooklyn. He was seventy-eight by then, with emphysema, and he was tethered to an oxygen machine. "On the first day of shooting, he left his hotel at 7:30 A.M. and was on the set in time to supervise detail after detail after detail," I wrote in my remarks at his memorial service, read by Jack Nicholson. "By the time the first shot was taken, everybody else around Huston looked frazzled. Not him. He looked quietly joyous." I had never seen him in better spirits. Anjelica Huston won the 1985 Oscar for Best Supporting Actress for her performance in the film. She now directs and writes screenplays in addition to acting, as does her younger brother, Danny Huston. The last film directed by John was *The Dead*, based on the James Joyce story, with a screenplay by Tony Huston. It was released in 1987, shortly after John's death, and is considered by many people to be John Huston's greatest film.

About a week before John died, he telephoned me at home. I was not there, and he left a message on the answering machine for me and my son, Erik.

"I just want to reas*sure* you," he said, in his familiar, inimitable, melodic actor's voice, "I am quite all *right*. Good night, darlings. Good-bye."

—LILLIAN ROSS

2002

PICTURE

TO THE NEW YORKER

Throw the Little Old Lady
Down the Stairs!

THE making of the Metro-Goldwyn-Mayer movie *The Red Badge of Courage*, based on the Stephen Crane novel about the Civil War, was preceded by routine disclosures about its production plans from the columnist Louella Parsons ('John Huston is writing a screen treatment of Stephen Crane's classic, *The Red Badge of Courage*, as a possibility for an M-G-M picture); from the columnist Hedda Hopper ('Metro has an option on *The Red Badge of Courage* and John Huston's working up a budget for it. But there's no green light yet'); and from *Variety* ('Pre-production work on *Red Badge of Courage* commenced at Metro with thesp-tests for top roles in drama'), and it was preceded, in the spring of 1950, by a routine visit by John Huston, who is both a screen writer and a director, to New York, the headquarters of Loew's, Inc., the company that produces and distributes M-G-M pictures. On the occasion of his visit, I decided to follow the history of that particular movie from beginning to end, in order to learn whatever I might learn about the American motion-picture industry.

Huston, at forty-three, was one of the most admired, rebellious, and shadowy figures in the world of motion pictures. I had seen him a year before, when he came here to accept an award of a trip around the world for his film contributions to world unity. He had talked of an idea he had for making a motion picture about the nature of the world while he was going around it. Then he had flown back to Hollywood, and to the demands of his employers, Metro-Goldwyn-Mayer, and had made *The Asphalt Jungle*, a picture about a band of criminals engaged in pursuits that Huston described somewhere in the dialogue of the movie as 'a left-handed form of human endeavour'. Now, on this visit, shortly after the sudden death, in Hollywood, of his father, Walter Huston, he telephoned

me from his Waldorf Tower suite and said he was having a terrible
time trying to make The Red Badge of Courage. Louis B. Mayer and most
of the other top executives at M-G-M, he said, were opposed to the
entire project. 'You know something?' he said, over the telephone.
He has a theatrical way of inflecting his voice that can give a com-
monplace query a rich and melodramatic intensity. 'They don't
want me to make this picture. And I want to make this picture.' He
made the most of every syllable, so that it seemed at that moment to
lie under his patent and have some special urgency. 'Come on over,
kid, and I'll tell you all about the hassle,' he said.

The door of Huston's suite was opened by a conservatively attired
young man with a round face and pink cheeks. He introduced himself as Arthur Fellows. 'John is in the next room getting dressed,' he
said. 'Imagine getting a layout like this all to yourself! That's the
way the big studios do things.' He nodded with approval at the
Waldorf's trappings. 'Not that I care for the big studios,' he said. 'I
believe in being independent. I work for David Selznick. I've worked
for David for fifteen years. David is independent. I look at the picture
business as a career. Same as banking, or medicine, or law. You've
got to learn it from the ground up. I learned it from the ground up
with David. I was an assistant director on Duel in the Sun. I directed the
scene of the fight between two horses. Right now, I'm here temporarily on publicity and promotion. David —' He broke off as Huston
strode into the room. Huston made his entrance in the manner of an
actor who is determined to win the immediate attention of his
audience.

'Hel-lo, kid,' Huston said as we shook hands. He took a step back,
then put his hands in his trouser pockets and leaned forward intently. 'Well!' he said. He made the word expand into a major
pronouncement.

Huston is a lean, rangy man, two inches over six feet tall, with
long arms and long hands, long legs and long feet. He has thick
black hair, which had been slicked down with water, but some of the
front strands fell raffishly over his forehead. He has a deeply creased,
leathery face, high cheek-bones, and slanting, reddish-brown eyes.
His ears are flattened against the sides of his head, and the bridge of

his nose is bashed in. His eyes looked watchful, and yet strangely empty of all feeling, in weird contrast to the heartiness of his manner. He took his hands out of his pockets and yanked at his hair. 'Well!' he said, again as though he were making a major pronouncement. He turned to Fellows. 'Art, order some Martinis, will you, kid?'

Huston sat down on the arm of a chair, fixed a long brown cigarette in one corner of his mouth, took a kitchen match from his trouser pocket, and scraped the head of the match into flame with his thumbnail. He lit the cigarette and drew deeply on it, half closing his eyes against the smoke, which seemed to make them slant still more. Then he rested his elbows on his knees, holding the cigarette to his mouth with two long fingers of one hand, and looked out of the window. The sun had gone down and the light coming into the suite, high in the Tower, was beginning to dull. Huston looked as though he might be waiting – having set up a Huston scene – for the cameras to roll. But, as I gradually grew to realize, life was not imitating art, Huston was not imitating himself, when he set up such a scene; on the contrary, the style of the Huston pictures, Huston being one of the few Hollywood directors who manage to leave their personal mark on the films they make, was the style of the man. In appearance, in gestures, in manner of speech, in the selection of the people and objects he surrounded himself with, and in the way he composed them into individual 'shots' (the abrupt close-up of the thumbnail scraping the head of a kitchen match) and then arranged his shots into dramatic sequence, he was simply the raw material of his own art; that is, the man whose personality left its imprint, unmistakably, on what had come to be known as a Huston picture.

'I just love the light at this time of the day,' Huston said as Fellows returned from the phone. 'Art, don't you just love the light at this time of the day?'

Fellows said it was all right.

Huston gave a chuckle. 'Well, now,' he said, 'here I am, spending the studio's money on this trip, and I don't even know whether I'm going to make the picture I'm here for. I'm auditioning actors at the Loew's office and talking production up there and doing all the

publicity things they tell me to do. I've got the Red Badge script
O.K.'d, and I'm going down South to pick locations for the picture,
but nothing is moving. We can't make this picture unless we have
six hundred Confederate uniforms and six hundred Union uniforms.
And the studio is just not making those uniforms for us. I'm beginning to think they don't want the picture!'

'It's an off beat picture,' Fellows said politely. 'The public wants
pictures like Ma and Pa Kettle. I say make pictures the public wants.
Over here,' he said to a waiter who had entered with a tray holding
six Martinis in champagne glasses. 'No getting away from it, John,'
Fellows went on, handing Huston a drink. 'Biggest box-office draws
are pictures catering to the intelligence of the twelve-year-old.'

People underestimated the intelligence of the twelve-year-old,
Huston said. He said he had an adopted son in his early teens, a
Mexican-Indian orphan, Pablo, whom he had found while making
Treasure of Sierra Madre in Mexico a few years ago, and his boy had
excellent taste in pictures. 'Why, my boy Pablo reads Shakespeare,'
he said. 'Do you read Shakespeare, Art?'

'Television, John,' said Fellows. 'The junk they go for on
television.'

Huston asked him vaguely what the talk was in New York about
television.

Television was booming, Fellows said, and all the actors, singers,
dancers, directors, producers, and writers who hadn't been able to
get work in Hollywood were going into television in New York. On
the other hand, all the actors, singers, dancers, directors, producers,
and writers who had gone into television in New York were starving
and wanted to go back to Hollywood. 'Nobody really knows what's
happening,' said Fellows. 'All I know is television can never do what
pictures can do.'

'Well just make pictures and release them on television, that's all.
The hell with television,' Huston said. 'Do you kids want the lights
on?' The room was murky. It made a fine tableau, Huston said.
Fellows and I agreed that it was pleasant with the lights off. There
was a brief silence. Huston moved like a shadow to a chair opposite
mine and lit another brown cigarette, the quick glow from the
match lighting up his face. 'Been to the races out here, Art?' he asked.

A few times, Fellows said, but David Selznick had been keeping him so busy he hadn't had much time for horses.

'The ponies have me broke all the time,' Huston said. 'You know, I can't write a cheque for five hundred dollars. I am always broke. I can't even take an ordinary vacation. But there's nothing I'd rather spend my money on than a horse, especially when the horse is one of my own. There's nothing like breeding and raising a horse of your own. I've got four horses racing under my colours right now, and in a couple of years I'll have more, even if I have to go into hock to support them. All I want is one good winner of my own. Everybody I know is conspiring to take my horses away from me. Someday I'll have one good winner, and then I'll be able to say, "Well, you bastards, this is what it was all about!"'

Financial problems, Huston said, had prevented him from taking the trip around the world. Although his M-G-M salary was four thousand dollars a week while he was making a picture, he had had to get the company to advance him a hundred and fifty thousand dollars, which he was paying off in instalments. He was bound by his contract to make at least one picture a year for the next three years for M-G-M. He was a partner in an independent company, Horizon Pictures, which he had started a couple of years before with a man named Sam Spiegel, whom he had met in the early thirties in London. Huston had directed one picture, *We Were Strangers*, for Horizon, and he was scheduled to direct another – *The African Queen*, based on the novel by C. S. Forester – as soon as he had completed *The Red Badge of Courage* for M-G-M. Huston said he thought *The African Queen* would make money, and if it did, he would then make some pictures on his own that he wanted to make as much as he did *The Red Badge of Courage*. The reason L. B. Mayer and the other M-G-M executives did not think that *The Red Badge of Courage* could be a commercial success, Huston said, was that it had no standard plot, no romance, and no leading female characters, and, if Huston had his way in casting it, would have no stars. It was simply the story of a youth who ran away from his first battle in the Civil War, and then returned to the front and distinguished himself by performing several heroic acts. Huston, like Stephen Crane, wanted to show something of the emotions of men in war, and the ironically thin line between cowardice and heroism. A few months earlier, Huston and an M-G-M producer named Gottfried Reinhardt, the son of the late Max Reinhardt, had suggested to Dore Schary, the studio's vice-president in charge of production, that they make the picture.

'Dore loved the idea,' Huston said. 'And Dore said he would read the novel.' A couple of weeks later, Schary had asked Huston to write a screen treatment – a rough outline for the detailed script. 'I did my treatment in four days,' Huston said. 'I was going down to Mexico to get married, so I took my secretary along and dictated part of it on the plane going down, got married, dictated some more after the ceremony, and dictated the rest on the plane trip back.' Schary approved the treatment, and the cost of making the picture was estimated at a million and a half dollars. Huston wrote the screenplay in five weeks, and Schary approved it. 'Then the strangest things began to happen,' Huston said. 'Dore is called vice-president in charge of production. L. B. is called vice-president in charge of the studio. Nobody knows which is boss.' His voice rose dramatically. 'We were told Dore had to O.K. everything. We got his O.K., but nothing moved. And we know that L. B. hates the idea of making this picture.' His voice sank to a confidential whisper. 'He just hates it!'

For the role of the Youth, Huston said, he wanted twenty-six-year-old Audie Murphy, the most-decorated hero of the Second World War, whose film career had been limited to minor roles. Huston said he was having some difficulty persuading both Schary and Reinhardt to let Murphy have the part. 'They'd rather have a star,' he said indignantly. 'They just don't see Audie the way I do. This little, gentle-eyed creature. Why, in the war he'd literally go out of his way to find Germans to kill. He's a gentle little killer.'

'Another Martini?' Fellows asked.

'I hate stars,' Huston said, exchanging his empty glass for a full one. 'They're not actors. I've been around actors all my life, and I like them, and yet I never had an actor as a friend. Except Dad. And Dad never thought of himself as an actor. But the best actor I ever worked with was Dad. All I had to tell Dad about his part of the old man in *Treasure* was to talk fast. Just talk fast.' Huston talked rapidly, in a startling and accurate imitation of his father. 'A man who talks fast never listens to himself. Dad talked like this. Man talking fast is an honest man. Dad was a man who never tried to sell anybody anything.'

It was now quite dark in the room. We sat in the darkness for a while without talking, and then Huston got up and went over to the light switch. He asked if we were ready for light, and then snapped the switch. He was revealed in the sudden yellow brightness, standing motionless, a look of bewilderment on his face. 'I hate this scene,' he said. 'Let's go out and get something to eat.'

Huston finished his drink in a gulp, set the glass down, and put a grey Homburg on his head, and the three of us rode down in the elevator. It was a warm, drizzly evening. The Waldorf doorman got us a cab, and Huston told the driver to take us to '21'. He raised one of the jump seats and rested his knees against it. 'You know, I just love New York when summer is coming in,' he said, emphasizing each word possessively. 'Everything begins to slow down a little. And later on, the clatter and hassling sort of comes to a stop. And the city is quiet. And you can take walks!' he said in a tone of amazement. 'And you pass bars!' he said, as though this were even more astonishing. 'And the doors of the bars are open,' he said, holding up his hands, palms toward each other, framing a picture of an open door. 'You can go anywhere alone, and yet you're never alone in the summer in New York,' he said, and dropped his hands to his lap.

Huston first came to New York in 1919, when he was thirteen, to spend the summer with his father, who had been divorced from his mother several years before. John was born in the town of Nevada, Missouri, and had spent the better part of his childhood with his mother, first in Weatherford, Texas, and then in Los Angeles. His mother, who died in 1938, had been a newspaperwoman. For three years before coming to New York, Huston had been bedridden with what was called an enlarged heart, and he also suffered from an obscure kidney ailment. When he recovered, he went to visit his father. He had a marvellous birthday in New York the summer he turned eighteen, he said. He had come East again from Los Angeles, where he had won the amateur lightweight boxing championship of California, and he had moved into a small fourth-floor apartment on Macdougal Street; the apartment above was occupied by Sam Jaffe (the actor who, years later, played the part of the German safecracker in The Asphalt Jungle). Huston's father, who was appearing on Broadway in Desire Under the Elms, came to the birthday celebration. Jaffe had asked John what he wanted as a present, and he had said a horse. 'Well,' he said, 'Sam' (and there was great affection in his pronouncing of the name), 'the kindest, most retiring guy in the world, had gone out and bought the oldest, saddest, most worn-out grey mare. It was all wonderful. The best birthday I ever had. Art, don't you just love New York in the summer?'

Not to live in, Fellows said, and Huston said, with a sigh, that it would be difficult to keep horses in New York, and besides, when you came right down to it, he really liked the way of life in the motion-picture world.

'It's the jungle,' he said. 'It appeals to my nature. Louella Parsons and her atavistic nonsense. I really like Louella. She's part of the jungle. It's more than a place where streets are named after Sam Goldwyn and buildings after Bing Crosby. There's more to it than pink Cadillacs with leopard-skin seat covers. It's the jungle, and it harbours an industry that's one of the biggest in the country. A closed-in, tight, frantically inbred, and frantically competitive jungle. And the rulers of the jungle are predatory and fascinating and tough. L. B. Mayer is one of the rulers of the jungle.' He lowered his voice impressively. 'I like L. B. He's a ruler now, but he has to watch his step or he'll be done in. He's shrewd. He's big business. He didn't know a thing about horses, but when he took up horses, he built up one of the finest stables in the country. L. B. is tough. He's never trying to win the point you're talking about. His aim is always long-range – to keep control of the studio. He loves Dore. But someday he'll destroy Dore. L. B. is sixty-five. And he's pink. And healthy. And smiling. Dore is about twenty years younger. And he looks old. And sick. And worried. Because L. B. guards the jungle like a lion. But the very top rulers of the jungle are here in New York. Nick Schenck, the president of Loew's, Inc., the ruler of the rulers, stays here in New York and smiles, watching from afar, from behind the scenes; but he's the real power, watching the pack closing in on one or another of the lesser rulers, closing in, ready to pounce! Nick Schenck never gets his picture in the papers, and he doesn't go to parties, and he avoids going out in public, but he's the *real* king of the pack. And he does it all from New York!' He uttered an eerie, choked laugh through clenched teeth. 'God, are they tough!'

The taxi drew up before '21'. 'Mr Huston!' the doorman said, and Huston shook hands with him. 'Welcome back, Mr Huston.'

It was close to midnight when Huston and Fellows and I emerged. Huston suggested that we walk, because he loved to walk at that time of the night. The drizzling rain had stopped and the air was clear, but the street was wet and shining. Huston said he wanted to go over to Third Avenue, because he liked to see into the bars there and because nobody over there looked like a studio vice-president. We headed for Third Avenue.

As we walked down Third Avenue, Huston started to take fast, important strides. 'You know what I like about making this picture, Art?' he said. 'I'm going to be out in the country. On location.' Walking along, he glanced into shop windows displaying silver plate and paintings. He stopped for a moment in front of the dusty window of an art shop and looked at the reproduction of a painting. 'Modigliani,' he said. 'I used to spend hours in this town looking at Modiglianis.' He had once done considerable painting himself, he said, but in recent years he had done little. We moved on, and suddenly, in the middle of the wet, glistening walk, we saw a man lying motionless, face down. He had one arm in the sleeve of a torn, brown overcoat, and the other arm was underneath him, the empty sleeve of the coat folded back over his head. His shoes were scuffed and ragged and they were pointed in toward each other. Half a dozen spectators stood gazing silently at the figure on the sidewalk. Huston immediately took charge. Putting his hands in his trouser pockets, he gave a peculiar quarter twist to his body. He took just a moment to push his hat back on his head, then squatted beside the motionless figure. He let another moment go by without doing anything, while the group of spectators grew. Everyone was very quiet. Huston lifted the hand in the overcoat sleeve and felt for the pulse. The Third Avenue 'L' rattled noisily by overhead, and then there was silence again. Huston held the man's wrist for quite a long time, never looking up at the crowd. Then he took quite a long time putting the man's arm back in its original position. Huston rose slowly to his feet. He fixed his hat forward. He put his hands back in his pockets. Then he turned to the audience, and, projecting his words with distinct care, he said, 'He's – just – fine!' He gave a thick, congested laugh through his closed teeth. He tapped his hat forward with satisfaction, and jauntily led us away. It was a scene from a Huston movie.

Five weeks later, Huston was back at the Waldorf, in the same suite. When he telephoned me this time, he sounded cheerful. During his absence, *The Asphalt Jungle* had opened in New York and had been reviewed enthusiastically, but he didn't mention that; what he felt good about was that he had just bought a new filly from Calumet Farms. When I went over to see him that evening, he was alone in his suite. Two days before, he had found a superb location for *The Red Badge of Courage* outside Nashville.

When Huston had returned to the studio after his Eastern trip, he told me, he had found that no preparations at all were under way for *The Red Badge of Courage*. 'Those uniforms just weren't being made!' he said with amazement. 'I went to see L. B., and L. B. told me he had no faith in the picture. He didn't believe it would make money. Gottfried and I went to see Dore. We found Dore at home, sick in bed. The moment we entered, he said, "Boys, we'll make this picture!" Maybe it was Nick Schenck who gave Dore the go-ahead sign. Anyway, that night Dore wrote a letter to L. B. and said in the letter he thought M-G-M ought to make the picture. And the next morning L. B. called us in and talked for six hours about why this picture would not make any money. You know, I like L. B. He said that Dore was a wonderful boy, that he loved Dore like his own son. And he said that he could not deny a boy who wrote that kind of letter to him. And when we came out of L. B.'s office, the studio was bubbling, and the uniforms were being made!' Huston chortled. He picked up a pad of paper and started sketching horses as he talked. He and Reinhardt, he said, had found a marvellous actor named Royal Dano to play the part of the Tattered Man, and Dano had that singular quality that makes for greatness on the screen. Charlie Chaplin and Greta Garbo have that quality, he said. 'The screen exaggerates and magnifies whatever it is that a great actor has,' he said. 'It's almost as though greatness is a matter of quality rather than ability. Dad had it. He had that something people felt in him. You sense it every time you're near it. You see it in Audie Murphy's eyes. It's like a great horse. You go past his stall and you can feel the vibration in there. You can feel it. So I'm going to make the picture, kid. I'm going to direct it on horseback. I've always wanted to direct a picture on horseback.'

The expenses at the Nashville site, he said, would be less than at the one he had originally hoped to get, in Leesburg, Virginia, and its terrain lent itself perfectly to the kind of photography he wanted – a sharply contrasting black-and-white approximating the texture and atmosphere of the Brady photographs of the Civil War.

'Tell you what,' Huston said, in his amazed tone. 'I'm going to show you how we make a picture! And then you come out to Hollywood and you can see everything that happens to the picture out there! And you can meet Gottfried! And Dore! And L.B.! And everybody! And you can meet my horses! Will you do it?'

I said I would.

Several weeks later, Huston telephoned again, this time from California. He was going to start making *The Red Badge of Courage* in a month, and the location was not going to be in Tennessee, after all, but on his own ranch, in the San Fernando Valley. He didn't sound too happy about it. 'You'd better get out here for the fireworks,' he said. 'We're going to have the Civil War right here on the Coast.'

When I arrived on the West Coast, Huston set about arranging for me to meet everybody who had anything to do with *The Red Badge of Courage*. The day I met Gottfried Reinhardt, the thirty-nine-year-old producer of *The Red Badge of Courage*, he was sitting in his office at the Metro-Goldwyn-Mayer studio, in Culver City, studying the estimated budget for the picture. It would be the fifteen-hundred-and-twelfth picture to be put into production since Metro-Goldwyn-Mayer was founded, on 24 May 1924. The mimeographed booklet containing the estimate was stamped 'Production No. 1512'. (The estimate, I learned later on, informed Reinhardt that the picture would be allotted nine rehearsal days and thirty-four production days; the footage of the finished film was expected to come to 7,865 feet; the total cost was expected to be $1,434,789.) Reinhardt's office was a comfortable one. It was a suite, which included a small bath and a conference room furnished with leather armchairs. A brass plate engraved with his name was on the door. In his private office, in addition to a desk and several green leather armchairs and a green leather couch, he had a thick brown carpet, a bookcase with a set of the Encyclopaedia Britannica, and a potted plant six feet high. The walls were hung with old prints. On his desk, near several large cigarette lighters, a couple of ball-point pens, and a leather cigar box, stood a framed photograph of Max Reinhardt. The elder Reinhardt had a look of gentle but troubled thoughtfulness. There was a considerable resemblance between father and son.

'Where you have your office is a sign of your importance,' Reinhardt told me as we sat around talking. 'I'm on the first floor. Dore Schary is two floors up, right over me. L. B. is also two floors up. I have a washbasin but no shower in my office. Dore has a shower but no bathtub. L. B. has a shower and a bathtub. The kind of bath facilities you have in your office is another measure of the worth of your position.' He smiled sardonically. 'An important director is almost as important as a producer,' he continued, getting up and straightening one of the prints. 'John's office is a corner one, like mine.'

Reinhardt is a paunchy man with a thick mane of wavy brown hair; in his cocoa-brown silk shantung suit, he looked like a Teddy bear. There was a cigar in his mouth and an expression of profound cynicism on his face. A heavy gold key chain hung in a deep loop from under his coat to a trouser pocket. He speaks with a German accent but without harshness, and his words come out pleasantly, in an even, regretful-sounding way. 'We promised Dore we would make our picture for one million five or under, and that we would make it in about thirty days,' he said, sitting down at his desk again. He put a hand on the estimate and sighed heavily. 'The producer's job is to save time and money.' He bobbed his head as he talked. A strand of hair fell over his face. He replaced it and puffed at his cigar in a kind of restrained frenzy. Then he removed the cigar and, bobbing his head again, said, 'When you tell people you have made a picture, they do not ask, "Is it a good picture?" They ask, "How many days?"' He tapped the ash from his cigar tenderly into a tray and gave another heavy sigh.

Reinhardt, who was born in Berlin, arrived in the United States in 1932, at the age of nineteen, for a visit. He had been over here a few months when Hitler came to power in Germany, and he decided to stay. Ernst Lubitsch, who had worked with the elder Reinhardt in Europe, offered Gottfried a job, without pay, at Paramount, as his assistant on a film version of Noël Coward's *Design for Living*, starring Fredric March, Miriam Hopkins, and Gary Cooper. In the fall of 1933, Reinhardt moved to Metro, as a hundred-and-fifty-dollar-a-week assistant to Walter Wanger, then a producer at that studio. Not long afterward, Wanger left and Reinhardt was made assistant to Bernard Hyman, who was considered a right-hand man of Irving Thalberg. Reinhardt became first a film writer (*The Great Waltz*) and then, in 1940, a producer (*Comrade X*, with Clark Gable and Hedy Lamarr; *Rage in Heaven*, with Ingrid Bergman and Robert Montgomery; *Two-Faced Woman*, with Greta Garbo, the last picture she appeared in). In 1942, he went into the Army. He worked on Signal Corps films for four years, and then returned to Metro and produced pictures featuring some of the studio's most popular stars, including Clark Gable and Lana Turner. His recent pictures, however, had not been regarded as box-office hits by the studio. At the age of seventy-two, Reinhardt's mother, a celebrated German actress named Else Heims, is still appearing in plays in Berlin. His father, who died eight years ago, came to Hollywood in 1934 to direct a stage production of *A Midsummer Night's Dream* at the Hollywood Bowl. (The production became famous because it presented an unknown young woman named Olivia de Havilland, who had never acted in public before, as a last-minute replacement for the star, who for some reason or other, was unable to go on.) Max Reinhardt was then invited by Warner Brothers to direct a movie production of *A Midsummer Night's Dream*. This picture was not a hit. For the next five years, he ran a Hollywood school known as Max Reinhardt's Workshop; for a short while in 1939, John Huston conducted a course in screen writing there. Max Reinhardt never got another directorial job in the movies. For many months he tried to obtain an appointment with L. B. Mayer, but Mayer was always too busy to see him.

At Metro-Goldwyn-Mayer, Gottfried Reinhardt had witnessed a succession of struggles for power among the executives at the studio. He had learned many lessons simply by watching these battles, he told me. 'M-G-M is like a medieval monarchy,' he said. 'Palace revolutions all the time.' He leaned back in his swivel chair. 'L. B. is the King. Dore is the Prime Minister. Benny Thau, an old Mayer man, is the Foreign Minister, and makes all the important deals for the studio, like the loan-outs of big stars. L. K. Sidney, one vice-president, is the Minister of the Interior, and Edgar J. Mannix, another vice-president, is Lord Privy Seal, or, sometimes, Minister without Portfolio. And John and I are loyal subjects.' He bobbed his head and gave a cynical laugh. 'Our King is not without power. I found, with *The Red Badge of Courage*, that you need the King's blessing if you want to make a picture. I have the King's blessing, but it has been given with large reservations.' He looked at me over his cigar. 'Our picture must be a commercial success,' he said flatly. 'And it must be a *great* picture.'

There was a stir in Dave Chasen's Restaurant in Beverly Hills when Dore Schary walked in. Chasen's is run by the former stage comedian whose name it bears, and it is popular with people in the motion-picture industry. The restaurant is divided into several sections. The first one, facing directly upon the entrance, contains semicircular booths. This section leads to a long bar opposite another section of booths. There are additional sections behind and to the sides of the first two. The head waiter immediately led Schary to a front booth. Two waiters took up sentry-like positions there, facing each other across the table. All the other patrons focused their attention on Schary. They seemed to be looking around at everybody except the people they were with and with whom they were managing to carry on conversations.

'I'll read you Ben's letter,' a man near us was saying. 'He writes, "Whenever I think of Byzantium, I remember you. I hope you survive the court intrigues of Hollywood's twilight, and when the place crumbles, may you fall from a throne."'

'I have news for you,' said his companion. 'It's not twilight yet. It's only smog.'

'I have news for *you*,' the first man said, staring without restraint at Schary. 'Ben will be back here. He *likes* the court intrigues.'

Schary was not a bit self-conscious. He had an aura of immense self-assurance, as though he had reached a point where he could no longer be affected by anything that might happen in Chasen's. He is an optimistic man, and he was talking to me optimistically about the movies. He respected foreign movies, he said, but he believed that the American picture industry provided more entertainment and enlightenment than any other movie-makers in the world. 'Our scope is international,' he said. 'Our thinking is international, and our creative urges and drives are constantly being renewed with the same vigour that renews so many things in the American way of life.' The motion-picture community generically referred to as Hollywood, he told me, is no different from any other American community that is dominated by a single industry. 'We're the same as Detroit,' he said. 'We just get talked about more, that's all.' He was almost the only man in Chasen's who was not at that moment looking around at someone other than the person he was talking to.

Dave Chasen, a small, solemn man with soft, wistful eyes, came over and told Schary how happy he was to see him there.

'How are you, doll?' Schary said.

'You're looking good,' Chasen said sadly.

Schary gave him a genial grin and went on talking to me about the picture industry. A man who seems to be favourably disposed toward the entire world, Schary has a chatty, friendly, homespun manner reminiscent of the late Will Rogers, but there is in it a definite hint of a firm-minded and paternalistic Sunday-school teacher. He is six feet tall, and he has a big head, a high, freckled forehead, and a large nose, shaped like a Saint Bernard's. He spoke earnestly, as though trying to convey a tremendous seriousness of purpose about his work in motion pictures. 'A motion picture is a success or a failure at its very inception,' he told me. 'There was resistance, great resistance, to making *The Red Badge of Courage*. In terms of cost and in other terms. This picture has no women. This picture has no love story. This picture has no single incident. This is a period picture. The story – well there's no story in this picture. It's just the story of a boy. It's the story of a coward. Well, it's the story of a hero.' Schary apparently enjoyed hearing himself talk. He was obviously in no hurry to make his point. 'These are the elements that are considered important in determining success or failure at the box office,' he said, and paused, as if he felt slightly bewildered by the point he was trying to make. He finally said that there had been successful pictures that did not have these so-called important elements. Crossfire, which he had made, was one, and All Quiet on the Western Front was another. 'Lew Ayres was the German equivalent of our boy,' he said. 'I'll almost bet you that Remarque knew The Red Badge of Courage. In the main, when you set out to make a picture, you say, "I just have a hunch about this picture." And that's what I felt about this one. Call it instinct if you will. I felt that this picture is liable to be a wonderful picture and a commercial success.'

A man who had been standing at the bar picked up his Martini and strolled over to a front booth near us. 'I have a great story for you,' he said to the group seated there. 'This actor comes back from a funeral and he's bawling and carrying on, the tears streaming down his face. So his friend tells him he never saw anybody take a funeral so hard. The actor says, "You should have seen me at the grave!"' The story-teller gave an explosive burst of self-appreciation. He took a sip of his Martini and caressed the stem of the glass. 'This old actor dies,' he said, his eyes moving away from his audience as Walter Pidgeon entered with a large party and was seated in the front section. 'The other old actors come to see him laid out in the coffin. "Joe looks terrific," says one. "Why not?" says the other one. "He just got back from Palm Springs!"'

Schary began talking about L. B. Mayer. 'I know Mayer,' he said. 'I know this man. I know Mayer because my father was like him. Powerful. Physically very strong. Strong-tempered and wilful. Mayer literally hits people. But my father made this guy look like a May party.' He gave me an easy grin.

Just then, a young man rushed over to the table, grabbed Schary's hand, and cried, 'Dore! Wonderful to see you, Dore!' He held on to Schary's hand, giving him an incredulous, admiring stare. 'You look wonderful, Dore! You look wonderful!'

'Sweetie, how are ya?' Schary said amiably.

The young man continued to stare at Schary; he seemed to be waiting for confirmation of something. Then he said, 'You remember me, Dore! Dave Miller!'

'Of course, doll,' Schary said.

'R.K.O.!' Miller announced, as though he were calling out a railroad stop, and in the same tone he announced that he was directing a picture at Columbia. Schary gave him a broad, understanding grin.

Miller shook his head unbelievingly several times and then, reluctantly, started to back away. 'You're doing wonderful things now, Dore. Wonderful! The best of everything to you, Dore,' he said. 'The best.'

The maze of paths followed by all the individuals at M-G-M who work together to make a motion picture led inexorably to the office of Louis B. Mayer, and I found him there one day, behind a series of doors, talking to Arthur Freed, a producer of musicals for the studio. Mayer's office was about half as large as the lounge of the Music Hall, and he sat behind a huge cream-coloured desk overlooking a vast expanse of peach-coloured carpet. The walls of the office were panelled in cream-coloured leather, and there was a cream-coloured bar, a cream-coloured fireplace with cream-coloured fire-irons, cream-coloured leather chairs and couches, and a cream-coloured grand piano. Behind Mayer's desk stood an American flag and a marble statue of the M-G-M lion. The desk was covered with four cream-coloured telephones, a prayer book, several photographs of lions, a tintype of Mayer's mother, and a statuette of the Republican Party's elephant. The big desk hid most of Mayer, but I could see his powerful shoulders, decked in navy blue, and a gay polka-dot bow tie that almost touched his chin. His large head seems set upon the shoulders without an intervening neck. His hair is thick and snow-white, his face is ruddy, and his eyes, behind glasses with amber-coloured frames, stared with a sort of fierce blankness at Freed, who was showing him a report on the box-office receipts of his latest musical, then playing at the Radio City Music Hall.

'Great! I saw it!' Mayer said, sweeping Freed back with his arm. 'I said to you the picture would be a wonderful hit. In here!' he cried, poking his index-finger at his chest. 'It wins the audience in here!' He lifted his snowy head and looked at the cream-coloured wall before him as though he were watching the Music Hall screen. 'Entertainment!' he cried, transfixed by what he seemed to see on that screen, and he made the face of a man who was emotionally stirred by what he was watching. 'It's good enough for you and I and the box office,' he said, turning back to Freed. 'Not for the smart alecks. It's not good enough any more,' he went on, whining coyly, in imitation of someone saying that winning the heart of the audience was not good enough. He pounded a commanding fist on his desk and looked at me. 'Let me tell you something!' he said. 'Prizes! Awards! Ribbons! We had two pictures here. An Andy Hardy picture, with little Micky Rooney, and *Ninotchka*, with Greta Garbo. *Ninotchka* got the prizes. *Blue ribbons! Purple ribbons!* Nine bells and seven stars! Which picture made the money? Andy Hardy made the money. Why? Because it won praise from the heart. No ribbons!'

'Hah!' Mr Freed said.

'Twenty-six years with the studio!' Mayer went on. 'They used to listen to me. Never would Irving Thalberg make a picture I was opposed to. I had a worship for that boy. He worked. Now they want cocktail parties and their names in the papers. Irving listened to me. Never satisfied with his own work. That was Irving. Years later, after Irving passed away, they still listened. They make an Andy Hardy picture.' He turned his powerful shoulders toward me. 'Andy's mother is dying, and they make the picture showing Andy standing outside the door. *Standing.* I told them, "Don't you know that an American boy like that will get down on his hands and knees and pray?" They listened. They brought Mickey Rooney down on his hands and knees.' Mayer leaped from his chair and crouched on the peach-coloured carpet and showed how Andy Hardy had prayed. 'The biggest thing in the picture!' He got up and returned to his chair. 'Not good enough,' he said, whining coyly again. 'Don't show the good, wholesome, American mother in the home. Kind. Sweet. Sacrifices. Love.' Mayer paused, and by his expression demonstrated, in turn, maternal kindness, sweetness, sacrifice, and love, and then glared at Freed and me. 'No!' he cried. 'Knock the mother on the jaw!' He gave himself an uppercut to the chin. 'Throw the little old lady down the stairs!' He threw himself in the direction of the American flag. 'Throw the mother's good, home-made chicken soup in the mother's face!' He threw an imaginary plate of soup in Freed's face. '*Step* on the mother! Kick her! That is *art*, they say. Art!' He raised and lowered his white eyebrows, wiggled his shoulders like a hula dancer, and moved his hands in a mysterious pattern in the air. 'Art!' he repeated, and gave an angry growl.

'You said it,' said Freed.

'Andy Hardy! I saw the picture and the tears were in my eyes,' Mayer said. 'I'm not ashamed. I'll see it again. Every time, I'll cry.'

'In musicals, we don't have any of those phony artistic preten-sions,' Freed said.

Mayer gave no sign that he had heard Freed. 'Between you and I and the lamp-post,' he said, straightening his bow tie, 'the smart alecks around here don't know the difference between the heart and the gutter. They don't want to listen to you. Marie Dressler! Who thought you could take a fat old lady and make her a star? I did it. And Wally Beery. And Lionel Barrymore.' He leaned back in his chair, one hand tucked into his shirt, his eyes squinting, his voice turning into the querulous rasp of Dr Gillespie informing Dr Kildare of his diagnosis of the disease. Then, resuming his natural manner, he said, 'The audience knows. Look at the receipts. Give the audience what they want? No. Not *good* enough.' He paused.

'Thoreau said most of us lead lives of quiet desperation,' Freed said quickly. 'Pictures should make you feel better, not worse.'

Again Mayer did not seem to hear. '*The Red Badge of Courage,*' he said. 'A million and a half. Maybe more. What for? There's no story. I was against it. They wanted to make it. I don't say no. John Huston. He was going to do *Quo Vadis.* What he wanted to do to the picture! No heart. His idea was he'd throw the Christians to the lions. That's all. I begged him to change his ideas. I got down on my hands and

knees to him. I sang "Mammy" to him. I showed him the meaning
of heart. I crawled to him on hands and knees. "Ma-a-ammy!"
With tears. No! No heart! He thanked me for taking him off the
picture. Now he wants The Red Badge of Courage. Dore Schary wants it.
All right I'll watch. I don't say no, but I wouldn't make that picture
with Sam Goldwyn's money.'

In the few days remaining before rehearsals started, Huston had
to attend budget and production conferences, he had to examine,
with his cameraman and technical crew, the exact spots on his San
Fernando Valley Ranch where the battle scenes for the picture would
be shot, and he had to make a number of revisions in the screenplay,
including some suggested by the Production Code Administrator of
the Motion Picture Association of America, which had come to him
in a copy of a letter addressed to Mayer:

Dear Mr Mayer:
We have read the script for your proposed production The Red Badge of
Courage, and beg to report that the basic story seems to meet the requirements of
the Production Code. Going through the script in detail, we call your attention to the
following minor items.
Page 1 A: Here, and throughout the script, please make certain that the expression
'dum' is pronounced clearly, and does not sound like the unacceptable expletive
'damn'.
Page 21: The expression 'damn' is unacceptable.
Page 41: The same applies to the exclamation 'Lord', the expression 'I swear t'
Gawd'.
Page 42: The same applies to 'Lord knows' and the exclamation 'Gawd'.
Page 44: The exclamation 'Good Lord' is unacceptable.
Page 65: The expression 'hell to pay' is unacceptable.

Joseph I. Breen, the writer of the letter, stated that three other uses of
the word 'Lord' in the script were unacceptable, along with one 'in
God's name', two 'damns', and three 'hells', and, before signing
off – cordially – reminded Mr Mayer that the final judgement of the
Code Administrator would be based upon the finished picture.

Hedda Hopper, in the Los Angeles *Times*, headlined one of her daily columns with the news that Audie Murphy would star in *The Red Badge of Courage*. 'The happiest and most appropriate casting of the year took place at M-G-M yesterday when Dore Schary gave Audie Murphy, the most decorated hero of World War II, the leading role in *The Red Badge of Courage*, with John Huston directing,' she wrote. 'For a change, we'll have a real soldier playing a real soldier on the screen. It couldn't happen at a better time.'

The administrative headquarters for the M-G-M studio is a U-shaped white concrete building identified, in metal letters, as the Irving Thalberg Building. The steps leading to the Thalberg Building, between broad, shrub-bordered lawns, are wide and smooth, and they shone whitely under the midsummer sun, as cool and as stately as the steps to the Capitol in Washington, as I headed for them one morning. A taxi drew over to the kerb and jerked to a halt. The door opened and Huston leaped out. He plunged a hand into a trouser pocket, handed the driver a wadded bill, and rushed toward the steps. He had stayed in town the night before, he said, at one of his three places – a small house in Beverly Hills he rented from Paulette Goddard – and he had expected his secretary to telephone him and wake him up. She had not telephoned, and he had overslept. He seemed angry and tense. 'Audie's waiting for me,' he said irritably.

We went into a large reception room with grey-chequered linoleum on the floor, and Huston strode across it, nodding to a young man seated at a semicircular desk between two doors. 'Good morning, Mr Huston,' the young man said brightly. At once, the catches on both doors started clicking, and Huston opened the one on the right. I hurried after him, down a linoleum-floored corridor, whose cream-coloured walls were lined with cream-coloured doors. On each door was a slot holding a white card with a name printed on it. At the end of the corridor, we turned to the right, down another corridor, and at the end of that we came to a door with his name on it, engraved in black letters on a brass plate. Huston opened it, and a young lady with curly black hair, seated at a desk facing the door, looked up as we came in. Huston turned immediately to a bench adjoining the entrance. Audie Murphy was sitting on it. He stood up.

'Hello, Audie. How are you, Audie?' Huston said gently, as though speaking to a frightened child. The two men shook hands. 'Well, we made it, kid,' Huston said, and forced an outburst of ho-ho-hos.

Murphy gave him a wan smile and said nothing. A slight young man with a small, freckled face, long, wavy reddish-brown hair, and large, cool grey eyes, he was wearing tan twill frontier riding pants, a matching shirt, open at the collar, and Western boots with pointed toes and high heels.

'Come in, Audie,' Huston said, opening the door to an inner office.

'Good morning,' the secretary behind him said. 'Publicity wants to know what do you do when you hit a snag in writing a script?'

'Tell publicity I'm not here,' Huston said in a tone of cold reproach. Then, his voice gentle again, he said, 'Come in, Audie.'

Huston's office had oak-panelled walls, a blue carpet, and three windows reaching from the ceiling to the floor. There was a long mahogany desk at one end of the room, and at the opposite end, facing it, was a blue leather couch. Several blue leather armchairs were scattered around the office.

'Sit down, guys,' Huston said, and himself sat down behind the desk, in a swivel chair with a blue leather seat. 'Well,' he said, clenching his hands and resting his chin on them. He swung from side to side in his chair a few times, then leaned back and put his feet on the desk on top of a stack of papers.

Murphy sat down in an armchair facing one of the windows and ran a forefinger across his lower lip. 'I've got a sore lip,' he said. ''Bout six this morning, I went riding on my colt. I went riding without my hat, and the sun burned my lip all up.' He spoke with a delicate plaintiveness, in the nasal, twangy drawl of a Texan.

'I've got the same thing, kid,' Huston said, pursing his lips. 'Tell you what, Audie. Bring your colt out to my ranch. You can have your colt right there with you, any time you want to ride while we're making the picture.'

Murphy fingered his sore lip, as if trying to determine whether

Huston's pleasant offer did anything for his affliction. Apparently it didn't, so he looked sadly out the window.

'We'll do a lot of riding together, kid,' Huston said. 'That's good riding country there in the hills, you know.'

Murphy made a small, sighing noise of assent.

'I want you to hear this, Audie,' Huston said, nervously unfolding a sheet of paper he had taken from his jacket. 'Some new lines I just wrote for the script.' He read several lines, then laughed appreciatively.

Murphy made another small noise of assent.

Huston continued to laugh, but his eyes, fastened on Murphy, were sombre. He seemed baffled and worried by Murphy's unresponsiveness, because usually actors were quick to respond to him. He took his feet down from his desk and picked up a slip of blue paper one heel had been resting on. 'Interoffice Communication,' he read aloud, and glanced quickly at Murphy to get his attention. 'To Messrs Gottfried Reinhardt, John Huston ... SUBJECT: Hair for RED BADGE OF COURAGE Production. As per discussion this morning, we are proceeding with the manufacture of: 50 Hook-on Beards at $3.50 each, 100 Crepe wool Moustaches at 50c. each, 100 Crepe wool Falls at $2.50 each – for Production No. 1512 – RED BADGE OF COURAGE. These will be manufactured in the Make-up Department.'

Huston stopped reading, looked at Murphy, and saw that he had already lost his attention. 'Well, now,' Huston said, 'let's go get some breakfast. I haven't had any breakfast yet.'

The door opened, and a stoop-shouldered young man with enormous, eager-looking eyes came in. He was introduced as Albert Band, Huston's assistant. Huston moved toward the door.

'Where you going?' Band asked, blinking his eyes. His eyelashes descended over his eyes like two dust-mops.

'Breakfast,' said Huston.

Band said that he had had his breakfast, but he would come along and watch Huston have his.

We went out a side door to the studio gates, where a policeman in a stone hut looked carefully at each of us as we filed through. 'Mr Huston,' he said.

'Good morning,' Huston said, giving full weight to each syllable.
We went down a narrow street between low, grey-painted buildings of wood or stucco, which had shingles identifying them as
'Men's Wardrobe', 'International Department', 'Casting Office',
'Accounting Department', and 'Danger 2300 Volts'. Farther along
the street were the sound stages, grey, hangar-like buildings. We
passed a number of costumed actors and actresses, and people in
casual summer dress who exchanged nods with Huston and looked
piercingly at Murphy, Band, and me.

A portly gentleman in a grey pin-striped suit stopped Huston and
shook hands with him. 'Congratulate me,' he said. 'My picture opens
next week in New York.'

'Music Hall?' Huston asked.

'I have news for you,' the man said in a dry tone. 'Dore Schary
personally produces a picture, it gets into the Music Hall. I got
Loew's State.'

The M-G-M commissary is a comfortable restaurant with soft
lighting, cream-coloured walls, an aquamarine ceiling, and modern
furnishings. When Huston, Murphy, Band, and I entered, about a
third of the tables were occupied, and most of the people sitting at
them stared at our party without restraint. We took a table, and
Huston ordered orange-juice, a hard-boiled egg, bacon, and coffee.
Murphy fingered his sore lip.

'How about some coffee, amigo?' Huston asked him.

Murphy nodded wistfully.

'Gottfried told me a great story yesterday,' Band said, batting his
enormous eyes at Huston. 'Two producers come out of the projection room where one has just shown the other his picture and he
asks, "Well, how did you like the picture?" "Great," the other
producer says. "What's the matter – you didn't like it?" the first
producer asks. Isn't that a great story?' Band said with a short laugh.

'A great story, Albert,' Huston said, putting a brown cigarette in
one corner of his mouth.

'I've got another one,' Band said. He took a kitchen match from
his pocket, scraped the head of it with his thumbnail, and held the
flame to Huston's cigarette. 'This producer doesn't like the score

that has been composed for his picture. "The music isn't right," he says. "It's a picture about France," he said, "so I want a lot of French horns." ' Band laughed again.

'Got a newspaper, Albert?' said Huston. Band said no. 'Get me a paper, Albert,' said Huston. 'I want to see the selections.' He did not look up as Band went out. Drawing deeply on his cigarette, he looked down through the smoke at the table and brushed away some shreds of tobacco.

Murphy fixed his gaze on the windows along the far wall. Huston looked at him. 'Excited, kid?' he asked.

'Seems as though nothing can get me excited any more – you know, enthused?' he said. 'Before the war, I'd get excited and enthused about a lot of things, but not any more.'

'I feel the same way, kid,' said Huston.

The waitress brought Huston's breakfast and Murphy's cup of coffee. Huston squinted at Murphy over his drooping cigarette and told him that his hair looked fine. 'You might taper the sideburns a bit, kid,' he said, taking the cigarette from his mouth and resting it on an ashtray. 'That's all we need to do, kid.' He took a few sips of orange juice and then pushed the glass aside, picked up the hard-boiled egg, and bit into it. 'Audie, ever been in Chico, up north of San Francisco, near the Sacramento River?' he asked expansively. 'Well, now, we'll be going up there on location to do the river-crossing scene and other stuff for the picture. And while we're there, we'll go fishing, kid.'

Band returned and handed Huston a newspaper. Huston took a couple of quick swallows of coffee and pushed his breakfast aside. Opening the paper on the table, he said that his filly Tryst was running that day and that he wanted to know what the handicappers had to say about her. He picked up the paper and held it in front of his face. The headline facing us read, 'CHINESE REPORTED AIDING FOE'.

Murphy stared vaguely at the paper. 'I'd like to go fishing,' he said.

From behind the newspaper, Huston grunted.

'You going fishing?' Band asked.

From behind the newspaper, Huston grunted.

'When we get to Chico,' said Murphy.

At an adjoining table, a young man was saying loudly, 'He comes out here from Broadway and he thinks he's *acting* in movies. Today on the set, I'm doing a scene with him, and he says to me, "I don't feel your presence." "So reach out and *touch* me," I said.'

'Look, I know you're busy, I don't wanna butt in, but this I gotta tell you,' a roly-poly little man said, going up to the young man's table. 'I'm at Sam Goldwyn's last night and he says he's got a new painting to show me. So he takes me over to the painting and points to it and says, "My *Toujours Lautrec*!"'

Huston closed the newspaper and folded it under his arm. 'Let's get back, guys,' he said. He instructed Band to place a token bet on Tryst for him, and Band walked off.

Back in the Thalberg Building, Huston invited Murphy and me to see a number of test shots he had made on his ranch for *The Red Badge of Courage*. He had seen the tests and, with Reinhardt and Schary, had made the final decisions on the leading players in the cast. In addition to Audie Murphy as the Youth, there would be Bill Mauldin as the Loud Soldier, John Dierkes as the Tall Soldier, and Royal Dano as the Tattered Man. We trooped downstairs to a carpeted lounge in the basement and went into a projection room that contained two rows of heavy, deep leather armchairs. Beside the arm of one of the centre chairs was a board holding a telephone and a mechanism called a 'fader', which controls the volume of sound. The first shot showed the Youth, who had returned to his regiment after running away from battle, having his head bandaged by his friend, the Loud Soldier. Mauldin, dressed in Union blue, his ears protruding horizontally from under a kepi, said as he bound a kerchief around Murphy's head, 'Yeh look like th' devil, but I bet yeh feel better.'

In the audience, Murphy said in a loud whisper, 'I was biting my cheek so hard trying to keep from laughing.'

'Yes, Audie,' said Huston.

The next scene showed Murphy carrying a gun and urging some soldiers behind him to come on. 'Let's show them Rebs what we're made of!' Murphy called fiercely, on the screen. 'Come on! All we got to do is cross this here field! Who's with me? Come on! Come on!' Murphy advanced, and Huston's voice came on the sound track, laughing and saying, 'Very good.'

'I was biting my cheek so hard my whole cheek was sore,' Murphy said.

'Yes, Audie,' Huston said.

Next there was a scene between Murphy and the Tall Soldier, played by John Dierkes. The Tall Soldier died, his breath rasping and then ceasing, and his hair blowing long and wild. The Youth wept.

The lights came on. 'We're going to be just fine,' Huston said.

Back in his office, where we found Band waiting for us, Huston, taking another cigarette, said that Dierkes would be just wonderful in the picture.

'Just great,' said Band.

Murphy was back in his armchair, staring out the window as though lost in a distant dream. Huston gave him a sharp glance, then sighed and put his long legs up on the desk. 'Well, now, Audie, we're going to have such fun making this picture on my ranch!' he said. 'Let me tell you kids all about the ranch.' There was a compelling promise in his tone. He waited while Murphy shifted his gaze from the window to him. Huston deliberately took his time. He drew on his cigarette, and blew the smoke away. He began by telling us that he had four hundred and eighty acres – rolling fields, pasture, a brook, and hills harbouring mountain lions and jaguars. He had paddocks and stables for his horses, a pen for eight Weimaraner puppies, dog-houses for the Weimaraner parents and three other dogs (including a white German shepherd named Paulette, after Paulette Goddard), and a three-room shack for himself, his adopted son Pablo, and a young man named Eduardo, who managed the ranch. Huston's wife, the former Ricki Soma, and their infant son lived at Malibu Beach, and Huston commuted between the two establishments. At the ranch, Huston had a cowboy named Dusty, and, with a good deal of laughter, he described Dusty's gaunt and leathery face and his big, black ten-gallon hat. 'Oh, God!' he said, with a shake of his head, 'Dusty wants to be in the picture.' He coughed out a series of jovial ho-ho-hos.

Murphy, who had given him a quiet smile, developed the smile into hollow-sounding laughter. Huston seemed satisfied that he had finally got a response out of Murphy.

The door opened and Reinhardt stood there, an expression of cynical bewilderment on his face, a large cigar between his lips.

'Come in, Gottfried,' said Huston.

'Hello, Mr Reinhardt,' Murphy said, standing up.

Reinhardt took a few steps forward, bobbing his head paternally at everyone. 'There's going to be trouble, John,' he said, in a tone of dry, flat amiability. He chewed his cigar around to a corner of his mouth to let the words out. 'The production office thought the river for the picture was a stream. In the script, it says, "The regiment crosses a *stream*." Now they want to know what you mean you need hundreds of men to cross the Sacramento River?' He bobbed his head again.

'Ho! Ho!' Huston said, crossing his legs on top of his desk. Murphy sat down again. Band paced the carpet in front of Huston's desk.

'Trouble!' Reinhardt said.

'Well, now, Gottfried, you and I are used to trouble on this picture,' Huston said. He put a brown cigarette in his mouth. Band held a kitchen match to it. Huston cocked his head over the flame and gave Murphy a wry smile. 'They're afraid the soldiers will get their little tootsies wet,' he said, with a titter.

Murphy smiled sadly. Band laughed and batted his eyes first at Huston, then at Reinhardt.

'Now, Albert wouldn't be afraid to cross the river, would you, Albert?' Huston asked.

Murphy smiled.

'I have news for you,' Band said. 'I'm going to cross it. You promised me I could have a part in this picture.'

Reinhardt laughed, the upper part of his body bouncing energetically. As Band continued pacing in front of Huston's desk, Reinhardt fell in ahead of him, and the two men paced together. Reinhardt's gold key chain looped into his trouser pocket flopped noisily as he paced. 'Everybody in Hollywood wants to be something he is not,' he said as Huston watched him over the tips of his shoes. 'Albert is not satisfied to be your assistant. He wants to be an actor. The writers want to be directors. The producers want to be writers. The actors want to be producers. The wives want to be painters. Nobody is satisfied. Everybody is frustrated. Nobody is happy.' He sighed, and sat down heavily in a chair facing Murphy. 'I am a man who likes to see people happy,' he muttered through his cigar.

The door opened, and John Dierkes entered. 'Hi, John! Hi, everybody,' he said cheerfully, in a rasping drawl. He had a thick shock of stringy orange hair. 'Hi, sport!' he said to Murphy. 'Hedda sure likes you, sport. Didja see what she said about you today?'

'Did you let your hair grow?' Reinhardt asked him.

'Sure did, Gottfried,' said Dierkes. 'It's been growin' and growin' for weeks.' He sat down, clasped his hands between his knees, and beamed at Murphy. 'You learnin' your lines, sport?' he asked.

Huston recrossed his legs impatiently and said that he had just seen Dierkes' screen test. 'You look like an ugly bastard,' Huston said. 'You're the only man I know who is uglier than I am.'

Dierkes dropped his long chin in an amiable smile. 'That's what you said the first time we met, John,' he said. 'In London. I was in the Red Cross and you were sure spiffy in your major's uniform. 1943.'

'I was on my way to Italy,' Huston said. 'That's when we made The Battle of San Pietro.'

Reinhardt turned to Murphy. 'Did you ever see the picture K-Rations and How to Chew Them?' he asked in a loud voice. He tilted his cigar to a sharp angle and pointed a finger at himself. 'Mine,' he said.

'England was just wonderful in the war,' Huston said. 'You always wanted to stay up all night. You never wanted to go to sleep.'

Reinhardt said, 'I'll bet I'm the only producer who ever had Albert Einstein as an actor.' Attention now focused on him. He said that he had been making an Army film called Know Your Enemy – Germany, the beginning of which showed some notable German refugees. 'Anthony Veiller, a screen writer who was my major, told me to tell Einstein to comb his hair before we photographed him. I said, "Would you tell Einstein to comb his hair?" He said no. So

we photographed Einstein with his hair not combed.' Reinhardt
bounced merrily in his chair and laughed.

'God, those English bootmakers!' Huston said. 'The love and
affection they lavish on their boots! Whenever I go to London, I
head straight for Maxwell and order boots made.'

Reinhardt got up and went to the door, saying that in the afternoon there was going to be a conference of the key members of the
crew assigned to the picture. The cost of making a picture depended
largely on the time it took, he observed. The director and his actors
might work together only three hours of an eight-hour day; the
balance of the time would be spent waiting for scenes to be prepared. Reinhardt wanted to discuss what he called the leapfrog
method, which meant having an assistant director line up shots in
advance, so that Huston could move from one scene to another
without delay. 'We bring this picture in early, we will be real
heroes,' Reinhardt said.

'Don't worry, Gottfried,' Huston said.

'I will see you later?' Reinhardt asked.

'I'll be there, Gottfried. Don't worry,' Huston said.

Huston gave me a copy of the script for The Red Badge of Courage and
left me alone in his office to read it. The script was a mimeographed
booklet in a yellow paper cover, which was stamped with the seal
of M-G-M. Also on the cover were the words 'Production No. 1512'
and the names of the film's producer, Gottfried Reinhardt, and its
director, John Huston. A notation on the flyleaf stated that the
number of pages was ninety-two. Each shot described in the script
was numbered. I turned to page 92. The last shot was numbered
344, and its description read:

CLOSE TRUCKING SHOT — THE YOUTH

As he trudges from the place of blood and wrath, his
spirit changes. He is rid of the sickness of battle. He lifts
his head to the rain, breathes in the cool air, hears a sound
above him.

CAMERA PANS UP to a tree and a bird is singing.

FADE OUT

I turned to page 73, one the Breen Office had found unacceptable expressions on:

> CLOSE SHOT — LIEUTENANT
> Lieutenant
> Come on, men! This is no time to stop! In God's name, don't just stand there! We'll all get killed. Come on! I never seed sech lunkheads! Get movin', damn yeh – Oh, yeh cowards – Yeh rotten little cowards!

I turned back to the beginning and settled down to read:

> FADE IN:
> MED. LONG SHOT — EMBANKMENT ACROSS A RIVER — NIGHT
> Low fires are seen in the distance, forming the enemy camp. Trees and bushes. A LOW WHISTLE IS HEARD from across the river.
> MED. SHOT — THE OTHER SIDE OF THE RIVER
> Moonlight reveals some bushes and trees, and a sentry walking into view. Crickets sing in the still night. The low whistle is repeated. The sentry puts his rifle to his shoulder, stands staring into the gloom.
> CLOSE SHOT — SENTRY — IT IS THE YOUTH
> The Youth
> Who goes there?
> MED. LONG SHOT — ACROSS THE RIVER
> Southern Voice
> Me, Yank – jest me. . . . Move back into the shadders, Yank, unless you want one of them little red badges. I couldn't miss yeh standin' there in the moonlight.

The script took me a couple of hours to read. It included several scenes written by Huston that did not appear in the novel, but for the most part the screenplay indicated that Huston intended to embody in his picture the Youth's impressions of war exactly as Crane had described them.

After finishing the script, I went into a sort of back room of Huston's office, used as a conference and poker room, where I found Mrs Huston. Mrs Huston had not seen her husband for several days. She is a striking girl with an oval face and long, dark hair drawn back tight from her face, parted in the middle, and done up in a bun in back. She was formerly a ballet dancer in New York, and is now an actress. She showed me around the room. There were a sofa and several chairs covered in brown leather. There were photographs of horses on the walls. There was a framed picture, clipped from a magazine, showing Huston with his father and captioned, 'John Huston – for the last three years a major in the Army's Signal Corps – has produced an important and engrossing documentary film, *Let There Be Light*. His father, Walter Huston, does an equally fine narration for this picture on the crackup and treatment of neuropsychopathic soldiers.' There were certificates of awards – the One World Flight Award for Motion Pictures, and the Screen Writers Guild Award to Huston for his *Treasure of Sierra Madre*, which was described in the citation as 'the best-written Western of 1948', and two Motion Picture Academy statuettes – one for the best screenplay of 1948, the other for the best-directed film that year. A silver tray on a corner table was inscribed 'To John Huston, One Hell of a Guy. The Macadamized Award from all the Members of the Asphalt Jungle.'

Albert Band came into the room. He said there ought to be a lot of fun with the new picture, especially when the company went on location at Chico.

Mrs Huston said that she was going along to Chico, where she would do some fishing. 'I just love fishing,' she went on, as if trying to convince herself.

Huston entered, greeted his wife, and announced that everybody ought to have a drink. He called his secretary in and told her that the key to the liquor was under one of the Oscars.

'How's the young man?' Huston asked his wife.

The baby was fine, she said.

'Did you bring my car, honey?' he asked.

The car was outside.

'Tryst is running today, honey,' Huston said tenderly.

'I have news for you,' Band said. 'Tryst ran out of the money.'

Huston looked astonished and, after a moment, laughed in a strained way. 'Albert,' he said, 'get over to Gottfried's office and find out when that goddam meeting is supposed to start.'

Since most of the film was to be shot about thirty miles from Hollywood, on Huston's ranch, in the San Fernando Valley, Huston arranged to look over the terrain one day with Reinhardt and the production crew. I arrived at the ranch about eleven o'clock in the morning, and a few minutes later the crew drove up in a large black limousine. Houston came out of his ranchhouse to greet us, dressed in a red-and-green checked cap, a pink T-shirt, tan riding pants flapping out at the sides, tan leggings, tan braces, and heavy maroon shoes that reached to his ankles. Included in the crew were the camerman, Harold Rosson, a short, stocky, gum-chewing, middle-aged man with a sharp face; the unit manager, Lee Katz, a heavy-set man in his late thirties, with thin blond fuzz on his head, a brisk, officious manner, and a perpetual ingratiating smile; the 'leapfrog' director, Andrew Marton, a serious, pedantic Hungarian-American with a heavy accent and a nervous, solicitous manner, whose job it would be to arrange things so that Huston would not have to wait between scenes; the art director, Hans Peters, a stiff, formal German with cropped hair, who also had a heavy accent; another assistant director, Reggie Callow, a harassed-looking man with a large red face, a bowl-shaped midriff, and the gravelly voice of a buck sergeant; and the technical adviser, Colonel Paul Davison, a retired Army officer with a moustache, dark glasses, and a soldierly bearing. All were carrying copies of the script.

Rosson clapped Huston on the shoulder. 'Happy birthday, pal,' he said.

'I almost forgot,' Huston said. 'Thanks, Hal. Thanks very much, kid.'

Reinhardt and Band drove up in a grey Cadillac convertible with the top down. Reinhardt had a navy-blue beret on his head and a cigar in his mouth. He came over and pumped Huston's hand. 'Happy birthday, John,' he said.

'Oh, yes. I almost forgot,' Huston said. 'Well, gentlemen, let's get started.'

Everybody was wearing rough clothes except Reinhardt, who wore neat gabardine slacks of bright blue and a soft shirt of lighter blue. Band had on Russian Cossack boots, into which were tucked ragged cotton pants. Marton wore dungarees and a khaki bush jacket, which, he said, he had brought from Africa, where he had recently worked as co-director of *King Solomon's Mines*. Colonel Davison wore Army fatigues.

Dusty, the Huston-ranch cowboy who wanted to play in the picture, stood around while the crew got organized. He went into the stables and returned leading a large black horse, saddled and bridled. Huston mounted it, and then Dusty brought out a white-and-brown cow pony.

'I'll ride Papoose, pal,' Rosson said to Huston, and heaved himself aboard the cow pony.

'He was once married to Jean Harlow,' Band said to Colonel Davison, pointing to Rosson.

'Let's go, gentlemen!' Huston called, waving everybody on. He walked his horse slowly down the road.

'John can really set a saddle,' Dusty said, watching him go.

Rosson started after Huston. Reinhardt and Band followed in the Cadillac. The rest of us, in the limousine, brought up the rear of the cavalcade.

Marton peered out the window at Rosson, rocking along on the cow pony. 'He used to be married to Jean Harlow,' he said thoughtfully. 'Reggie, what do we do first?'

Callow said that they were going to stop at the location for the scene showing the Youth's regiment on the march, to determine how many men would be needed to give the effect of an army on the march. It was Scene 37. All the script had to say about it was 'MEDIUM LONG SHOT — A ROAD — THE ARMY ON THE MARCH — DUSK'.

'The mathematics of this discussion is important,' Callow said.

Katz, whose primary job was to serve as a liaison man between the crew and the studio production office, was sitting up front. He turned around and said, smiling, 'Mathematics means money.'

'Everything is such a production,' said Marton. 'Why can't they just turn Johnny loose with the camera?'

Colonel Davison, who was sitting in a jump seat next to Peters, cleared his throat.

'What, what?' Katz said to him.

'Warm today,' the Colonel said, clearing his throat again.

'Nothing,' Marton said. 'In Africa, we had a hundred and fifty degrees in the shade.'

'That so?' said the Colonel.

Katz turned around again. There were beads of perspiration on his forehead and in the fuzz on his head. 'You boys are going to have a time climbing these hills today,' he said cheerily. 'Hot, hot.'

Peters said, without moving his head, 'Very warm.'

'It's going to be a tough war,' Callow said.

The road for the MEDIUM LONG SHOT was a dirt one curving around a hill and running through sunburned fields. A large oak tree at the foot of the hill cast a shadow over the road. Huston and Rosson sat on their horses near the top of the hill, waiting for the rest of the party to struggle up to them through dry, prickly grass. Reinhardt was carrying a sixteen-millimetre movie camera. A hawk flew overhead, and Reinhardt stopped, half-way up the hill, and trained his camera on it. 'I like to take pictures of birds,' he said. When everyone had reached Huston and was standing around him, Huston pointed to the bend in the road.

'The Army comes around there,' he said commandingly. He paused and patted the neck of his horse 'Colonel,' he said.

'Yes, sir!' Colonel Davison said, coming to attention.

'Colonel, how far apart will we put the fours?' Huston asked.

'About an arm's length, sir,' said the Colonel.

'Get away from my script!' Callow said to Huston's horse, who was attempting to eat it.

Huston gave Callow a reproachful look and patted the horse's neck. 'Never mind, baby,' he said.

'Gentlemen,' Rosson said, 'keep in mind we must not have these Western mountains in what was primarily an Eastern war.' He dismounted and gave the reins of his pony to Band, who clambered clumsily into the saddle. The pony started turning in circles.

'It's only me, little baby,' Band said to it.

'Albert!' Huston said. Band got off the pony, and it calmed down.

'Gentlemen,' Huston said. 'The finder, please.'

Marton handed him a cone-shaped tube with a rectangular window at the wide end. It would determine the kind of lens that would be needed for the shot. Huston looked at the road through the finder for a long time. 'A slow, uneven march,' he said dramatically. 'The Union colonel and his aide are leading the march on horseback. Looks wonderful, just wonderful. Take a look, Hal.' He handed the finder to Rosson, who looked at the road through it.

'Great, pal!' Rosson said, chewing his gum with quick, rabbit-like chomps.

'Doesn't it look like a Brady, kid?' Huston said to Rosson.

'Great, pal,' said Rosson.

The two men discussed where the camera would be set up, how the shot of the column of soldiers would be composed, when the shot would be taken (in the early morning, when the light on the troops would be coming from the back). They also discussed the fact that the scene, like most of the others in the picture, would be photographed as if from the point of view of the Youth. Then they got to talking about how many men would be needed for the scene.

'How about four hundred and fifty?' said Katz.

'Eight hundred,' Huston said immediately.

'Maybe we could do with six hundred and fifty,' Reinhardt said, giving Huston a knowing glance.

Katz said that the column would be spaced out with horses and caissons, and that they could get away with less than six hundred and fifty infantrymen.

Huston gave Colonel Davison a sly glance and winked.

The Colonel quickly cleared his throat and said, 'Sir, to be militarily correct we ought to have a thousand infantry.'

'God!' Reinhardt said.

'Never, never,' Katz said.

'Make the picture in Africa,' Marton said. 'Extras cost eighteen cents a day in Africa.'

'That's exactly fifteen dollars and thirty-eight cents less than an extra costs here,' Callow said. 'We could change it to the Boer War.'

'Is it to be six hundred and fifty, gentlemen?' Huston said impatiently.

'If that's the way you want it,' Katz said. 'Anything I can do you for.'

We went from one site to another, trudging up and down hills and breaking paths through heavy underbrush. The afternoon sun was hot, and the faces of the crew were grimy and wet, and their clothes were dusty and sprinkled with burs and prickly foxtails. Only Reinhardt seemed unaffected by his exertions. His blue slacks were still creased; and a fresh cigar was in his mouth as he stood beside Huston examining the site for a scene – to be shot some afternoon – that would show the Youth coming upon a line of wounded men, who would be moving down a path on a slope. Huston and Reinhardt looked at a grassy slope that led down to a road and a patch of trees. The distance from the top of the slope to the road was two hundred and seventy yards, Callow told Huston and Reinhardt. The three men estimated that they would need a hundred extras to make an impressive line of wounded men.

Huston looked through the finder at the slope. 'The Youth sees a long line of wounded staggering down,' he said, in a low voice.

'We've got to have something for these men to do in the morning,' Katz said. 'We can't have a hundred extras on the payroll and have them stand around with nothing to do for half a day.'

Huston lowered the finder. 'Let's just put the figures down as required for each shot, without reference to any other shot,' he said coldly.

Katz smiled and threw up his hands.

'And if we find we need twenty-five more men –' Huston began.

'I will appeal to Mr Reinhardt,' Katz said.

'You have great powers of persuasion,' said Huston.

Reinhardt bobbed his head and laughed, looking at his director with admiration.

Callow sat by the side of the path, laboriously pulling foxtails out of his socks. 'I'm stabbed all over,' he said. 'I fought the Civil War once before, when I was assistant director on *Gone with the Wind*. It was never this rough, and *Wind* was the best Western ever made.'

Reinhardt was aiming his camera at a small silver-and-red airplane flying low overhead.

'That's no bird; that's Clarence Brown,' said Band.

'Clarence is up there looking for gold,' Marton said.

'There is a great story about Clarence Brown,' Reinhardt said. 'A friend says to him, "What do you want with all that money, Clarence? You can't take it with you." "You can't?" Clarence says. "Then I'm not going."' Band and Marton agreed that it was a great story, and Reinhardt looked pleased with himself.

Katz was saying that the first battle scene would have four hundred infantrymen, fifty cavalrymen, and four complete teams of artillerymen and horses, making a total of four hundred and seventy-four men and a hundred and six horses.

'More people than we ever had in *Wind*,' Callow said.

Huston, now on his horse, leaned forward in the saddle and rested the side of his face against the neck of the horse.

'We accomplished a lot today,' Reinhardt said.

Huston said, with great conviction, 'It looks just swell, Gottfried, just wonderful.'

'It must be a great picture,' Reinhardt said.

'Great,' Band said.

Huston wheeled his horse and started across the slope at a canter. He approached a log on top of a mound of earth, spurred his horse, and made a smooth jump. Reinhardt trained his camera on Huston until he disappeared around a wooded knoll.

That night, John Huston celebrated his forty-fourth birthday at a formal dinner party in Hollywood attended by a couple of dozen of his closest friends and associates. The party was given by Reinhardt, in the private dining room of Chasen's Restaurant. The host stood near the door. He looked cynical, and scornful of everything about him as he pumped the hand of each arriving guest, but he managed, with a half-smoked cigar fixed firmly in a corner of his mouth, to beam with delight. The guests all exuded an atmosphere of exclusiveness and intimacy. It seemed to have nothing to do with Huston's birthday. The birthday, apparently, was merely the occasion, not the cause, of the guests' effusions. Good will was stamped on the faces of all, but there was no indication as to whom or what it was directed toward. As they entered, the guests exchanged quick glances, as though they were assuring each other and themselves that they were there.

At one end of the room, a couple of bartenders had set up a double file of champagne glasses on the bar. Waiters circulated with platters of canapés. Reinhardt's wife, a slender, attractive, sardonic-looking lady with large, brown, sceptical eyes and a vaguely Continental manner, moved with a sort of weary impishness among the guests. She was wearing a gossamer blue dinner gown embroidered with silver. The other ladies at the party – all wives of the friends and associates – were almost as festively adorned, but there was about many of them an air of defeat, as though they had given up a battle for some undefined goal. They stood around in groups, watching the groups of men. Mrs Reinhardt, with the air of one who refuses to admit defeat, bore down on Edward G. Robinson, John Garfield, and Paul Kohner, who was Huston's agent. Robinson, who had recently returned from abroad, was talking about his collection of paintings. Garfield was acting exuberant. Kohner was a genial, tolerant onlooker. At Mrs Reinhardt's approach, Robinson abandoned his paintings and, starting to hum, fixed on her a broad smile of welcome. 'Silvia,' he said, and continued to hum.

'There is a rumour making the rounds,' she said, pronouncing each syllable slowly and emphatically. 'The men are going to play poker after dinner, and the ladies will be given the brush. You know what I am talking about?'

Robinson smiled even more broadly.

Garfield said, 'The girls can go to a movie or something. Eddie, you buy any paintings in Europe?'

'Julie, you are *not* playing poker,' said Mrs Reinhardt to Garfield.

'I have news for you,' said Garfield, 'I am. Eddie?'

'Not this trip,' Robinson said, without ceasing to grin at Mrs

Reinhardt. 'In New York, a Rouault. The time before in Europe, a Soutine.'

'Last night, I met somebody owned a Degas,' said a tall and glamorous-looking but nervous girl with red hair, who had detached herself from a group of ladies and was now at Robinson's elbow. Mrs Reinhardt and the three men did not bother to acknowledge her remark. 'This Degas,' the red-haired girl said miserably, 'it's getting out of the bathtub, for a change, not in.'

'You are playing, too, Paul?' Mrs Reinhardt asked Kohner as the red-haired girl, still ignored, moved back to her group.

'Maybe I'll go to Europe, Eddie,' Garfield said. 'I think I need Europe.'

Mrs Reinhardt joined her husband. 'Gottfried! Did they make the crêpes Hélène, Gottfried?'

'Yes, darling. I personally showed them how,' he said, giving his wife a pat on the head. 'Mingle with the wives. You must mingle.'

'I won't mingle,' said Mrs Reinhardt. 'I have an odd interior climate.' She wandered off.

Huston, very sunburned, arrived with his wife. In the lapel of his dinner jacket, he wore the ribbon of the Legion of Merit, awarded to him for his work on Army Signal Corps films in the war. 'Well!' he said, looking oppressed, and slightly alien to the overflowing intimacy that was advancing toward him.

'John!' Reinhardt said, as though it had been a couple of years instead of a couple of hours since they had last met. 'Ricki!' he said, greeting Mrs Huston with the same enthusiasm.

As Huston confronted the party about to envelop him, his face was contorted, like a baby about to explode into tears; then he relaxed into a slouch and went forward to meet his celebrators.

'Johnny!' someone said, and he quickly became the hub of a wheel of admirers. Mrs Huston, looking tremulous and beautiful, started uncertainly after him but stopped behind the circle, which included a director, William Wyler; a writer, Robert Wyler; Huston's lawyer, Mark Cohen; and Paul Kohner. As Mrs Huston joined a group of wives, there was a good deal of laughter in the circle around her husband. Cohen, a scholarly-looking gentleman with pince-nez, laughed good-naturedly at everything everybody said. Robert Wyler, William's elder brother and husband of an actress named Cathy O'Donnell, laughed at everything William said. Huston laughed without waiting for anything to be said.

'God love ya, Willie!' Huston said to William Wyler, putting a long arm all the way around his friend's shoulders and shaking him.

Wyler, a short, stocky, slow-speaking man with a self-absorbed expression, drew back and looked up at him. 'Johnny, you're getting older,' he said.

Laughter, led by Robert Wyler, thundered around the circle.

'Ho! Ho! Ho!' Huston said, forcing each laugh out with tremendous care. 'I've had nine lives so far, and I regret every one of them.'

At the door, Reinhardt greeted Sam Spiegel, Huston's partner in Horizon Pictures, and Spiegel's wife, Lynne Baggett, a tall, statuesque actress with fluffy blonde curls piled up on top of her head.

'So, Gottfried, you start rehearsals next week,' Spiegel said, his eyes flickering busily around at everybody except the man he was talking to. Spiegel, whose professional name is S. P. Eagle, is a stout, hawk-nosed man in his late forties with sad, moist eyes, an expression of harried innocence, and a habit of running his tongue swiftly along his upper lip. He was born in Austria, came to America in 1927, was working in Berlin for Universal Pictures when Hitler came to power, in 1933. He met Huston later that year, when both were looking for work in the British motion-picture industry. In 1947, learning that Huston was looking for fifty thousand dollars, Spiegel got the money and gave it to him in exchange for a promise to found an independent motion-picture company – Horizon Pictures – and to put half the money into it. Spiegel had then promoted, from the Bankers Trust Company in New York, a loan of nine hundred thousand dollars for Horizon's first film. He had gone on to promote for himself an extensive knowledge of what all the other producers in Hollywood were up to, and a proprietorship over Huston that most of them were jealous of. Reinhardt beamed at him as warmly as he had at the other guests. Mrs Reinhardt welcomed the Spiegels with an intensely playful air of surprise at their presence. Spiegel lingered at the door, stared at the admirers surrounding Huston, and told Reinhardt, without being asked, that he had just finished producing a Horizon film starring Evelyn Keyes, Huston's third wife (the present Mrs Huston is his fourth), and that he planned to make two more pictures while he was waiting for Huston to complete his Metro assignment with Reinhardt. 'Then John will make *The African Queen* with me,' Spiegel said. 'I get him next, Gottfried.'

'Fine,' Reinhardt said, bouncing up and down like an amiable bear.

'*The African Queen* can be a commercial success. It will give John the kind of commercial hit he had when he made *The Maltese Falcon* in 1941,' Spiegel said blandly.

'Fine,' Reinhardt said, ignoring the implication that *The Red Badge of Courage* would be a commercial failure.

'When do we start the poker game?' Spiegel asked.

'Fine,' said Reinhardt, still bouncing.

'Gottfried,' Spiegel said, 'when is the poker?'

'Gottfried!' Mrs Reinhardt said.

'Poker?' Reinhardt said. 'After dinner.'

Mrs Spiegel spoke for the first time. 'What do we do?' she asked.

'You go to a movie or something, baby,' said Spiegel. 'A nice double feature.' He tapped her arm, and they moved on into the room.

Mrs Reinhardt, watching them go, gave a cry of mock hysteria. 'Gottfried, nobody ever listens to anybody else!' she said. 'It's a condition of the world.'

'Fine,' Reinhardt said to her, and turned to greet a couple of late-comers. They were Band and his wife, a pert, slim girl, formerly a photographer's model, whose picture had appeared twice on the cover of a magazine called *Real Story*. The Bands were late because they had stopped to pick up a present for Huston. The present was a book of reproductions of French Impressionists.

'I believe in friendship,' Band said to Reinhardt, then made his way to Huston and delivered the present.

Huston unwrapped his present. 'This is just swell, amigo – just wonderful,' he said to Band. He closed the book and took a cigarette box out of his pocket. It was empty. 'Get me some cigarettes, will ya, kid?' he said.

Band rushed off for cigarettes.

Dave Chasen came into the room, sucking at a pipe, and asked Reinhardt if everything was all right.

'Fine,' said Reinhardt.

'I'll stay a minute,' Chasen said, and sighed. 'What I have to listen to out there! And everybody wants to sit in the front. If I put everybody in the front, who will sit in the back?' He went over to Huston, saying 'John!'

'Dave! God love ya, Dave!' Huston said, giving the restaurateur his long-armed embrace.

'Dave!' half a dozen voices called. 'Dave! Dave!' Everybody seemed to make it a point to sound his name, but only Mrs Reinhardt appeared to have anything to say to him. She told him that she was worried about her black French poodle. 'Mocha is so neurotic, Dave, he refuses to eat. Dave, he wants lobster. Can I take home some lobster for Mocha, Dave?'

Chasen said all right, sighed again, and returned to his duties.

At dinner – before the men started their poker game and the women went to a movie – the guests sat at circular tables seating six, and between courses they moved from table to table, discussing the party as compared to other parties. Everybody was talking about the decline of big parties. People were cutting down on the big parties, they said. When did Nunnally Johnson give that big tent party? Four years ago. The tent alone, put up over his tennis court, had cost seven hundred dollars. The tent was of Pliofilm, and you could look up and see stars in the sky through it. You hardly ever found a party any more where the host rented a dance floor from that company that rented terrific dance floors. It was easier, and less expensive, to give a party at Chasen's.

'We entertain each other because we never know how to enjoy ourselves with other people,' Reinhardt said to the guests at his table. 'Hollywood people are afraid to leave Hollywood. Out in the world, they are frightened. They are unsure of themselves. They never enjoy themselves out of Hollywood. Sam Hoffenstein used to say we are the croupiers in a crooked gambling house. And it's true. Every one of us thinks, You know, I really don't deserve a swimming pool.'

The guests did not seem to mind what he had said, but on the other hand, there was no indication that anyone had listened to him.

Everything Has Just Gone Zoom

THE week before rehearsals started on *The Red Badge of Courage*, Reinhardt and Huston found it a little hard to believe that they actually had a starting date (25 August 1950) and a work schedule (nine rehearsal days and thirty-four shooting days). As the rehearsals approached, Reinhardt kept repeating to Huston that they would make 'a *great* picture'; the picture would be profitable to Loew's, Inc., and at the same time it would duplicate the quality of the Stephen Crane novel and be *great* artistically. Huston, in turn, kept repeating that the picture had 'a wonderful cast, with wonderful faces'. Whenever Huston or Reinhardt received an inter-office communication from one of the thirty-two departments involved in the production of their picture, he was able to reassure himself of the reality of the project by noting that on the memo the 'Subject' was described, convincingly, as 'Production No. 1512' and that copies were going to all the key executives, including Schenck himself, in New York. If a memo went to Schenck, it was real. A couple of times, when Huston was looking over a memo, he said to Reinhardt, 'You know, we're really going to *make* the picture.'

On the eve of the first rehearsals, I dropped in on Reinhardt and Huston at Reinhardt's house, where they were working on the script. Reinhardt lived in Bel Air, on a winding narrow road high in the hills overlooking Beverly Hills. The house was in a hollow, and it resembled the English mansion in the movie version of *Wuthering Heights* – gabled, dark, and forbidding. I found the two men in a study that had deep leather armchairs, two loveseats, and a green-tiled fireplace, in which stood a couple of tropical plants. Beyond a wide archway was a gloomy, cavernous room where the outline of a grand piano was visible. Reinhardt, holding a copy of the script, was pacing back and forth in front of an armchair in which Huston, comfortably dressed in a pink-checked cotton shirt, grey flannel

slacks, and loafers, lay sprawled, his long legs stretched out and a
copy of the script on his lap. Reinhardt's collar was unbuttoned and
his necktie hung loosely around his shoulders. A long strand of
hair had fallen over his right eye, and the stub of a cigar was in his
mouth. He explained to me that they were devising dialogue for a
scene in which the Youth and his comrades, marching to their first
battle, are taunted by battle-scarred veterans.

'You got anything?' Reinhardt asked Huston, stepping over his
legs. Albert Band, Huston's assistant, entered the room and started
pacing behind Reinhardt. Huston was rhythmically banging his
chin against his chest. Then, after drawing little sketches of Reinhardt in the margin of his script, he scribbled some words. 'Write
this down, Albert,' he said. '"Hang your clothes on a hickory limb,
and don't go near the battle!"'

'Good,' Band said, writing it down. 'Very good.'

'Now!' Reinhardt said, standing still for a moment. 'We need
words for Scene 1 1 0. Or you can ad-lib it on the set.'

Huston turned the pages of the script, a mimeographed booklet
stamped on the cover with the words 'Production No. 1 5 1 2', to the
scene:

MEDIUM SHOT — BACK OF THE LINE OF FIRING MEN

A private is fleeing, screaming, from his place in the line.
He is met and stopped by the captain of the reserves who
grabs him by the collar. The private is blubbering and
staring with sheeplike eyes at the captain, who is pounding
him.

Huston said, 'I think this would be good if it's not said. Just have
this little bit of action.'

'You have to say *something*,' Reinhardt said.

'We'll do it on the set,' said Huston. 'I want to see how it looks
first.'

Reinhardt rotated the cigar stub in his mouth. 'Albert, go tell
the cook we'll eat in half an hour,' he said, and Band left the
room.

Huston shifted to a loveseat and lay back, his hands clasped behind his head. He seemed lost in some remote thought. Suddenly he jerked his head in a conspiratorial way at Reinhardt and, taking a piece of paper from his pocket, said he wanted to read something aloud. On 23 April 1863, he said, his great-grandfather, Colonel William P. Richardson, received a silver-sheathed sword from the non-commissioned officers and privates of the 25th Regiment, Ohio Volunteer Infantry, and he was going to put the sword in the movie; it would be worn by the actor playing the part of the Youth's general. 'We ought to put this kind of talk in the picture, too,' he said. 'Listen. This is from the speech my great-grandfather's superior officer made when he presented it to him: "Wealth, influence, or favouritism might procure such a gift as this, but the esteem and confidence of brave men cannot be bought." Jesus, Gottfried, people don't talk like that any more!'

Reinhardt nodded, then glanced impatiently at his script.

'My mother had that speech copied,' Huston said. 'He was her grandfather. I've got a Brady of him.'

'Your mother would have been pleased to know that you're making The Red Badge of Courage,' Reinhardt said. He looked rather taken with his own adroitness in bringing his director back to the task of the hour.

'Nothing I ever did pleased my mother,' Huston said.

Band came back, and Reinhardt said that they would have to work on the script every night after rehearsals. Huston told him they were farther ahead than he seemed to think.

'We accomplished a lot today,' Band said.

'We really must finish,' Reinhardt said, with restrained desperation.

'Don't worry about it, amigo,' said Huston.

'Remember that night in this room when we both said we wanted to make the picture?' Reinhardt said. 'I said to you, "What about making The Red Badge of Courage?" And you said, "That's my dream." And we shook hands.' Reinhardt looked very serious. 'L. B. begged me not to do this picture,' he said. 'He was like a father to me.'

Mrs Reinhardt came in, wearing black jersey ballet tights and shirt, and ballet slippers. She had a black apron tied over the tights, and the apron strings floated behind her like a tail. She was accompanied by Mocha, her black French poodle. Band started to sit down in an armchair, but Mocha beat him to it.

'Today, Mocha ate four bananas,' Mrs Reinhardt said.

Reinhardt did not look at her. He said to Huston, 'L. B. called me into his office and talked for hours about the kind of pictures that make money. He said he was telling me for my own good. I thought he would weep.'

'L. B. is *weeping*?' Mrs Reinhardt said.

'He didn't want us to make the picture, honey,' Huston said.

Mrs Reinhardt said, 'Gottfried, should I let Mocha eat strawberries?'

Reinhardt said, 'L. B. told Dore if he thought we should make the picture, to go ahead and make it.'

'Hang yourselves, boys, in other words,' Huston said cheerfully.

Reinhardt looked at him shyly and laughed. 'Now L. B. puts Dore on the spot with this picture,' he said. 'He has his arm around Dore. And he says he loves Dore.' He laughed, and then he looked serious. 'Frankly, I'm worried,' he said. 'The book is about the thoughts of the Youth. Will we show what really goes on inside the boy?'

'Audie Murphy will show it, Gottfried,' Huston said.

'You wanted Audie,' said Reinhardt.

'Yes,' Huston said in a patient tone.

'Montgomery Clift – ' Reinhardt began.

'Don't worry, Gottfried,' Huston said.

'This must be a *great* picture,' Reinhardt said.

'Don't worry, Gottfried,' Huston said.

Around the same time, Huston's agent, Paul Kohner, submitted the script to a local psychologist for reassurance that the theme of *The Red Badge of Courage* – that of a boy who runs away from his first battle and then, when he returns to his comrades, performs heroic acts in his next battle – was valid. The psychologist turned in a typewritten report stating that the script told the story of a soldier who surmounts his fear complex and becomes a hero, in accordance with the established theory that a courageous action can be a direct reaction to cowardice. 'Of course, it is presupposed dramaturgically that the psychosis of fear is taken as a fact,' he wrote. 'And so automatically the question arises as to whether such a conception can be generalized. . . . Since the motives of his heroism are of purely psychopathic origin it should be stated that the filmic description of the psychological evolution fails to convince at the important moments. This is a cardinal fault in regard to the conception of the matter.' He then suggested several additional scenes that would explain the Youth's change from cowardice to heroism in battle. 'These differentiated psychological Zwischentöne have to be plastically formed,' he wrote, and added that if his suggestions were followed 'the picture could be the outstanding one of the year'.

Huston and Reinhardt read the analysis, exchanged bleak looks, and had it filed.

The morning of the day rehearsals were to start, on Huston's ranch, Huston, a red-and-green-checked cap on his head, a brown cigarette in his mouth, and his arms folded on the top bar of a white rail fence separating a small ranchhouse from his stables, watched his adopted son, Pablo, saddle a big black horse. It was the horse from whose back Huston intended to direct the picture. The horse moved impatiently under the saddle.

'All right, baby,' Huston said soothingly.

'Take it easy, baby,' said Pablo. 'Dad, you want me to walk him a little bit?'

'Just hold him there, Pablo,' said Huston, and exhaled a stream of cigarette smoke with an expression of happy fulfilment. He mounted the horse, and with a quick, dramatic gesture, he pulled his cap down farther over his forehead, and then, taking the reins in both hands, he sat facing the dry rutty dirt road leading away from the stables. The big horse stood motionless. Huston sat in silence, staring grimly ahead for a moment. 'Well now, Pablo,' he said, with intense emphasis on each syllable. 'Keep an eye on everything back here, amigo.' Then he started the horse down the road (MEDIUM SHOT) at an easy, rocking walk, stirring up a cloud of dust in his wake.

Huston stopped his horse beside a large oak tree next to a dry, barren, yellow field. Studio limousines and a large studio bus were parked in the field. A pyramid of rifles was stacked near the bus. Under the oak tree sat Harold Rosson, the cameraman, with Reggie Callow, assistant director; Lee Katz, unit manager; Andrew Marton, the 'leapfrog' director; Colonel Paul Davison, the technical adviser; and Albert Band.

Callow stepped forward and gave a brisk salute. 'The troops are in good shape, Mr Huston, sir,' he said. 'Been drilling them for an hour.'

'Very good, amigo,' Huston said.

'Rough day,' Katz said. 'Hot, hot.'

A dozen of the studio's stock actors, in blue uniforms and kepis, lounged about on the grass. Not far from them was another group, consisting of a script clerk, a still photographer, a few assistant and second assistant directors, a few assistant and second assistant cameramen, grips (the movie equivalent of stagehands), and property men. The leading members of the cast, all in blue uniforms, sat in a circle on the ground playing poker: Audie Murphy, the Youth; Bill Mauldin, the Loud Soldier; John Dierkes, the Tall Soldier; Royal Dano, the Tattered Man; and Douglas Dick, the Lieutenant.

'All right, lads,' Huston said. He dismounted, tied his horse's reins to a branch of the tree, and spent the next hour conferring with Rosson on camera problems. The stock players lolled about, blank-faced and resigned. They were being paid a hundred and seventy-five dollars a week, and audiences wouldn't notice them enough to remember their faces. Some were on the way up; that is, they were being given work more and more regularly. Others were on the way down. All of them had the manner of men who expected no major surprises. The leading actors made a great show of casualness and boredom, and then became genuinely bored, genuinely casual, and gave up the poker game. Bill Mauldin, his kepi pushed back and a cigarette holder stuck jauntily in his mouth, held the others' attention for a while with a series of jokes.

'Hell, this is ditch-diggin' work,' Mauldin remarked at one point. 'I'm just here raisin' scratch, so's I can go back home and work on my play.' He started to roll a cigarette.

Dano took a pack from his pocket and held it out.

'Hell,' Mauldin said, 'I was rollin' my own when you was in three-cornered pants.'

'Gosh, Bill,' Dierkes drawled. 'You talk just like the Loud Soldier.'

'Hell,' Mauldin said, looking proud and pleased, and ducked his head.

Dano remarked amiably that working in pictures was fine with him. He seemed at ease and as well suited to the role of the Tattered Man as Mauldin was to the Loud Soldier. He was unshaven and gaunt – so skinny that his bones protruded. He had large dark eyes, long lashes, and black hair, which was hanging raggedly over his ears. His uniform was torn and his shirt-tail was outside his trousers. He looked as though he had always worn tatters. He yawned, stretched out on the ground with his head on a rock, and went to sleep.

Dierkes turned to Murphy, who, with a troubled expression, was staring at the top of a tree, and asked him how he felt.

Murphy said that his malaria was acting up again, that he had had an attack of nausea while driving out to the ranch, and that he was going to lie down in Huston's ranchhouse.

As Murphy walked slowly away, Dierkes shook his head and said to Mauldin that he was amazed whenever he realized that Murphy was the most-decorated soldier of the last war. 'When the war ended, he wasn't even old enough to vote,' he added. In a tone of deep respect, Dierkes, who had an enormous interest in other people, said that Murphy was one of nine children of a Texas share-cropper who abandoned his family when Murphy was fourteen. The mother died two years later. Murphy was working in a radio-repair shop when the war came. He tried to enlist in the Marines and then in the paratroops, but was turned down because he was underweight. He finally got into the infantry. Among his decorations were the Medal of Honour, the Distinguished Service Cross, the Silver Star, the Legion of Merit, the Bronze Star, the Croix de Guerre, and the Purple Heart. 'Now look at the little sport,' Dierkes said.

'Hell, amigo, he's in a war picture, ain't he?' Mauldin said.

'All right, lads!' Huston called. They woke Dano up, and the first rehearsal began.

The rehearsals concentrated less on the acting than on preparations for getting the actors photographed. Huston studied his actors from various points through a finder, and conferred with Rosson about the placing of the camera, composing the basic plan of each scene with the meticulous care of a painter at work on a picture. A scene in which the Loud Soldier was to run up to a group of comrades and shout that the Army was moving into battle would have to look as if it were near a river where, in the previous scene, the Loud Soldier had heard the news. The latter scene would be filmed at the Sacramento River location, near Chico, California, several hundred miles north of the ranch. At the end of the nine-day rehearsal period, the company would go up to Chico for several days of additional rehearsal and shooting.

After a couple of hours, the cast and crew had lunch, provided by an M-G-M catering truck, in the field. Lee Katz told Huston that in the course of making the picture ten thousand five hundred box lunches would be served, at a cost to Metro of $15,750 – one of the smaller items in the picture's budget. During lunch, a prop man brought Huston a box containing old-fashioned watches of several styles and asked him to choose one for a scene in which the Loud Soldier, fearing that he will be killed in battle, gives his watch to the Youth. Another prop man carried over three small, squealing pigs and asked Huston to choose the one that would be stolen from a farm girl in a scene featuring a soldier pillaging a farmyard. Huston chose a watch and cast a pig, and then called for a rehearsal of a scene between Murphy and Mauldin just before their first battle.

Murphy sat under an oak tree, and Mauldin sat several yards behind the tree. Huston and Rosson squatted in front of them. Callow, his script open to the scene, stood behind Huston. The script clerk, whose name was Jack Aldworth, conferred with Callow about time schedules. Colonel Davison sat at the roadside with Marton, who began to tell how he had narrowly escaped death at the hands of African natives while making King Solomon's Mines. The stock players lolled nearby.

'All right, Billy, come on down,' Huston said to Mauldin, putting the finder to his eyes. Through it he watched Mauldin come down and lean over Murphy's shoulder, saying, 'Why, hello, Henry. Is it you? What yeh doin' here?'

'Oh, thinkin',' said Murphy.

Huston did not seem to be paying any attention to the performances of the actors. Occasionally, he interrupted to ask them to look in this direction or that, and he discussed with Rosson where the camera should be placed and how much of the tree should be in the picture.

After the rehearsal of the scene was over, Huston made his first comment on the acting. He drew Murphy aside and told him that there was a humorous aspect to the Youth's fear. 'Fear in a man is something tragic or reprehensible, you know, Audie?' he said. 'But fear in a youth – it's ludicrous.'

Murphy nodded solemnly.

'All right, amigo,' Huston said, clapping him on the shoulder. 'You just work it out for yourself.'

'Here comes the producer, boys!' someone shouted. 'Act busy!'

Reinhardt plodded slowly across the sun-baked, yellow field. A fresh cigar was in his mouth, and a blue beret was on his head. He shook Huston's hand and asked him how things were going.

'Wonderful, Gottfried,' said Huston. 'Just wonderful.'

As the rehearsals progressed, Huston seemed to show a greater interest in the acting of some scenes, and he was particularly interested in one in which Murphy discovered his comrade the Tall Soldier, Dierkes, in the line of wounded men straggling away from the battle the Youth had run away from. Dano, the Tattered Man, trudged along a dirt road, one arm dangling at his side. Murphy came from behind a clump of bushes and fell in with him. The Tattered Man looked fervently at him. 'Th' boys ain't had no fair chanct up t' now, but this time they showed what they was,' Dano said. 'I knowed it'd turn out this way. Yeh can't lick them boys. No, sir! They're fighters, they be. Where yeh hit, ol' boy?' Dierkes came shuffling past them. Murphy started after him, calling his name, and put a hand on his arm.

At this point, Huston fell into step with Murphy and Dierkes, his face signalling grotesque and terrible emotions, which were not apparent in the faces of the actors. Band brought up the rear, following the lines in the script.

'I was allus a good friend t' yeh, wa'n't I, Henry?' Dierkes said, in a kind of delirium. 'I've allus been a pretty good feller, ain't I? An' it ain't much t' ask, is it? Jest t' pull me along outer th' road? I'd do it fer you, wouldn't I, Henry?'

Murphy tried to get Dierkes to lean on him for support.

'No, no, no, leave me be,' Dierkes said, pulling away.

Huston elbowed Dierkes aside and put Murphy's hand on his own arm. 'When you say "No, no, no, leave me be," start to go down and make him let go of you,' he told Dierkes. He stumbled and fell forward, loosening Murphy's grip. 'All right, try it again – by yourselves this time.'

Huston lit a brown cigarette as the actors moved back up the path to do the scene again. Inhaling deeply, as though in anger, he said that Dano was wonderful. 'That boy is an *actor*,' he said. 'He's a great actor. I don't have to tell him a goddam thing. The only other actor I've known who had that was Dad. But Dierkes will be wonderful in the picture. That face! Even when an actor is limited in his acting experience, you can cover for him. You can get him to do things that don't require acting.' He threw his cigarette down and ground it out. 'You make him let go of you as you start to go *down*,' he said to Dierkes in a soft voice.

Dierkes looked puzzled. 'Don't I pull my arm away from him?'

'Do whatever you want to do with your goddam arm,' said the director. 'The point is you *make* him let go of you by falling.'

Dierkes looked more puzzled. 'I see, John,' he said.

'Once more,' Huston said crisply.

There were only a few days left of the allotted rehearsal time. The company had become tense. With a certain air of impatience with the problem, Huston had tried to communicate to the others his ideas and feelings for composing the various shots, and he had talked about the way things might eventually look on the screen. The others had tried to demonstrate that they understood just what he was driving at. But the strain was beginning to tell. One joke that made the rounds of the cast and crew was 'This is getting to be a long war'. The most popular one was 'Did you hear about the coward who quit M-G-M to join the Army?'

Reinhardt was becoming dissatisfied with the script. He acted like a man under pressure. He lost weight, and smoked more cigars every day. Huston showed no sign of being under any pressure. He was able to turn from one thing to another with ease, good humour, and concentration. In a single hour one day, he did the following: When Dusty, the official cowboy on Huston's ranch, wanted to know when he would be given a part in the picture, Huston entered into a long, involved discussion with him about why it was necessary for a man to choose between a career in pictures and life on the range, and how much better the latter was in the long run. From Dusty, he turned to Audie Murphy, and asked him to look through the finder at the hilltop where the Tall Soldier would die. 'He goes to die in the open, Audie,' Huston said. 'Do you feel the sense of expanse up there?' He went into a long, involved explanation of why a man chooses to die in the open. From Murphy, Huston turned to Rosson, to work out the details of placing the camera on a dolly, or wheeled platform, and of building dolly tracks for scenes in which the camera would have to roll along with moving actors. From Rosson, Huston turned to a telephone to take a call from Sam Spiegel, his partner in Horizon Pictures; he told Spiegel he might be free to work on Horizon's next picture, The African Queen, in four months. From the telephone, he turned to Hans Peters, the art director, to inquire whether a night scene filmed on a set at the studio would look as real as one filmed outdoors. From Peters, Huston turned to a newspaper photographer who wanted him to pose with Mrs Huston, who was watching rehearsals, for what he called a happy-go-lucky family shot, and he agreed to pose later that day. From the photographer, Huston turned to a tree branch lying in the road and demonstrated with it how a jockey twirls a whip. From the tree branch, Huston turned to his wife, who told him that he was expected to appear in an hour, in black tie, at a dinner party at the home of L. B. Mayer.

The operating budget for Production No. 1512 was by now complete. It showed that the total cost was supposed to come to $1,434,789, including:

Direction	$156,010
Story and Continuity	41,992
Cast	82,250
Departmental Overhead	238,000
Rent and Purchase Props	80,800
Extras	145,058
Cameramen	25,500
Sound	35,177
Cutters and Projectionists	15,650
Producer's Unit Charge	102,120
Production Staff	30,915
Stills and Stillmen	6,995
Picture Film and Dev.	17,524
Sound Film and Dev.	8,855
Music	12,620
Wardrobe	43,000
Make-up and Hairdressers	13,915
Auto and Truck Hire	49,125
Meals and Lodging	35,385
Travel and Transportation	6,360
Location Fees and Expenses	18,255
Misc.	23,850

In a breakdown of these figures, the estimate showed that Audie Murphy was scheduled for forty-seven working days at a salary of $2,500 a week; his cost to the production would be $25,000. Bill Mauldin, working the same number of days at $2,000 a week, would cost $15,667. John Dierkes would work thirty days at $600 a week and would cost $3,000; Douglas Dick, forty-six days at $800 a week, would cost $6,133; Royal Dano, twenty-four days at $750 a week, would cost $3,000. The Story and Continuity cost included $10,000 paid to the estate and the publisher of Stephen Crane for the rights to film the novel, and $28,000 paid to the writer of the screenplay – Huston. The Directorial charges included Huston's $4,000-a-week salary, totalling $137,334.

The Rent and Purchase Props included $33,370 for the use of horses and the services of their trainers. The figures for the battle scenes indicated that they would be violent as well as expensive: eighty thousand rounds of ammunition, at $110 per thousand, would come to $8,800; three caissons had to be reconditioned at $25 each; two hundred and fifty 45-70 rifles with bayonets and slings would come to $200. There would be ten Confederate flags ($65) and two Union flags ($13). Six dummy horse carcasses were to be bought at $275 each. Among the battle regalia that was being rented were two Union battle drums, at $5 each per week; two short bugles, at $3.50 each per week; twenty pairs of carbine boots, at $1.50 a pair per week; thirty nose bags, at one dollar each per week; a hundred infantry packs and blanket rolls suitable for foreground use, at $1.50 each per week; and twenty-five cavalry sabres, at $5 each per week. The Production Staff charge of $30,915 included the cost of Lee Katz ($8,718), of two assistant directors ($5,366, half of which represented Reggie Callow's cost to the picture), of two second assistant directors ($2,609), and of Jack Aldworth, the script clerk ($1,430). The estimate explained that Aldworth would be paid $160 a week while on location, and $140 a week at the studio. Of the money to be paid to the cameramen, Rosson, at a weekly salary of $750, would receive $11,250.

The Sound charges were broken down in this fashion: twenty-nine days of recording at the studio would cost $7,337; two days of playback, $506; the use of the public-address system for fifty-eight days, $4,002; and 30,000 feet of re-recording, or dubbing, at sixteen cents a foot, $4,800. The estimate for Picture Film and Dev. showed the expenses involved in buying and processing both negatives and positives, and that the job would take more than forty times as much film as was expected to appear in the final product. The 180,000 feet of black-and-white negative, at 4·1 cents a foot, would cost $7,380; the processing of 165,000 feet of black-and-white negative, at 2·5 cents a foot, would cost $4,125; 155,000 feet of black-and-white positive, at 1.283 cents a foot, would cost $1,989; and the processing of it, at 2·6 cents a foot, would cost $4,030.

The breakdown of the Wardrobe charges of $43,000 revealed that uniforms for officers would cost more than those for soldiers in both the Union and Confederate Armies. In addition to old uniforms on hand in the wardrobe department, there would be a hundred and twenty-five new ones for Union soldiers at $50 each ($6,250), twenty-five new Union officers' outfits at $75 each ($1,875), and ten Confederate officers' uniforms at the same price ($750). The cost of Music, including a thirty-five-piece orchestra, was figured on a basis of $600 an hour. Box lunches, as Lee Katz had pointed out, would cost $15,750.

The cost of extras and bit players was broken down scene by scene:

> EXT. Fording River (Chico)
> Sc. 65–66 – soldiers slide down bank, cross stream, and climb hill – $2,850
> EXT. Farm (Ranch)
> Sc. 43–47 – soldiers side with farm girl as she berates fat soldier for attempting to snatch pig

fat soldier	$150
girl	$150
ad-libs (4) @ $55	$220
extras – total	$2,431

One of the least expensive shots would show the body of a dead soldier in the woods. (The Youth would come upon the body after he had run away from the battle.) The only cost for this, other than the overhead and Murphy's salary, would be the wages of the extra who would play dead – $25. Extras who spoke lines would be paid an additional $23 for each day they spoke. The battle scenes would be the most expensive. The Confederate charge that causes many Union soldiers, including the Youth, to flee would cost $16,469.

Reinhardt, Huston, and the cast and crew of *The Red Badge of Courage* were accompanied to Chico, for the first shooting on the film, by Mrs Huston, Pablo, and Mrs Reinhardt. The Hustons, the Reinhardts, and the leading members of the cast were quartered in the Oaks Hotel there. (The other members of the company were scattered about the town.) The Oaks is a small, neat, rectangular building in the centre of a small, neat, rectangular town.

Late in the morning of the first day, Mrs Reinhardt sat gloomily in a high-backed chair in the lobby. She was wearing a high-necked dress of mossy-green sheer silk with a golden butterfly at the throat, and high-heeled black pumps. She looked chic and elegant. The other lobby-sitters were for the most part gentlemen dozing under ten-gallon hats. A newspaper lay in Mrs Reinhardt's lap; a black banner head stretched from one side to the other: 'AMERICANS SMASH RED ROADBLOCK.' Huston and Reinhardt were on the Sacramento River, eight miles away, with some stunt men who were trying to find a safe and cinematically attractive site for the scene in which the Youth's regiment would cross a river. The actors were rehearsing in a park four miles away. It was a twenty-four-hundred-acre park, and Mrs Reinhardt told me she did not have the faintest notion where to find anybody in it, even if she were dressed for the excursion.

'It's wilderness and you need trousers,' she said to me. 'Gottfried loathes me in trousers. The temperature outside is *one hundred and five degrees*. Have you read the news?' She opened the newspaper and pointed to a headline read-in, 'MOVING-PICTURE CREWS ARRIVE IN CHICO FOR FILMING OF CIVIL WAR DRAMA SHOTS'.

'We are famous,' Mrs Reinhardt said dryly. She closed the newspaper and sighed in utter despair. 'Why am I here?' she asked.

Huston was in an expansive mood. He was sitting behind the desk in a room in the Oaks Hotel, his chair tipped back and his heels resting on the desk, and looking over some local citizens who, in response to advertisements, were applying for bit parts in the picture. He loved to use the faces of non-professional actors in his pictures, he told me, and besides it cost less to hire bit-part players and extras – a couple of hundred men would be engaged at $10 a day each to appear as members of the Youth's regiment in the Union Army – locally than it would to transport them from Hollywood. The first applicant to come in was an eager, hard-breathing young man named Dixon Porter. He had a round, innocent face and an incongruously heavy black beard. Huston gave him a gracious nod. 'Nice beard you've got there, Dixon,' he said. He picked up a long pad of yellow paper and started making sketches of Dixon and various types of beards.

Reggie Callow, who was attending the audition, along with Colonel Davison and the other assistant director, Joel Freeman, said that beards were almost as important as talent for these bit parts.

'M-G-M offers a five-dollar bonus to every man with a good beard!' Callow said, in a raucous voice. 'Go ahead, Dixon. Read.'

Dixon Porter read, '"Ain't they a sight to behold, in their brand-new uniforms! Hang yer clothes on a hickory limb and don't go near the battle!"'

'Thank you, Dixon,' Huston said. 'Very good, Dixon. Thank you very much.'

'We'll let you know, Dixon,' Callow said mechanically, ushering the applicant out.

'That boy is good,' Huston said. 'Not tough but good. We'll find some use for him. Now let's get some real grizzled sons of bitches.' He went back to his sketching.

The next applicant was a thin young man with a long, dolorous face, horn-rimmed glasses, and a soft beard. He said he belonged to a local little-theatre group. After he had read and departed, Huston told Callow they needed tougher-looking men, tough as hell.

'Every time you get little theatre, you get these delicate fellas,' Callow said.

The third applicant, who was accompanied by his three-year-old daughter, explained earnestly that he hadn't been able to get a baby-sitter. Huston tore off the page he had been sketching on, crumpled it up, and threw it on the floor. The earnest father and the three-year-old went out again.

'Joel!' Huston said sternly to the other assistant director, a serious young man with a crew haircut. 'Joel, you go out tonight to the pool-rooms! To the gas stations! Find the tough guys and bring them back. We need guys who look tough.'

'You mean guys who look – ' Freeman began.
'Tough!' said Huston.

Reinhardt had finally pinned Huston down to the job of revising the script with him. They worked in Huston's hotel room, with Albert Band, making some changes requested by Joseph I. Breen, the Motion Picture Production Code Administrator. Huston lay on the bed, his back resting against the head-board, and sketched thoughtfully on a yellow pad as Band read off the lines that were considered objectionable.

'"Gawd, he's runnin',"' Band read.
'"Look, he's runnin',"' Huston said in a bored voice.
'"It'll be hell to pay,"' Band read.
'"It'll be the devil to pay,"' said Huston.
'You can't say that,' Reinhardt said.
Huston said, 'The hell you can't.'
'Joe Breen – ' Reinhardt began.
'All right,' Huston interrupted. '"It'll be the dickens to pay."'
'"Damn tobacco,"' Band continued.
'Take "damn" out,' said Huston.
'That takes care of your censor problem for now,' said Band.
Reinhardt directed him to make copies of the changes and send them to Metro's Script Department. Then he looked uncertainly at Huston. 'You don't like to write?' he asked.
'When I put pencil to paper, I find myself sketching,' Huston said. 'I can't write alone – I get too lonely. I have to dictate.'
Reinhardt asked him to try to write some dialogue for the Youth's officers just before the regiment went into action, to give the audience an idea of the position of the Youth's regiment in relation to the battle. Reluctantly, Huston set to work. Reinhardt went to his own room for a cigar. When he returned, Huston said. 'Here's a speech. The Colonel rides up behind the lines and says to the Captain, "Captain, the Rebs are on that hill over there. We're goin' to try an' push them off. Maybe we will, maybe we won't. Anyway, take positions on that road down there and hold it whatever happens!" Captain says, "We'll stand, Colonel, sir!"'
'Good!' Reinhardt said explosively.

'It's got to be kept simple,' Huston said, looking pleased.

'Good!' Band said explosively.

The telephone rang. Band answered it and told Huston it was Sam Spiegel, calling from Hollywood. Huston said to say he wasn't in. Reinhardt bit off the end of his cigar and smiled happily.

Late in the afternoon of the day before the shooting of the picture was to start, Huston asked Harold Rosson if he wanted to go fishing. Rosson said no, adding that he had been bitten by a wasp, burned by the sun, and exhausted by tramping through underbrush in search of locations, and besides, he had a bad dust cold; he was going to bed. Undaunted, Huston said that he was going fishing. Pablo escorted Mrs Reinhardt on a shopping trip, from which she returned with an outfit, recommended by Pablo, to wear on location – a pair of Army suntans, a green T-shirt, and a green pork-pie hat. At the Oaks, Andrew Marton passed around a copy of the *Hollywood Reporter* in which the column 'Trade Views', written by W. R. Wilkerson, the paper's owner, was devoted entirely to the leapfrog method being used in making *The Red Badge of Courage*. (This was a reference to Marton's job of getting scenes lined up for Huston so that they could be shot without delay.) The column said, 'Reinhardt and Huston are trying to make the picture with as little cost as possible. Such activity is to be congratulated and given every encouragement.'

At two o'clock in the morning of the day the shooting was to start, Reinhardt sat down and wrote a letter to Huston:

Dear John:

Well – today is the day! After all the cliffs and shallows we have had to circumnavigate, it seems almost miraculous that this day should have come at all and so soon. How well I remember that night in my house, when at two o'clock we suddenly, enthusiastically, almost recklessly decided on The Red Badge of Courage *! Well, the first phase is completed. We didn't 'run'. However, taking a leaf from our book, that isn't enough. We now must prove that we are real heroes. Or better, you must prove it. For I, the more or less unarmed lieutenant, can merely egg you on. It is you who will have to engage the enemy from today on, and I know that you will give a wonderful account of yourself. To that end* you have my very best wishes, my unshakeable confidence, and, if you want, my help.

I needn't tell you that the course ahead will be far from an easy one. The deep waters we have reached offer far greater dangers than the petty little political cliffs and financial shallows we were able to avoid. And they require much more than your amazing talents (which are a pleasure to watch) or whatever circumspection I was able to lend our venture. They require your constant, untiring watchfulness.

Let me – on this day – point out the main problems as they come to mind one by one:

(1) Audie Murphy. He needs your constant attention, all your ingenuity (photographically and directorially), all the inspiration you can give him. He shouldn't be left alone for a single second. Nothing should be taken for granted. At the risk of making myself a tremendous bore, CONCENTRATE ON AUDIE MURPHY! I watched him. I believe he will be good. How good (and the whole picture depends on the degree) depends entirely on the support you give him.

(2) Variety. Change of pace. At the speed you are going to do this in all respects terribly difficult picture and the crazy continuity you will shoot it in, there is the danger of losing the rhythm of the continuity; the tempo might become too even, the moods too similar. In view of the general sameness of the background and the subtlety and introspectiveness of the development, I beg you to examine and re-examine every scene in the light of what precedes and follows the action. This may sound like childish advice. But I know how easy it is to get bogged down in the physical difficulties alone.

(3) Humour. Wherever you see the opportunity, bring it out; wherever you can, inject it!

(4) Geography. I know you are aware of that. But I repeat: it is imperative that we always know where we are. Especially the transitions from one locale to another must be smooth and clear.

(5) Script. Every hour you can spare (and I know this is going to be tough from now on) you ought to spend on the script until, from beginning to end, it is in a shape to your own satisfaction. Needless to say, I am at your disposal all the time. You have no idea – or maybe you have – how the days and hours you spent on the script (away from the set) in the last few weeks improved it.

That is all. Regarding the last point, I must add that you made me very unhappy last night. You know I was waiting for you. But it wasn't so much your failure to tell me that you went fishing which disturbed me (although it wouldn't have hurt if you had done it), but I know we would have accomplished a lot, maybe finished the

script, if you had kept our appointment. Now that the shooting starts it will be twice
as difficult. After all, that is the main reason why I came. If we can't get together, I
might as well pack up and go home. I hope you won't mind my frankness in telling
you this. You asked me once to be your 'boss'. I can't do that. I can only be your
accomplice and friend. And in those capacities, I am anxious and ready to lend you
whatever assistance I can.

And now, good luck! I have a feeling something quite extraordinary is likely to
come out of all this. But whatever will be the outcome, I can tell you one thing
already: it has been a great experience to be associated with you. And somehow I am
quite calm: we will steer our ship safely and proudly into port.

Always,
Gottfried

Reinhardt's letter was not the only one Huston received in the
morning. At breakfast with Murphy and Mauldin, he read a letter
from Dore Schary that said, 'Today's your day, and with it goes all
my best to you. I'm sure, John, we'll get a damned good movie
out of Red Badge – one that we'll all be proud of. Good luck and
good shooting. Sincerely, DORE.' Joe Cohn, the head of Metro's
Production Office (logistics, budgets, etc.), wired Huston,
'YOU ARE DOING A WAR PICTURE. SHOOT – SHOOT –
SHOOT.'

The atmosphere at the breakfast table was one of readiness.
Murphy and Mauldin, the two leading men, had on their blue uniforms and kepis. They listened abstractedly as Huston, putting his
correspondence aside and playing nervously with a couple of
quarters, told them about Nate Leipsig, who he said was the greatest
coin manipulator in history. Then Huston, who was wearing
regulation Army suntans, stood up, put a Mexican straw hat on, took
a gulp of coffee, and said he would see the boys outside. A few
minutes later, Huston and Reinhardt, who wore blue cotton slacks
and a matching knit shirt and was carrying a pith helmet, came out.
Both men were looking grim. 'I want to ride out with you, Gottfried,'
Huston was saying. Reinhardt nodded benignly and clapped the
helmet on his head.

The first scene to be shot, No. 72, read:

MEDIUM SHOT − NEW ANGLE

The regiment encounters the body of a dead soldier and the ranks open covertly to avoid the corpse.

It was being set up on a dirt road running through the thickly wooded park. A couple of hundred Chicoans, many of them sporting five-dollar-bonus beards and all of them dressed in Union blues and carrying rifles or swords, were lined up on the road in a column of fours. Near the head of the column stood Dixon Porter, wearing the sword and red sash of a lieutenant; he was one of the extras. A long dolly track, with wooden rails, had been laid beside the road. The camera, fixed on a tripod, stood on a rubber-wheeled dolly at one end of the track. The trees lining the road arched high over the heads of the warlike array. Everybody in Huston's crew seemed, with a harassed awareness of the dollar value of every minute, to be rushing everyone else. Rosson, standing on the dolly and peering through the camera at the line of soldiers, gave hurried signals to assistants helping him get the camera in position. Huston and Reinhardt made a hasty inspection of the Chicoan army. Marton dashed at Mauldin, collared him, and thrust him into the Union ranks behind Murphy and Dierkes. The time was 8.38 a.m.

In the road, ahead of the troops, lay a soldier, face down, his uniform dishevelled, a rifle under his limp arm, his legs sprawled. Callow was arranging and re-arranging the legs. A still photographer aimed a Speed Graphic at the dead man; his flash bulb popped, and he quickly turned his camera on the waiting troops. Band arrived and began to tag after Huston, who walked over to the camera.

'Good morning, boys,' Huston said to Rosson and his assistants. 'Good luck, gentlemen!'

Jack Aldworth was writing in a hard-covered notebook. The first page was headed 'LOG − PROD. NO. 1512 − HUSTON.' Under the heading, he had already written:

7.45–8.00 − *Travel to location*
8.00–8.20 − *Spot equip. and unload trucks*
8.20–8.32 − *Line up dolly shot with soldiers*

He now wrote:

8.32–8.40 – *Set up camera with it on dolly – meanwhile reh and drill soldiers*

Aldworth would submit his daily log to Reinhardt and to Callow, who would submit it to Lee Katz, who would submit copies of it to Joe Cohn, Dore Schary, and L. B. Mayer, in Culver City, and to Nicholas Schenck, in New York. (Along with the daily log would go a daily report on the time the crew left for location, the time shooting started and finished, the number of scenes filmed, and the number of extras used.) Reinhardt was standing beside the camera, reading a letter that had just been handed to him by a messenger:

Dear Gottfried:
   Well, we're off! And we're off to a good start. I'm certain it will be good, Gottfried, damned good. We'll make it so. Good luck and my best.
                                                              Sincerely,
                                                                 Dore

The rehearsal began. Callow yelled, 'Here we go, boys! Get in line!' The troops started marching towards the man lying in the road. Callow told them to pause and look down at the body as they passed it. Huston peered into the camera and watched the procession, then called to the troops that this was the first dead man they had ever seen, and told them to keep this in mind when they looked down at the body. The time was 8.56.
   For all the tension, hurry, and confusion, it was very quiet. At Callow's command, the Union soldiers, having passed the body, moved back to their starting point. They were silent, and their silence was respectful. A smoke machine mounted on a truck, which had been hidden in the woods off the road, started up with a clatter, and smoke drifted slowly among the trees in the almost windless heat of the morning.
   Huston moved about quickly and smoothly. He strode over to the dead man in the road and called for a bucket of water. A prop man scurried off, and was back with it in a few seconds. Huston quickly mussed the man's hair and sprinkled dirt over his hair, face, and knapsack. Reinhardt looked down with a cynical smile as Huston mixed a handful of earth with water and daubed mud over

the man's face and hands. Huston stood up. Aldworth was holding out a clean white handkerchief. Huston wiped his hands on it and called for blood. A make-up man sprinted over with a tube of 'panchromatic blood' – mineral oil with vegetable colouring. Huston, thumbs hooked in the back of his belt, directed the bloodying process. Callow rushed up and said, 'Mr Huston, have the troops lost their knapsacks by this time, or haven't they?' Huston, thoughtfully staring at the dead man, said they still had knapsacks. He sprinkled another handful of dirt over the man. Marton hurried up and asked whether the troops still had their knapsacks on, and Huston gave him the same answer he had given Callow. It was 9.10.

Colonel Davison came up to tell Huston that the drummer boys in the column looked too naked with only their drums. Huston directed a prop man to put packs on the boys. Aldworth was writing:

8.40–9.12 – Cont. line up dolly shot

A make-up man fussed with Mauldin's wig under his kepi until it covered the better part of his neck. Huston saw the wig and said it was all wrong. The wig was removed, and a smaller one was substituted. Smoke now lay over everybody and everything. The smoke machine sounded like a couple of steam shovels. 'Kill that motor!' Callow bawled.

A man carrying a loudspeaker box on his shoulder and a microphone in his hand walked over to Huston. 'All right,' Huston said in a dramatically calm voice into the mike. 'All right, boys.' Everybody looked at him. 'The idea is these troops are coming into a battle area,' he said. 'This is the first time you have heard gunfire. I'm going to fire a revolver. This will be the first shot you have ever heard. Each soldier as he passes the dead man will slow down. This is the first dead man you have ever seen. All right.' The time was 9.26.

There was a brief silence – a lull before a battle. Huston told a smoke man not to make smoke, because this would be a rehearsal. Callow reminded the troops that they were not to step over the dead man but pass around him. Huston went over to the camera and called for action. Callow told the men to get going. They began to shuffle toward the dead man. The camera trained on them rolled on ahead, pulled along the dolly track by grips. Huston walked backward behind the dolly, looking intently at the faces of the troops. He gave the Chicoans a menacing look, and slowly raised the revolver over his head. He fired the revolver, still watching grimly, then fired again. The troops shuffled uneasily around the body of the dead man. Callow called 'About face!' and the men returned to their starting position. Huston went over to the dead man and sprinkled more dirt on him. Reinhardt laughed. 'How he loves to do that!' he said.

The time was 9.35. Jack Aldworth was writing:

9.12–9.35 – Reh

Katz said to Reinhardt, 'Joe Cohn asked me last night when you were coming back.'

'I wish I knew,' Reinhardt said.

'Consider the whole thing unasked,' said Katz. At the end of each day, he told Reinhardt, the film that had been shot would be flown back to Culver City for developing.

Reinhardt said he wanted to see each day's film – called rushes, or dailies – the following day. He didn't want to wait two or three days. 'I don't care how they feel about spending the money,' he added.

'May I quote you?' Katz asked, smiling.

'It's important,' said Reinhardt.

'Let me just find my studio notes,' Katz said, digging in his pockets.

'If we can get them two *hours* sooner, I want them,' said Reinhardt.

Katz took out his notes and studied them. 'It would mean a difference of ten or twelve dollars a night,' he said. 'I'll talk to Joe Cohn about it.'

'All this for two lines in the script,' Albert Band said. 'Would television go to all this trouble for two lines in a script?'

Callow announced that everyone was to be very quiet, because they were going to start shooting. A prop man was chalking on a small slate:

Huston   Scene 72

Prod 1512   Set 01

EXT ROAD AND DEAD SOLDIER

The smoke machine started again. Aldworth wrote:

9.35–9.40 – *Put in smoke effect in BG* [background]

Pistol in hand, Huston knelt directly in front of the camera.

'Quiet and roll it!' Callow shouted.

The camera buzzed. The prop man held his slate in front of the camera for a moment.

'*Action!*' Huston said. The soldiers moved forward. The camera moved ahead of them.

Reinhardt looked at Huston with a long sigh. 'Now there is no turning back,' he said. 'We are committed.'

On their fourth encounter with the body since the shooting had begun, the troops apparently gave the performance Huston wanted. 'Cut! That's it,' he said. 'Print it!'

Aldworth wrote down:

9.40–10.00 – *Shoot four takes (Takes* 1–2–3 – *NG* [no good] *action)*

The dead man got up and wiped a muddy palm over his muddy face. He asked Band whether he would be paid extra for lying in the road a couple of hours.

'Over Joe Cohn's dead body,' Band said.

At 2.30 p.m., the temperature in the woods was a hundred and eight. Eight Chicoans had collapsed while Huston was rehearsing a scene that required some troops to run off the road and into the forest and start digging ditches, as the Lieutenant of the Youth's platoon, played by Douglas Dick, walked toward the camera, smoothing his moustache, youthfully arrogant as he looked forward to his first taste of battle. At 2.32, Huston ordered his crew to print the shot of the troops.

At 4.02, Huston began working on a close-up of Dick smoothing his moustache. Huston lifted his own shoulder slightly to signify youthful arrogance, and encouraged Dick to imitate him. At 4.28, after seven takes, Huston said, 'That's it.'

At 4.45, Huston started working on close-ups of the soldiers digging in.

'Do we expect an attack?' Dixon Porter asked him.

'You don't know what the hell to expect. That's why you're digging,' said Huston.

Katz came over and said he didn't want to rush anybody, but the film had to be flown out of Chico at 6.30. Huston nodded curtly.

Huston directed the camera to be set up behind an elderly Chicoan who was digging in. The man had a long, deeply lined face. Kneeling alongside the camera, behind the man, Huston ordered him to relax and said he would tell him exactly what to do. 'Action!' he called. 'All right, sir. Move a little forward, sir. Now turn around and look behind you, slowly. That's right. Now dig. With your scabbard. Hard at it. Now with your plate! Hard. Harder. Very good. Cut!' He thanked the man and looked very happy. It was a face he liked.

Huston was rehearsing a group of soldiers in a digging scene when Rosson told him that they were fighting a losing battle with the sun. In the scene, Arthur Hunnicutt, an actor with a care-worn face, was leaning on his rifle, watching half a dozen comrades dig a hole. 'I don't hold with layin' down and shootin' from behint a little hill,' he was saying. 'I wouldn't feel a bit proud doin' it. I aim t' do my fightin' standin' up.' One of the soldiers digging said, 'If yeh want t' get shot that's yer own business.' Hunnicutt said, 'Well, I ain't goin' t' lay down before I'm shot – and that's all there is to it!'

'Light's going!' Rosson cried. 'Let's take it.'

Jack Aldworth wrote:

6.10–6.17 – *Moving camera and actor to get sunlight*

At 6.20, Huston took his last shot of the day. Then he walked over to a rotting log and sat down. He put his elbows on his knees and cupped his face in his hands.

Jack Aldworth noted in his report – a copy of which would be in Nicholas Schenck's New York office the next day – that eleven scenes had been shot for *The Red Badge of Courage*, out of a total of three hundred and forty seven.

On the second day of shooting, John Dierkes, the Tall Soldier, arrived at the day's location ahead of the other actors. A dusty dirt road wound through patches of wood and brush to the location, which was a broad, level, barren field beside the Sacramento River. Near the river bank, grips were working on a twenty-five-foot-high tower of steel scaffolding, from which the camera would shoot scenes of the Union soldiers drilling on the field. A dolly track ninety feet long ran across the field at right angles to the river. On the track was the camera, which was to photograph a scene of soldiers drilling before a row of Army tents. Dierkes walked to the far end of the dolly track and sat down on one of the rails. He rubbed the back of one hand over an orange stubble of beard, and with the other he unbuttoned the stiff, high collar of his tunic. He took his kepi off and put it on the ground. With a crumpled bandanna, he wiped the perspiration from his neck. The sun was already hot in the clear sky, and the morning air was humid and buzzing with swarms of giant flies. Two trucks were lumbering past, manned by eight grips, who all had wrestlers' muscles. Dierkes stood up and saluted them. The grips did not return the salute. They seemed detached and superior, impervious to heat, humidity, flies, and isolation, fixed as though forever in one another's company, and completely absorbed in their truckloads of tools, ladders, ropes, reflectors, two-by-fours, and tripods. The trucks stopped. The head grip shouted that some small trees were needed. The grips took saws and axes, and headed for a patch of woods. A sound truck was being manoeuvred into position near the camera. As it came to a halt, a young man jumped out and set up a microphone boom by the camera. In a little while, a property truck came up. The barrel-chested man in charge of it was stripped to the waist, revealing tattoos on his arms, chest, and back. Cheerfully, he let the truck's tailboard bang down; inside were stacks of rifles, swords, kepis, and extra uniforms. A few minutes later, buses arrived with the blue-coated army of Chicoans, and they lined up to get their rifles from the prop man. Then the studio limousines brought the other leading players and Huston.

Huston made a brisk tour of inspection past the row of tents, their pyramids of rifles stacked in front of them. Behind Huston came Reinhardt, his pith helmet pulled down over his forehead, and behind him, under another pith helmet, came Band. Huston conferred briefly with Reinhardt, then walked towards Audie Murphy.

Dierkes slapped his kepi back on and went over to one of the studio's limousines and put his head in at the window. The driver was dozing over a newspaper.

'They workin' ya hard, Ferd?' Dierkes asked the driver.

Ferd looked up. 'Am I burned up!' he said. 'I was all set to get a couple of guys tomorrow and drive to Reno and hit them everlovin' crap tables. Then I hear they got news for me. We work. On Sunday.'

'Gosh, Ferd,' said Dierkes.

'Sunday is supposed to be a day of rest,' said Ferd.

'I guess they don't want the picture to get behind schedule,' said Dierkes.

'Behind schedule is all I hear,' Ferd said, and returned to his paper.

Over the loudspeaker, Callow was bellowing for the actors to form ranks preparatory to drilling. Dierkes, on his way to pick up a rifle, walked past the camera dolly. Huston was standing on it, talking to the cameraman. Dierkes stopped, took off his kepi, and mopped his face again. Huston kept on talking to the cameraman. Dierkes got his rifle and took the long way around to the drill field, past the dolly again. He waited a moment, then said good morning to Huston and the cameraman. Huston returned the greeting exuberantly but mechanically. Then, as though something had just occurred to him, he stepped down from the dolly and motioned Dierkes to come closer with one of his conspiratorial gestures. The two men squatted on the ground. 'I just want to tell you how glad I am to have you in the picture,' Huston said, with slow, dramatic emphasis. 'I just know you'll be good, John.'

The orange stubble of beard appeared to redden as Dierkes said, 'Thanks.' Then he added, 'I sure wish the picture was shot.'

'It'll be over before you know it,' said Huston. 'It always is. Too soon.'

'A picture, if it is a hit, is the director's hit,' Reinhardt said over dinner that night. 'If it is a flop, it is the producer's flop.' He was confident that The Red Badge of Courage would not be a flop, that it would, in fact, be both a work of art and a commercial success. The film shot the first day had been developed, and M-G-M's head cutter, Margaret Booth, whose official title is Executive Film Editor, had telephoned to tell him she had seen the first rushes.

'Margaret says everything looks fine,' Reinhardt reported to Huston. 'The march into the forest she loves. She says the trees look terrific, and Audie, too. The dead-man shot is very interesting, she says.'

'That's something if this dame says it's good,' said Huston. 'People put more stock in what she says than anybody else. She's tough as hell.'

'And she told Dore,' Reinhardt said.

On the third day of shooting the picture, the nervous excitement that had permeated the company at the start abruptly disappeared. Even the army of Chicoans seemed suddenly to lose all their eager anticipation. 'Pretty cheap outfit, M-G-M,' said one during a break in marching around on the hot drill field. 'Ten dollars a day, and it turns out to be work.'

Dixon Porter said to a friend, 'I suppose out of all this chaos comes order eventually.'

His friend said, 'All this hurry up and wait. It's just like the Army.'

Reinhardt had brought along a 16-millimetre motion-picture camera, and he was shooting his private movie of the making of the movie. 'Mine will be in Technicolor,' he told me. His wife arrived on the set wearing her newly purchased trousers and porkpie hat. Reinhardt groaned when he saw her outfit. 'Gottfried!' she announced, 'I will keep you supplied with bottles of soda pop.'

Mrs Reinhardt put a brown cigarette in the corner of her mouth.

'Silvia!' Reinhardt cried in horror.

'We are in a constant state of osmosis,' Mrs Reinhardt said, paying no attention to Reinhardt's agitation. 'Osmosis has been going on for a very long time. A liquid of a lesser density flowing towards a liquid of a greater density through a thin membrane.' She uttered a shrill, hopeless laugh and gave a hitch to her Army suntans.

Reinhardt wiped his face with a large silk handkerchief. It was immediately soaked with perspiration. He looked morosely at the wet silk as Katz came over to him, smiling gaily. 'This is a scorcher, in case you haven't noticed,' Katz said. 'Anything I can do you for?'

Reinhardt asked him whether the studio had given permission for the army to ford the Sacramento River.

'Insurance men are studying the river for safety,' Katz said. 'They're going into it themselves.'

'I will go in with them,' Reinhardt said.

'Good, good,' said Katz.

Huston came along and asked about the river crossing.

'Maybe if I were made head of the studio, I would go to you and say, "No river crossing!"' Reinhardt said.

'Watch out, or that may happen,' said Huston. He gave his choked kind of laugh.

'Then let's do the river crossing quickly,' said Reinhardt.

A few minutes before midnight that night, I accompanied Huston and Reinhardt to the Vecino Theatre, on Main Street, in Chico. The marquee was flashing the current attraction in electric lights – Jack Carson in The Good Humour Man. Waiting under the marquee were Rosson, Marton, Callow, and Band. After the regular programme was over, we were going to see the first rushes of The Red Badge of Courage. The rushes were being returned in forty-eight, rather than twenty-four, hours.

'This is it, pals,' Rosson said in a low voice as we joined them.

For a few moments, nobody said anything. The men looked at one another nervously. They seemed held together by the same tense expectancy that had marked the first day of shooting. 'Let's go, guys,' Huston said finally.

We followed Huston into a roaring darkness; on the screen several men and a girl were hitting each other over the head with sticks. We found seats in the rear. On the screen, a donkey kicked a man, and the crashes on the sound track mixed with the crashing laughter of the audience. Then Jack Carson was holding a girl in his arms, there was a final blast of music, and the house lights went on. 'Christ!' Huston said. He stared blankly at the audience making its way out of the theatre.

Katz came in, and Reinhardt, sitting on the aisle, started to rise to let him pass.

'Sit yourself still,' Katz said, and sat down behind him.

'Cigarette, Albert,' Huston said. Band quickly gave him one and lighted it.

'You gentlemen ready?' a man called from the projection booth.

'Go ahead,' Huston said, in a voice that sounded very loud in the now empty theatre. He slumped in his seat, putting his long legs over the back of the seat in front of him. Reinhardt knocked the ash off his cigar and sighed deeply. The house lights went off.

On the screen, the Chicoan army shuffled along the road; the faces reflected the feeling of tense expectancy that had marked the entire first day's shooting, and somehow the effect on the screen was just right dramatically. After the raucousness of Jack Carson, the shuffling of soldiers' feet sounded weirdly subdued. There was a cut to a close-up of the dead man in the road and then to one of Audie Murphy, starting at the sound of Huston's revolver. The scene of the column scattering into the woods was followed by two close-ups of Douglas Dick smoothing his moustache. In the first one, Dick held his shoulders rigid, and the fingers he passed over his moustache seemed unsure of where they were going, of where the moustache was. In the second scene, he lifted one shoulder arrogantly, in an approximation of the way Huston had shown him how to play it. Huston exhaled some smoke and changed his position so that his knees pressed against the seat in front of him. 'We use the second one, Albert,' he said. 'Make a note.'

When the house lights came on, Huston and Reinhardt walked out of the theatre rapidly.

'Well, now, the stuff looks very good, very good, Gottfried,' Huston said.

Reinhardt agreed that most of the scenes looked good, but he did not like the shot of the regiment coming upon the dead soldier. There wasn't shock in the scene, he said. It didn't serve its purpose – to show the Youth's first frightening impression of war.

Huston said that the shot would be just fine – all it needed was a darker print. 'The body is too light, that's all,' he said impatiently.

Reinhardt still looked troubled. 'There is no *surprise*,' he said.

'It'll be fine, Gottfried,' Huston said.

Dixon Porter had been promoted from extra to bit player. He was now one of the ragged veteran soldiers taunting the Youth and the other recruits. Huston sprayed Porter's face with water, then threw dirt in his face, and finally told him to roll around in a puddle of mud, all of which was intended to make him look tough. Another veteran was the man who had played dead. He was a painter and steeplejack named Jack O'Farren, and while he was waiting for the shot to be taken, he handed out business cards reading 'The Sky's the Limit with Jack O'Farren' to all the recruits. Two of the other veterans, a real-estate salesman named Smith and a Chico State College art student named Feingold, rolled in patches of river moss, on their own initiative, after Huston had ordered them to roll in mud. They looked wonderful, he told them. He seemed exhilarated. He led the veterans in loud, boisterous laughter for their scene, slapping his knee and guffawing, and told the veterans they were great, just great; after the shot was taken, he led the spectators in applause for the performance.

With a good deal of zest, Huston then prepared to film the scene in which the Youth comes upon the body of a dead officer propped up against a tree at the edge of the woods. The effect, according to the script, was to be that of a cathedral interior, with the rays of the sun breaking through a thick haze of battle smoke. Huston showed . the extra playing the dead man how he should stare open-eyed in death at the tops of the tall trees, and then he showed Murphy how he should approach the sight and move back in slow, hypnotized fascination. Then Huston switched back to the role of the dead officer. He seemed to more than identify himself with the characters; the identification extended to the scene as a whole, including the tree. He sat against the tree, his hand clutching his sword, and again the look of death came into his eyes. Quickly he rose and strode back to the Youth's position, and again he demonstrated his idea of how one reacted when one came upon the horror of death. Reinhardt stood by watching. Huston did not talk to him.

That afternoon, Reinhardt appeared depressed. Because he was impatient to have a look at the latest rushes, he went to see them in the afternoon, while Huston was still shooting. I accompanied him to the theatre. Katz was standing outside. He told us to go on in and sit down, and said he would bring Reinhardt a soft drink.

'He'll bring the wrong thing, you'll see,' Reinhardt said to me. 'He'll bring me root beer and I hate root beer.'

Katz returned with a bottle of root beer, and the house lights dimmed. There were scenes of the soldiers drilling, of Dierkes marching with Murphy and Mauldin, and of Murphy running through the woods, and, at the end, another take of the dead-man shot that had disappointed Reinhardt. 'Much better,' Reinhardt said to me. 'I had them print this other take.' He seemed to be working himself toward a more cheerful evaluation of the picture. The drill field, he said, looked just like a Brady photograph. Great atmosphere, he told Katz, but they should have used more men in the scene.

'It looks like a lot of people,' Katz said. 'It looks almost *crowded*.'

Reinhardt did not argue the point. Dierkes looked wonderful, he said. Huston had certainly known what he was doing when he picked him. And in the second print the dead soldier *looked* like a dead soldier and produced a more startling, shocking effect. Murphy would be very good. 'John can charm anybody into anything,' he added.

When we returned to the set, Reinhardt told Huston that the rushes were wonderful. Huston seemed pleased. They walked to a shady spot and sat down.

'Tell me all about it, Gottfried,' Huston said.

'The dead soldier is all right now,' Reinhardt told him. 'If I had seen that take, I wouldn't have kicked at all.'

'It's all right now, then, Gottfried?' Huston asked, grinning at him for the first time since they had seen the first rushes together. Reinhardt laughed a relieved laugh and said yes. 'And it is really Virginia, because there is a cloud,' he said.

Mrs Huston and Mrs Reinhardt had gone back home. 'I leave in a great rush, in confusion, in a sudden gust of ambivalence towards Chico, actors, directors, producers, and the Civil War,' Mrs Reinhardt wrote in a terse note of farewell to me: 'I am returning to Mocha, who understands me.'

The Legal Department of M-G-M had finally given permission for two hundred and fifty uniformed, armed Chicoans to walk across the Sacramento River while two cameras turned. It was to be one of the most important scenes in the picture, Reinhardt told me, and it had been saved for the last day in Chico. At four that morning, Huston went fishing with Murphy. Four hours later, I drove out to the site of the river crossing with Reinhardt and Band. A hired motor launch took us across the river, and we landed near the spot where the camera had been set up, on a platform. Huston was not around. Rosson, wearing only a pair of swimming trunks, was hovering over his camera, surrounded by his assistants, and Callow was supervising the setting up of a fairly elaborate public-address system, over which he and Huston would call out orders to the men crossing the river. Reinhardt was getting his own movie camera ready for the big scene. 'I wish Dore could see this,' he said.

On the other side of the river, the soldiers were lining up.

'Everybody ready for D-Day?' one of the cameramen shouted.

Rosson said they had to wait for Huston. He stepped down from the camera platform and hunted around in the tall grass along the river bank, and there he came upon Huston, sound asleep. Rosson woke Huston, who followed him back to the camera, shaking his head sleepily. The director climbed on the platform and sat there, complaining that he and Murphy had not caught a single fish. He looked around glumly at the frenzied preparations for the crossing.

'Let's go, pals!' Rosson called.

'I'm scared to death,' Reinhardt said, putting his 16-millimetre camera to his eye.

Huston, over the public-address system, ordered the crossing to begin. The Chicoan army crossed the river and emerged soaked but triumphant. Huston stepped to the public-address system and told the men that they had been just great. 'When you see this picture, you're going to see one of the most impressive scenes ever filmed,' he said. 'Now we need some volunteers for another shot. It means going back into the river part of the way.'

'I'll go,' Dixon Porter said, right up front, as usual.

'Good boy, Dixon,' said Huston.

Porter brightened. 'Had to chop water all the way across the first time,' he said.

'You looked wonderful, just wonderful,' said Huston.

Albert Band turned up in a blue uniform, grabbed a rifle, and went into the river with the volunteers, as he had once warned Huston and Reinhardt he would. 'It felt wonderful,' he said when he came out.

During the day, a new joke made the rounds. Everybody told everybody else that the river-crossing scene would have to be reshot because one wig had been wrong. Reinhardt put in a call to Dore Schary as soon as he had returned to his hotel. The next time Reinhardt saw Huston, he said he had given Schary a full report on the river crossing.

'Dore said to me, "O.K., baby",' Reinhardt told Huston.

Jack Aldworth had made his final log note for the work in Chico ('Wrap up – return to hotels – crews start loading equipment for return to studio'), and the company was getting ready to go back to Los Angeles. Huston, Reinhardt, and Band were going to drive back in Reinhardt's convertible, and they offered me a lift.

Band seemed to have been highly stimulated by his recent military experience. 'One-hup-reep-foh-lelf-righ-lelf! One-hup-reep –' he chanted, marching in soldierly circles around Reinhardt.

'Albert!' Reinhardt said.

Band stopped and saluted.

'Get my camera, Albert,' said Reinhardt.

Band saluted again and went off, chanting his drill-field refrain. Huston showed up shortly afterwards, and read a newspaper while Band stowed the luggage. Reinhardt put his movie camera to his eye and focused on Huston reading the headline 'U.S. TROOPS ATTACK REDS'.

'Put the camera in the back seat, Albert,' said Reinhardt. He sighed and said he was fed up with taking his own movies. 'I've spent a fortune on this picture already,' he added.

Band climbed into the rear seat, and the rest of us sat up front.

'Well!' Huston said as we started off. 'How much ahead of schedule are we, Gottfried?'

'A day and a half,' said Reinhardt. 'Reggie says if we had done that shot of the river crossing in the tank at the studio, it would have cost twelve thousand dollars more than this did. Albert, the box of cigars. Under my coat next to you.'

'We can have the river crossing on the screen for a minute,' Huston said.

'That long?' asked Reinhardt, who was driving.

'It's worth it,' Huston said. He slumped down in his seat, arranging his long legs in a comfortable position. Reinhardt stepped on the gas. 'Don't rush,' Huston said, looking out at passing fields of haystacks. 'We're in no hurry, Gottfried. I like to see this kind of country. I just love to see this.'

Nobody spoke for a while, and then Huston said, 'I'm so happy about what we did in Chico.'

'It was not so bad, was it?' Reinhardt said.

'One-hup-reep-foh – ' Band said from the rear.

Huston sat up and said slowly, 'I made a mistake.'

Reinhardt started.

'On the veterans' close-ups,' said Huston. 'I forgot to dolly. The long shot was a dolly shot. I forgot that on the close-ups.'

Reinhardt closed his lips around the cigar. Maybe they could do some retakes when they returned to the ranch, Huston said. He closed his eyes and went to sleep. Reinhardt stepped on the gas.

One of the first things Reinhardt did when he got back to his office at Metro-Goldwyn-Mayer was to write a letter to Dore Schary:

Dear Dore:

Upon returning from the wilds of Chico, I find that in the heat of fighting the Civil War (and I mean 'heat'!) I missed your birthday so please let me send you my very best wishes belatedly today. Your presents are the rushes and the time in which they were shot.

With kindest personal regards,

Yours,

Gottfried

P.S. And I mean 'fighting'. I even forded single-footed the Sacramento River in order to convince the insurance man that it could be done without too big a risk. After all, what nobler gesture can a studio make than risk the lives of its producers?

The scenes that were shot at Chico had been pieced together in approximately the order they would follow in the finished picture, and Reinhardt had seen them in this form. Now Huston was looking at the film in a projection room at the studio, and Reinhardt was waiting for him in his own office. Schary had seen the film, too, he said, but Mayer would not see any part of the movie until it was previewed. 'Mayer really *hates* the picture,' he said. 'He will keep on hating it as long as he thinks we do not have a story. He would like to see us rewrite the script and give Stephen Crane's story a new *twist*.' He laughed sadly. 'It reminds me of the time Sam Hoffenstein was given a Tarzan picture to rewrite. He was told to give it a new twist. He rewrote it – he put it all into Yiddish.' He gave a shy smile. 'I love that story. It's a great story.'

Huston burst into the office, followed by Albert Band.

'The stuff looks awfully good, Gottfried,' Huston said. 'It'll cut like a cinch. I have very few criticisms.'

'What criticisms do you have?' Reinhardt asked.

'Well, practically nothing, *amigo*,' said Huston. He sat down and, tilting back, put his feet on Reinhardt's desk.

Reinhardt leaned back and put his feet up on the desk, too. 'This is an American custom I have embraced whole-heartedly,' he said. 'What criticisms?'

'I'll say right now Audie is superb,' said Huston. 'He's just marvellous. Sensitive. Alive. This boy is something.'

Reinhardt said. 'Will you do me a favour, John?'

'What?' Huston asked.

'Get Audie to smile in the picture,' Reinhardt said. 'Just once.'

'All right, Gottfried,' Huston said graciously.

A few days later, it was Huston, rather than Reinhardt, who seemed to have become dissatisfied. He was worried about the script for his picture. Specifically, he told Reinhardt that day, he was worried about the way the picture seemed to be turning into an account of the struggle between the North and the South in the Civil War. 'All we want to show is that what the Youth is doing has nothing to do with the big battle,' he said. 'The battle has gone on for three days and it's going to go on for another three days. The

Youth gets on the roulette wheel and stays for a little while and then
he's thrown off, and that's all we have to be concerned with. We
have to get something for the end that will show that.' All they had
at the end now, Huston said, was a scene in which the Youth's
regiment took a stone wall held by the Confederates, and that was
the last action scene in the picture. It bothered him, he said, that
there was no big scene at the finish. He felt that something was
missing.

Reinhardt said it was better not to strive for climaxes. 'Sometimes
the quiet ending is the more impressive,' he said. 'I always think of
the strong effect of the quietness of *Till Eulenspiegel*. The average
motion-picture guy would say that it is an anticlimax. I do not
think so.' Reinhardt seemed to be getting immense enjoyment out
of this kind of discussion.

Huston, ignoring the reference to *Till Eulenspiegel*, merely repeated
that they would have to get something new for the ending. 'I'd just
like the situation to be clarified,' he said. 'The Youth and his comrades have been fighting all that day and the day before. Now we
open the last battle by following the general on his white horse
riding along the lines. We go to the Youth and his regiment. They're
part of this big thing. They capture a fragment of the wall. We begin
with a big thing and end with a little thing. If the battle depended on
this wall, then we would know what the situation is. But we don't
know quite what happened.'

Reinhardt said, 'They take the wall. You think, This is the big
thing. They take prisoners. Suddenly they get a command to fall
in and march away, and they watch as another regiment is
committed.'

'I'd like to know from the standpoint of the battle itself
what's happening,' Huston said. 'And I don't know. I don't even
know.' He laughed, and said he would think of something.
'Another thing, Gottfried,' he said, at the end of the discussion,
'I don't like the dead soldier Audie finds in the woods. It looks
too stagy.'

Reinhardt protested that he liked the scene.

Huston said that he would do it over.

In his living room every night after dinner, Dore Schary ran the rushes of all the pictures in the production at M-G-M, and one night he invited me to come over and see the rushes of *The Red Badge of Courage*. Schary lives in Brentwood, a fashionable residential district, where he has a cream-coloured English stucco house. The doormat at the front door bears the words 'Schary Manor' – the name of his parents' Newark home, from which they ran a catering business. In the summer of 1950, Schary was forty-five – one year older than Huston, seven years older than Reinhardt, and twenty years younger than Mayer. He was born in Newark, the youngest of five children. He attended public grade school, quitting at the age of thirteen after an argument with a teacher about a problem in algebra. Six years later, having meanwhile worked off and on in the family business, been a necktie salesman, and tried other jobs, he returned to school and, by attending day and night, went through high school in a year. In 1928, he joined the Stuart Walker Stock Company in Cincinnati as an actor, and remained there for one season. He subsequently spent a summer as assistant recreation director at the Flagler Hotel in the Catskills (the director was Moss Hart), and from that he went on to play small parts in the Broadway productions of *Four Walls* and *The Last Mile*. Schary wrote a play that was not produced but was read by Walter Wanger, who signed him to a hundred-dollar-a-week contract as a writer at Columbia Studio in 1932. He took the job, but at the end of twelve weeks Wanger didn't pick up his option. Schary stayed on in Hollywood, and several months later he helped write the script of M-G-M's *Big City*, starring Spencer Tracy. Then, also for M-G-M, he collaborated on the writing of *Boys Town*, for which he won an Academy Award. He next collaborated on *Young Tom Edison* and *Edison, the Man*, and was given a job at M-G-M supervising a studio production unit, which made *Joe Smith, American*, *Journey for Margaret*, and *Lassie Come Home*. After this, Schary joined David O. Selznick's independent producing company, where he produced *The Farmer's Daughter* and *The Bachelor and the Bobby-Soxer*. The success of these films led to Schary's appointment as head of production at R.K.O., and for that company he made *Crossfire* and *Mr Blandings Builds His Dream House*. He returned to M-G-M in the summer of 1948, at the invitation of L. B. Mayer. Before long, in addition to serving as superintendent of production for the whole studio, he himself produced *Battleground*, starring Van Johnson, and *The Next Voice You Hear.* . . .

Schary met me at the door of his house with an easy-going, homespun grin and told me that he was just about to view the last of the day's rushes. He was wearing grey flannel slacks and a blue blazer with white buttons. He took me into a large sitting room. At one end of the room was his wife, who paints under the name of Miriam Svet, his three children (Jill, fifteen; Joy, thirteen; and Jeb, eleven), and M-G-M's chief cutter, Margaret Booth, a thin woman with a thin, bony face. Schary led me to a chair near them, and snapped his fingers. A wide panel in the wall at the opposite end of the room slid up, exposing a white screen, and the room was darkened. A projectionist in a booth behind us showed us *The Red Badge of Courage* scenes. These were followed by Technicolor scenes of Clark Gable and an Indian girl making love on a mountaintop. Schary told Miss Booth how he wanted the scenes trimmed, and the lights came on. The children thanked their father for being allowed to see the movies. He kissed them and sent them off to bed, adding that if they were good they could see the rushes the next night, too. Miss Booth said she had a date to go to a movie, and left. Mrs Schary excused herself, saying that she had to work on a painting.

Schary sat down. The rushes of *The Red Badge of Courage* had been magnificent so far, he told me. 'John and Gottfried have proved their point that they could make this picture,' he said. 'The original estimate on this picture was close to two million, and our estimators said it would take forty-eight days. John and Gottfried said they could do it in thirty and hold the cost down to a million five. Nobody believed it. But I believed it. I believe that no picture is like any other picture. So I believed the boys could do what they wanted to do. I believe that one of the most debilitating things is to have too large a frame of reference.'

Before production started, Schary said, Huston and Reinhardt had seemed almost overwhelmed with doubt, and he had had to steady them. They had come to see him at home, when he was ill. 'They were so concerned I went over the whole thing with them. I said, "I have no way of comforting you guys by telling you that this is going to be a great picture. I only know that John is a brilliant director. The script is wonderful. This can be an inspiring picture. I don't think anybody will be able to say it's a bad picture. Let's follow our first hunches and first instincts, and let's make the picture! Let's make it as efficiently and as economically and with as much enthusiasm as we can. Let's stop thinking about it as an if picture. It's to be made. That's all." From that time on, everything has just gone zoom.'

Schary gave me a candid look. 'I love John,' he said. 'That guy will live forever. He's a hearty, tough soul. When he wants something from you, he sits down next to you and his voice gets a little husky, and pretty soon you're a dead pigeon. He wanted Audie for the Youth, and he got him.' He shrugged benevolently. 'A creative man, when he wants to win a point, he uses effective and dramatic arguments.' Schary shrugged again. 'I love to do this imitation of John when he says hello to you,' he said. He did the imitation – getting up and giving a quarter twist to his body and saying 'hel-lo' – and then sat down and chuckled at his performance. 'I had visualized the Youth as a taller, blonder, freckle-faced kind of kid, sort of a younger Van Johnson,' he continued. 'I said, "John, you're a big ham. If you were twenty years younger, you'd love to play this part yourself." He said I was right. That's the kind of guy I had in mind – a guy with an odd, interesting kisser, with hair that falls down in front. But in the final test, I was sold on Audie. John never lost his hunch, and now he's got something there. Great guy, John. He's always flying back and forth. He goes here, there, everywhere, in a plane. A schlemiel like myself gets on a plane and it crashes. I love John.'

Schary grinned broadly. 'Show business!' he said. 'I'm crazy about show business. I'm crazy about making pictures. All kinds of pictures. But my favourites are the simple, down-to-earth pictures, the ones about everyday life. The Next Voice You Hear . . . was that kind of picture. I'm crazy about that picture. I love it.' Schary went on to say that he enjoyed seeing the rushes every night. 'I like to reaffirm myself,' he said. 'The biggest job is the transfer of an image to the screen. For The Red Badge of Courage I had an image in mind of dark-blue uniforms against light, dusty roads. This was an image that John moved successfully into the realm of production.' Schary gave a professorial nod. 'The boys are making an impressive picture. The only controversy about The Red Badge of Courage is whether it will be a success or a failure. It's as simple as that.'

Piccolos under Your Name,
Strings under Mine

THE RED BADGE OF COURAGE was a day and a half ahead on its thirty-four-day shooting schedule when, in September 1950, the cast and crew reported at Huston's ranch to start on the major battle scenes. In their two weeks at Chico, Huston and Reinhardt had completed eighty of the three hundred and forty-seven scenes outlined in the script – mostly shots showing the Youth drilling in camp, marching through woods, crossing a river with his regiment, and fleeing through a forest. Reinhardt had not entirely liked one scene that Huston wanted to keep (the Youth's regiment coming upon the body of a soldier in a road) and Huston had not entirely liked one scene that Reinhardt wanted to keep (the Youth coming upon a dead soldier seated upright in a forest), but for the most part the two men agreed that they had made a good beginning. The eighty scenes had been seen, and praised, by Schary, who said that the film indicated that The Red Badge of Courage would be an impressive and inspiring picture and that Reinhardt and Huston were fulfilling their promise to him to produce the movie at a maximum cost of $1,500,000, to finish it on schedule, and to try to make it a commercial success. Neither Mayer nor Schenck had seen any part of the film, but, by frequent long-distance telephone talks with Schenck, Schary kept in close touch with him about reports on Production No. 1512 that came to Schary's desk (duplicates of which came to Mayer's desk) at the studio; these showed that of the total cost of $1,434,789 estimated for the movie, $468,044 had been spent up to the time Huston prepared to shoot his first battle scene. (Other reports of around the same time revealed that the studio's musical film An American in Paris – Production No. 1507 – would have a thirteen-minute ballet sequence costing $400,000, and that Quo Vadis – Production No. 1312 – would cost $8,500,000 but was expected to show a net profit of $12,000,000.) The first battle scene, which would give the Youth his first sight of combat, was going to cost Loew's, Inc., $155,000.

The battle scene was filmed from the top of a long, steep hill that faced another hill, which was longer but not so steep. The hills ran down to a shallow ravine, and this ravine was where the Youth would encounter his first fighting. From the top of the steeper hill, he would see the clash of the Union and Confederate cavalry, amid bursting shells. Stuffed dummies of men and horses had been strewn over the battlefield. A studio ambulance was parked out of range of the camera; any actual casualties, it was announced, would be delivered to Los Angeles Hospital in forty minutes. Lee Katz, unit manager, the liaison man between Production No. 1512 and the studio Production Office, headed by vice-president Joe Cohn, climbed to the top of the hill and, panting, asked Huston if he was all ready for the battle. 'Some battle!' Katz said. 'It's costing a hundred and fifty-five thousand dollars.'

'Doesn't it look just wonderful?' Huston said.

A great many people were on hand for the battle. A couple of hundred extras in Union blue lounged around with rifles and waited to be assigned their places. (As the shooting of the picture progressed, most of the extras were scheduled to change into grey uniforms from time to time and fight as Confederate soldiers.) Bill Mauldin, John Dierkes, and minor character actors stood off to one side; along with Audie Murphy, they were to be placed so that one of the three cameras being used would register their reactions to the battle.

'The new Mike Romanoff's will have only one section,' one of the character actors was saying. 'All tables will be on a par with each other. Everybody will be equal.'

Andrew Marton, the 'leapfrog' director, seemed to have abandoned future battles for the one on hand. He thoughtfully examined the faces of the soldiers, and then thoughtfully examined the sight below, and nodded with approval. 'Johnny likes this sort of thing to look menacing and forbidding,' he said.

'This will be greater than Gone with the Wind,' said Albert Band.

Audie Murphy was off by himself studiously thrusting a bayonet into the ground. 'All set for the big battle?' Colonel Davison asked him. Murphy smiled politely and said yes.

Huston, who was wearing Army suntans and a red-and-green-checked cap, ran up and down the long hills without losing his wind; he was arranging the Union soldiers in jagged lines and hurrying back to check with Harold Rosson on how they looked through the camera.

'Where's your horse, pal?' Rosson asked, chewing gum rapidly.

Huston said that he had found directing the picture on horseback, as he had started out to do, too hard on his horse. 'Christ, Hal, doesn't it look great?' he said as he surveyed the troops.

'We're getting it to look like Brady, all right, pal,' Rosson said.

Huston laughed. The irony of the Youth's flight from his initial battle and his heroic deeds in a later battle must be made clear in the picture, he told the cameraman – his war in the movie must not appear to be a North v. South war, but a war showing the pointlessness of the Youth's courage in helping to capture, near the end of the picture, a fragment of wall. To bring this out, Huston said, he had written some additional scenes for the picture, including one in which soldiers from another regiment told the Youth that he had not fought in the major battle but only in a diversionary action. 'I think it will be very good, kid,' Huston said.

'O.K., pal,' Rosson said, grinning. 'Just tell me what you want.'

The man in charge of touching off explosions during the filming of the battle scenes was studying a large map; it showed the location of explosives buried on the field of battle. With his help, Huston and Reggie Callow were instructing the Union cavalry to charge where explosions couldn't injure them.

'It looks like the Civil War,' Reinhardt said. He was wearing a pith helmet and a shirt open at the collar, and he stood next to one of the cameras, his fists pressed to his sides.

'You mean the War Between the States,' said Band. 'The studio says you can't call it the Civil War in pictures.'

Reinhardt went over to Murphy and told him that this battle would look completely realistic. Murphy listened, shifting his bayonet from hand to hand, and then, in one of his rare talkative moments, said that the psychology in all wars was the same – that he believed the psychology of a raw recruit in the Civil War was the same as that of a young man in the World Wars.

'You think the German was a good soldier?' Reinhardt asked.

'We had respect for the Germans,' Murphy said. 'There was none of this blowing smoke rings in their faces stuff. It was a mistake to underestimate the German soldier.'

'Yes,' Reinhardt said, laughing. 'You know, there are three kinds of intelligence – the intelligence of man, the intelligence of the animal, and the intelligence of the military. In that order.'

Murphy kept on shifting his bayonet from hand to hand.

'Ready for the big battle, Gottfried?' Katz asked cheerfully. Reinhardt smiled and nodded.

A group of stunt men on horseback were all ready to make a Union cavalry charge across the battlefield. One of them, a young man named Terry Wilson, was riding a restless, snorting horse. A group of extras who were soldiers in the Union Army surrounded Wilson as he quieted his horse and told them that he was going to lead the charge. It would be the first of many services, which he called 'taking bumps', he would perform for Huston, including wrecking caissons, falling off horses, being dragged across battlefields by horses, making horses fall as though shot, and being blown up in the air by what would appear to be exploding shells. Wilson, an ex-Marine, and the other stunt men were rugged, and disdainful of the actor-soldiers, many of whom carried suntan lotion in their knapsacks. Wilson said that stunt men were willing to knock themselves out for a man like John Huston, 'He's all guy, you know,' he said to the extras. 'A guy's guy.'

'You get more dough in this war than in the Army,' one of the extras said.

'This war stuff doesn't pay so well,' Wilson said. 'I'll get four hundred dollars for wrecking a caisson and a hundred and fifty for getting blown up. A hundred and fifty for falling from a horse. Seventy-five for rearing a horse. Maybe four hundred and fifty dollars to fall with a horse. If I break my neck, I get thirty dollars a week compensation. I don't do it for laughs, but I'll give Mr Huston anything he wants.'

An elderly man with a full grey beard, who was working as an extra, muttered that Wilson ought to watch himself. 'I fought in every war there was in history since the Philistines,' he said. 'And I'm telling you this one looks the most dangerous. I was a weary foot soldier in the American Revolution. I fought the Philistines in *Samson and Delilah*. I was in the First World War in *Sergeant York*. I was with Errol Flynn in the suppression of the Irish Rebellion in *The Private Lives of Elizabeth and Essex*. I was in all the Napoleonic Wars and the Spanish-American War and the Second World War. I even fought the Civil War once before, in *Gone with the Wind*. I've been in all the wars, and I speak from experience – this war is going to be the roughest. You haven't seen anything yet.'

'If Mr Huston wants it that way, it'll be all right with me,' Wilson said.

'Quiet!' Callow bellowed over a public-address system. 'Everybody quiet. This applies to top brass and everybody.'

'Forward march!' Katz said to nobody in particular.

'The man from the Pentagon is trying to speed up operations,' Band said.

'Well, now!' Huston said, looking dazed and happy. He took off his cap and tossed it on the ground. Then he grasped the microphone and asked all the soldiers to be careful as they proceeded downhill; if anybody slipped, he said, he must be sure to protect the men in front from his bayonet. Then he called, 'Action!' There was a good deal of yelling and confusion. The Union cavalry charged down the hill. The explosives went off on the battlefield. The smoke-makers sent smoke drifting over the scene. The line of Union foot soldiers, with Murphy up front, his lips pressed grimly together, started moving downhill towards the battle. After about five minutes, Huston called 'Cut!' He laughed, and said it had all looked just wonderful.

The next day, an M-G-M publicity man came out to the ranch to get material on *The Red Badge of Courage*. After surveying the wreckage on the field of battle, he said, 'This is wonderful art. Too bad we can't use it. Battle stills don't sell tickets. Two things sell tickets. One, stars. Two, stories. No stars, no stories here. Can't sell Huston. Directors don't sell tickets, except DeMille. We'll think of *something*.'

Huston received from Margaret Booth, whose opinion was respected by every producer and director on the lot, an inter-office communication that read:

Dear Mr Huston:
   I haven't had a chance to tell you how wonderful I feel the dailies [rushes] are. Yesterday the scene between Audie Murphy and Royal Dano [the Tattered Man], where they come down the hill after John Dierkes' death, was simply wonderful. Also the scene of the Army walking down the hill was very fine; in fact, I could go on naming one after another that I felt was great. I hope to get out to the location soon.
                                                                              Margaret Booth

A few days later, Reinhardt told me he was going to see the first cut of the picture – a piecing together on film of all the scenes shot so far. He did not want Huston to know it was ready yet, he explained, because he wanted to see it with Margaret Booth and Benny Lewis, the cutter assigned by Miss Booth to the picture, before Huston saw it. I accompanied Reinhardt to a projection room in the basement of the Irving Thalberg Building, at the M-G-M studio, where we were joined by Lewis and Miss Booth. The cut began with the men drilling on the field at Chico. Miss Booth immediately asked why there was only one shot of the men marching.

'Huston said just one shot and a close-up as brief as we can make it,' Lewis said.

'Malarkey,' said Miss Booth. 'The marching is supposed to be funny, but it isn't funny now. You don't know what kind of marching this is.'

'Then let's build it up,' said Lewis. 'We'll put more of it in.'

'More of it back and forth; then it will be funny,' Miss Booth said impatiently.

'I could put in a piece where the fat fellow walks by,' said Lewis.

Reinhardt spoke for the first time. 'Put it in,' he said.

At the conclusion of the showing, Miss Booth criticized the scene that showed a group of veteran soldiers laughing at raw recruits; she said she didn't know what it meant. Reinhardt cleared his throat and explained that it wasn't plain because the long shot was a dolly shot; the close-ups were not. 'John shot it wrong. He forgot to dolly,' he said.

'Reshoot it,' said Miss Booth, and continued, 'That shot of the men digging – that's very dull to me. Cut it right down to the bone, Benny.'

'The old man with the lines in his face, turning around and looking over his shoulder?' said Lewis.

'What's he supposed to be looking at?' Miss Booth asked.

'John likes that,' said Reinhardt.

'What's he looking at?' Miss Booth asked again.

'At the producer,' said Lewis.

'He's a stockholder,' said Reinhardt.

'I have news for you,' said Lewis. 'He's looking at Mr Mayer. Well his looking days are over.'

'I don't get it, Gottfried,' said Miss Booth. 'All this individual digging.'

'John likes these faces,' said Reinhardt.

Miss Booth snorted. 'Cut it!' she said, standing up. 'I've got to go. Don't put anything back, Benny.'

When she had left, Reinhardt said to Lewis, 'For the time being, you can keep the shot of the old man turning around toward the camera. John is especially fond of that.' He stood up and, smiling sadly, he said to me, 'Let's go up to my office.' As we went upstairs, he said, 'This is how we make pictures. This will be recut thirty times. The digging scene will eventually come out. But we must go at it slowly. We cannot shock John by doing it all at once.'

Seated behind his desk, Reinhardt leaned back in his chair. 'Actually, every director should make the rough cut – the film as assembled from start to finish for the first time – himself,' he said, and bit the end off a cigar. 'But it's almost a physical impossibility. Once the director is through, you can usually do what you want with a picture.' He sighed and lit the cigar. 'When John sees the first cut, he may holler like hell,' he said. 'He may ask Benny Lewis to put it all back. But then he'll come around to the way Margaret Booth wants it. There's so much about pictures that has nothing to do with art.' He sighed again, and went on, 'To me, there are three terrible moments in making a picture. First, the rough cut. Second, the first preview. Third, knowing the picture has opened in New York. For John, the rough cut will be the most painful. I will say to him, "This is the best picture you have ever made." He will say to me, "This is the best picture *you* have ever made." John is like a race horse. You must keep him in a good mood all the time. John is a charmer, you know, but he is really very forlorn, a very lonely man. He is out of touch with human emotions.' He chewed on his cigar for a while. Then he said, 'I wish I had made John reshoot the dead man in the road. It doesn't make the point at all. I felt it when I saw the first rushes. No matter how enthusiastic we are about the script, the cast, and the director, the impact of the first rushes usually tells you whether the picture will be good or not. Once the first impact is gone, it is easy and customary to delude yourself. Subsequent rushes will seem good. Performances will seem extraordinary. Scenes will be effective. The tension, the pressure, the sense of self-preservation, the all-powerful urge of wishful thinking will help bury the first impression, and create hope – even confidence.' He smiled cynically and picked up a memorandum he had written to Schary about Tim Durant – a friend and riding companion of Huston's who, though not a professional actor, was playing the part of the General in *The Red Badge of Courage* – saying that Huston had thought it would be a nice gesture, since Durant was playing the General at a nominal salary, for M-G-M to give him a present of a hunting coat, to be made by the wardrobe department. On the memorandum, Schary had made a notation O.K.'ing the idea and instructing Reinhardt to order the coat. Reinhardt shook his head absently at the memorandum. 'It was different when I worked for Ernst Lubitsch,' he said. 'Lubitsch was a producer and director who did everything himself. The cutting. Every frame. And he was brutal with himself.' Reinhardt looked mournful, like a man who didn't know how to go about being brutal with himself.

Margaret Booth, Reinhardt went on, was very helpful to him. She had been Irving Thalberg's cutter, and she had known Reinhardt ever since he came to M-G-M in 1933. 'Margaret really saves me,' he said. 'She won't work this closely on a picture with all the producers. She feels like a mother to me.'

Several times each week, Reinhardt went out to Huston's ranch to see how the picture was progressing. He arrived one day as

Huston was preparing to shoot, as part of the first battle, a Confederate bayonet charge – the specific part of the battle that would cause the Youth to run away. 'Realism!' Reinhardt said to me as he watched Huston. 'How L. B. Mayer hates this!'

'It looks great,' Albert Band said.

'Yes,' Reinhardt said. 'You know, Mayer thinks that John's whole point of view is corroded. He thinks John represents stark realism, which he hates. He thinks I am an intellectual European and want to make pictures that won't go in Kalamazoo, Michigan. Mayer told me that I was making a big mistake with this picture. He begged me not to make this picture.' Reinhardt looked confidently around the set.

Huston, in dungarees and a torn blue shirt, was telling Rosson that he wanted a lot of smoke, to obliterate the charging enemy just as they reached the ditch along which the Youth and his comrades were deployed. He explained that the audience was not to see what happened after that. 'The Rebs come down at us with bayonets and then it's all blotted out by the smoke. Got it, Reggie?' he said to Callow.

'Yes, sir!' said Callow, and instructed the enemy to come down with bayonets, and then walked on quickly to talk to the smoke men.

'They either want you or they don't want you in this business,' Reinhardt went on, still watching Huston. He paused, as if he had just had a new thought. 'Me they don't want, but they got to have.' He laughed and, taking a white silk handkerchief from his trouser pocket, wiped his face. 'They are very cruel in this business when they decide they do not want you,' he said. 'All you have to do is watch the faces of your underlings. Suddenly your words don't mean anything any more to your underlings, and you find yourself standing in a corner saying to yourself, "What happened to me?" Why don't I buy a house out here, like everybody else? Because deep down I know I don't want to be tied here. I don't want to stay here. I will never buy a house in Hollywood.'

Abruptly, Reinhardt walked over and joined Huston at the camera, which was in a ditch behind the Youth and his comrades, to watch the filming of the charge. It was a fierce and frightening attack. The grey-clad soldiers started running across the wreckage-strewn field towards the camera, their bayonets pointed forward, and they leaped toward the Youth just as the smoke machine sent up a thick, impenetrable cloud. 'I would run from this,' Reinhardt said.

'So would I,' said Huston. He called 'Cut!' and strode away from the camera, his face blackened by smoke and his shirt and trousers stained with sweat and grime.

A visitor had just arrived on location – Sam Spiegel, Huston's partner in Horizon Pictures. As Huston emerged from the smoke of battle, Spiegel went up and slapped him on the back. 'How is the Yankee general?' he asked. Huston gave him a smile.

Spiegel was immaculate in brown suède shoes, orange-and-green Argyle socks, tan gabardine slacks, and a brown-and-white-checked sports shirt. He was carrying a bright-yellow cashmere jacket and he was smoking a pipe. 'Gottfried!' he cried. 'How is the commander of the forces?' He took the pipe from his mouth. 'How is the war, Gottfried?'

Reinhardt said that things were all right.

'Nice, very nice, Gottfried,' Spiegel said, looking around at everyone except the man he was addressing. 'How many feet have you shot, Gottfried?'

'About four thousand,' said Reinhardt. 'We're getting wonderful stuff. Terrific!'

'Bill!' Spiegel called. 'Bill Mauldin!'

Mauldin, lolling in the ditch, turned and waved.

'How do you like being an actor, Bill?' Spiegel called.

'Hell, Sam, it's O.K.,' said Mauldin.

'You remember the party you came to at my house, Billy?' said Spiegel.

'Sure thing, Sam!' Mauldin called. 'Helluva party!'

Spiegel put his head back and murmured a low, satisfied 'Ah-h-h.' Then he stared sadly at Huston, who was throwing a bayonet at a cigarette stub on the ground. 'So, Gottfried,' Spiegel said, keeping his eyes on Huston. 'The picture is all right, then?'

'It will be a great picture,' Reinhardt said.

'Nice,' said Spiegel. 'I get him next. For *The African Queen*. I like to get him when he is feeling good.'

Howard Strickling, studio publicity director of M-G-M, put out a mimeographed booklet outlining a promotion campaign for *The Red Badge of Courage*. 'It has BIGNESS. It has GREATNESS! First, last, and always, it is ENTERTAINMENT in the grand tradition!' the foreword stated. The booklet gave the gist of articles that were to be written by publicity-staff people for fan magazines, including 'The Audie I Know', by Bill Mauldin, and 'I Know Bill Mauldin', by Audie Murphy. Civil War stories, it was asserted in another section, had long made popular movies; *Gone with the Wind* had grossed millions of dollars and *The Birth of a Nation* had been the greatest grosser of all time.

The Red Badge of Courage might be a great picture, Strickling told me, and on the other hand you couldn't be sure. 'We'll know when Mr Mayer sees it,' he said. 'Dore is good. He's the nearest thing to another Irving Thalberg the studio ever had. He's idealistic, but that will be knocked out of him in time. The realist at the studio is Mr Mayer. He always shows what he feels. When he goes to a preview, if he hurries out without talking to anybody after he sees the picture, you know there's trouble. If he stays and chats, you know everything's O.K.'

One afternoon late in September, Reinhardt was in a projection room in the Thalberg Building, working with Benny Lewis on the cutting of the picture. Reinhardt's shirt collar was unbuttoned and his necktie was hanging loose. He paced up and down the room, puffing on a cigar; he was worrying about a scene that showed Dierkes, the Tall Soldier, running up to the top of a hill to die.

'We've got to delay him,' Lewis was saying. 'My God! A wounded man getting up the hill so fast! S. C. will grab him for the track team.'

'Start him up the hill,' Reinhardt said, pacing. 'Then cut to Audie and the Tattered Man chasing him. Then cut back to Dierkes. That will delay it.' He stopped beside a telephone and asked to be connected with his office. 'I don't want to be disturbed,' he told his secretary. He hung up and turned to Lewis. 'I've got to have the stuff by tomorrow morning,' he said. 'Bill Rodgers and Si Seadler are here from New York, and I must show them what I have. How much can we have to tomorrow morning?'

All the shots filmed at Chico, Benny Lewis said, plus some scenes showing battles and the death of Dierkes – about thirty-five hundred feet, or forty minutes, in all.

'I want it,' Reinhardt said. The two visitors, he told me later, were important figures in the New York office of Loew's, the company that produces and distributes M-G-M pictures. Rodgers was general manager in charge of sales and Seadler was Eastern advertising manager. Both were key assistants of Schenck. 'They can make or break a picture,' Reinhardt said, and resumed his nervous pacing.

The next morning, at the studio, there was a showing of *The Red Badge of Courage* that was attended by Rodgers and Seadler. Reinhardt introduced them to me. Nobody talked as the lights dimmed in the projection room, and nobody talked during the showing. The only sound during the brief intervals of quiet on the sound track came from Reinhardt; he was breathing heavily. As soon as the showing ended and the lights went on, he stood up and faced his guests.

'Impressive,' said Seadler, a wiry man with a constant look of worried amiability.

'Mmm,' said Rodgers. He was a dignified, courteous, white-haired man with eyes as cool as those of a box-office man in a theatre.

'Those death scenes are absolutely superb,' Seadler said.

Reinhardt said, 'Don't you think we ought to exploit Audie Murphy to the fullest?'

'Can we get his cooperation?' Rodgers asked.

'We're getting his cooperation,' Reinhardt said. 'And the Defence Department will be very, very grateful for whatever we do.'

'They'd cooperate to the fullest,' said Seadler.

'We should get this picture out in a hurry,' Reinhardt said. 'Take advantage of the current war situation. We must sell this picture. New York must sell this picture. This should be one of M-G-M's great pictures. Like *Gone with the Wind*.'

'There's no way of knowing,' said Seadler.

Reinhardt said. 'What about using drawings by Bill Mauldin for promotion? "Up Front with Bill Mauldin in the Civil War."'

'Mauldin's cartoons are too grim,' Seadler said. 'For this picture, you should concentrate on the beauty of the photography, and at the same time get over the power of the big battles.'

'Let's try everything,' Reinhardt said. 'We must bring the New York office strongly behind this picture. There's no Gable or anything in this picture. We must sell this picture as an important picture, in the great tradition. Like *Mutiny on the Bounty*. Like *The Good Earth*.'

'When Mr Schenck sees the picture in New York, we'll know how to sell it,' Seadler said.

'If this picture isn't *sold*, then all the money will be down the drain,' Reinhardt said.

Rodgers spoke up, courteously and slowly; he appeared to be considering the subject with detachment. 'We're compelled by law today to sell each picture alone,' he said. 'No picture of ours has ever gone out without being tested. We don't market them until they have been tried out. But you can be sure that it will be sold. Its greatness depends on how it is received by the public. But you can be sure that we are geared to do our part.'

Reinhardt seemed eager to take his cue from Rodgers. He said, 'This is an artistic picture, but, frankly, I'm not interested in that. I want to see this picture make money.' He seemed to be getting lost in his own salesmanship. 'I want to see this picture make millions.'

Rodgers smiled faintly. 'You can be assured that when we receive it, we'll get after it,' he said.

Seadler said, 'If the picture is good, I'll say so. I'm the kind of a guy in the company who will speak my piece. Even to Mr Schenck.'

'After you're through, you may think you have a great picture, but then the responsibility is *ours*,' Rodgers said.

'All I'm interested in is that the picture makes ten million dollars,' Reinhardt said.

Seadler said, 'We'll know how things stand when Mr Schenck sees it in New York.'

The assembled film of most of what had been shot of *The Red Badge of Courage* — pieced together by the cutters under Reinhardt's supervision — was shown a few nights later to Huston, Reinhardt, and Huston's aides, including Rosson, Colonel Davison, Marton, Callow, Katz, and Band. After the showing, Huston and the others looked pleased, and somewhat stirred. Everybody smiled at everybody else.

'Well, now, kid,' Huston said to Rosson, putting a hand on the cameraman's shoulder.

'I don't mind saying that the photography looks great, pal,' Rosson said, grinning.

'Doesn't it look just swell, kid?' said Huston.

Everyone went up to Reinhardt's office and sat down. Reinhardt's expression was solemn. 'I'll make a short speech,' he said. 'There will be no accolades. People thought this picture would not turn out the way we thought it would turn out. The mood has changed. The big shots from New York have come here, and they have seen the stuff and liked it.'

Now everybody's expression was solemn.

'We are doing a remarkable job,' Reinhardt continued. 'We are working with two hundred extras when we should have two thousand. Last night, someone saw the stuff at Dore Schary's house and asked how much would the picture cost. He was told one and a half million. He said, "It already looks like three million." That is the way our picture looks.'

Everybody grew even more solemn.

Reinhardt put a cigar in his mouth. Everybody waited for him to speak again. He lit the cigar and blew the smoke out, then said. 'If now we bring in the picture three or four days early, everyone will be not only an artist but a hero.'

The artists and potential heroes looked at each other.

Reminding Reinhardt that the schedule called for only twelve more days of shooting, Callow said, 'We can't bring it in in nine, Mr Reinhardt.'

'Then bring it in in ten,' said Reinhardt.

Huston said they hadn't saved any time with the leapfrog system, because they hadn't been able to put it into effect. 'We didn't have what we were supposed to have – substitute actors to stand in and do what the real actors were going to do,' he said. Callow said he hated to disagree, but the fact of the matter was that they had been held up by the smoke-makers, who hadn't been able to get the smoke on the battlefield at the right time and in the right way. 'We had bad luck with the wind,' he said. Huston repeated that the trouble was lack of men. 'If what we're interested in is days,' he added. Callow said that the leapfrog system wouldn't have worked, no matter how many men they had, because basically it was unsound – the only person who could know what kind of scenes Huston wanted was Huston himself. Then everybody started to talk at once. Reinhardt looked bewildered. When there was a momentary lull in the talk, Reinhardt said quickly, 'If you can't bring it in in ten days, bring it in in eleven. One day early. That's all I ask.'

A couple of days later, a long line of Union troops walked slowly across Huston's battlefield in a scene showing the Youth's regiment beginning a charge toward the enemy. They held their rifles low, bayonets fixed and pointed forward. The camera, on a dolly track, moved along with the line. Huston walked beside the camera on the other side of the dolly track and studied the line of soldiers as they started to walk faster and faster and finally broke into a run. Explosions went off at predetermined positions on the field, and soldiers in the line – chosen by Callow to have the honour of dying in action – clutched their midriffs, dropped their rifles, threw up their arms, and fell. Huston called 'Cut!', and with satisfaction said that the scene looked just great. He took some close-ups of the feet of the soldiers in the various stages between the slow walk and the run and then, as he was getting ready to take close-ups of falling men, he suddenly looked surprised and told Rosson to hold things a minute. 'I have an idea, Hal,' he said, in the amazed tone he sometimes uses. 'It might be something, kid.' He tossed his head in a conspiratorial gesture at one of the extras, a skinny young man with a long, thin face and a weak chin, who was wearing steel-rimmed spectacles. Huston squatted on the ground with the extra, in what appeared to be a deep, concentrated consideration of a problem. Then he nodded briskly. 'All right, amigo,' he said. 'Let's see you do it.'

The young man grinned bashfully; then he took a few steps forward, carrying his rifle, threw up his hands, dropping his rifle, and fell to the ground.

'That's the idea, *amigo*,' Huston said, and chortled. He held another brief conference with the young man, and again the young man grinned bashfully.

This time the young man knelt and handed his spectacles to Huston, who placed them on the ground before him. The young man blinked his eyes, groped for the spectacles, put them on, and then collapsed, as though in death.

Huston chortled again. 'Very good,' he said. '*Very good.*' He put a brown cigarette in his mouth, offered one to the young man, and then called to Rosson. 'I've got an extra little bit here, Hal,' he said cheerfully. He lighted the extra's cigarette and then his own, and proceeded to work with Rosson on setting up the camera to take the scene of a soldier who falls and puts on his lost spectacles before rolling over in death.

The next day Huston worked on a new scene he had written to point up the irony of the Youth's heroic action in the general scheme of the battle. This scene would take place just before the final battle, in which the Youth and his comrades capture the wall. Huston directed Tim Durant, as the General (who was wearing, in addition to the uniform provided by M-G-M, the sword that had belonged to Huston's great-grandfather), in a scene requiring him to ride his white horse along the line of raw recruits preparing to go into battle, stopping before each company and inviting the troops to have supper with him after they had won the battle, then pausing to chat with some ragged veterans of battle and, instead of offering them the spurious invitation, offering them a chaw of his tobacco. Durant spoke in a thin, almost nagging voice. As he was departing, one of the veterans called, 'Having supper with us tonight, General?' The General rode away, followed by friendly guffaws from the veterans. Huston grew more and more exuberant as he went on to direct Durant in a close-up – the General taking off his hat in prayer and muttering, 'Thy will be done, sir.'

'Very good, Tim,' Huston said, laughing, as he called 'Cut!'

'I now become one of the immortals of Beverly Hills,' Durant said.

'Ho! Ho! Ho!' Huston said.

Benny Burt, another friend of Huston's, had been given a part in the picture as a soldier in the Youth's regiment. He was a scrawny little man, with large, melancholy eyes. He talked out of the side of his mouth in a staccato manner, and he was not completely happy about his role. He had played a stool pigeon in Huston's *The Asphalt Jungle*, and he had played small parts in a number of pictures since then, including *Cry Danger*, *M*, *The Enforcer*, *The Lemon Drop Kid*, *Convicted*, and *Chain Gang*. He had hoped for something bigger in *The Red Badge of Courage*, but he was just an anonymous soldier. In his two weeks' work, he had lost several pounds, bringing his weight down to a hundred and eight. 'I want to sink my teeth in one good part and I'll set this town on fire,' he said.

Burt had been waiting for his opportunity since 1933, when he came to Hollywood. Before that, he had worked in vaudeville and burlesque in a Gus Edwards act called *Snuffy the Cab Man*. 'I was in burlesque when it was *burlesque*,' he told me. 'I'm not one of these Johnny-come-latelies. I do seven different dialects, including a pretty fair Chinaman. My Greek character would kill you. I used to kill Al Capone and all his boys with my Greek dialect when I worked for Capone's Royal Frolics, in Chicago. Every six weeks I wanted to quit, so they gave me a raise every time. Capone and his boys taught me how to bet the horses. They should drop dead for what they did to me. If it wasn't for the horses, though, I never would of met him,' he said, jerking a thumb at Huston, who was fussing over the camera. 'It was at the race track. I'm at the track, and I'm with three hoodlums from Chicago. I'm at the hundred-dollar window betting thirty-five hundred for those guys. He' – again he jerked his thumb at Huston – 'is behind me, and he says to me, "I always see you here." So I tell him to bet this horse. He did and the horse won. So he says, "Here's a hundred-dollar ticket for you." I say, "You owe me nuttin." So he says, "Then come have a drink with me." So we had a couple of drinks. Then he says, "What you doin' for dinner?" He wants me to have dinner with him. From then on I'm with him morning, noon, and night. I was with him the night his dad died. I told him, "John, don't you worry, I'll take care of you." All my life, nobody ever gave me nuttin, but from then on we were like brothers. I did everything for him. I drove him here, there. I let him hypnotize me. I took care of his clothes. His suits cost three hundred and fifty dollars apiece.

He has fifty pairs of shoes at fifty-five dollars a pair. It burned me up when Cholly Knickerbocker called him one of the worst-dressed men. I was with him on Thanksgiving and I was with him on Christmas. I was his family.'

Burt scratched his whiskered chin and put a brown cigarette in his mouth. Huston used to listen to his advice about betting on horses, he told me sadly, but now he didn't any more. 'All I do around here is swallow two tons of dirt in them battles,' he said.

Band, puffing on a long cigar, came over and told Burt that, one by one, the supporting actors who were soldiers were dying in the picture and that he was in charge of deciding which ones might live. 'Do you know Crawford? I just killed him off,' he said. 'One more off the payroll.'

'Albert, don't kill me,' said Burt.

'I'll just have you get wounded,' said Band.

'Don't do nuttin to me. Just let me keep on fightin',' said Burt. His face brightened. 'Hey, Albert!' he continued. 'You shoulda seen me when I worked in Slapsie Maxie's. I used to come on and yell, "Hey, Maxie! Jane Russell's out in front!" and he'd yell back, "She always was!"'

Band puffed importantly on his cigar, and then said that he might just have Burt shot in the leg.

'Don't do nuttin to me,' said Burt.

Huston strolled over, an unlit cigarette dangling from a corner of his mouth. Burt whipped out a match. 'Thank you, Benny,' Huston said.

'How you doin', boss?' Burt asked. 'Everythin' goin' all right?'

'Why, yes, thank you very much, Benny,' said Huston.

'You gonna rest up Bargin Lass?' Burt asked, referring to one of the four horses in Huston's racing stable.

'Uh-huh,' said Huston, his mind obviously on something else. 'Well, now, Benny, I need a close-up for the next shot. You might be good for it. You might be very good for it, Benny.'

Burt could not contain his delight. 'Sure, sure,' he said.

Huston laughed and told him to be on the alert for a call.

Sporadically, Huston received communications from Dore

Schary, cheering him on. 'There's been a little illness at the studio
and some people have been absent,' Schary wrote as the filming of
the picture approached its end. 'I've been working so darned hard
that on weekends I've had to kind of stay close to home, which
accounts for my inability to get up and see you and thank you and
everybody personally for a film that I think is going to work together
into a very important movie.'

Two days later, Huston heard from Schary again. 'The material
continues to look wonderful,' he wrote. 'However, I have two slight
concerns: (1) I think in some of the shots the dust is so heavy that
we lose some of the effectiveness. It is, of course, very likely that in
the cutting you plan to eliminate some of this and use the clearer
sections. (2) I think that the laughing of the regulars is a little over-
done when our new regiment walks past them after the fight. There
doesn't seem to be enough provocation or motivation for this, and
I am afraid that it sets up a general ambivalence that may hurt us,
and, rather than creating interest, will very likely create confusion.
The material with the General going past the men and the dinner
invitations is wonderful – very rich, real, and human. Again, my
best – and stay with it. Fondest, D. S.'

Huston was going to play a bit part in the picture, as he did in
many of his pictures. He had a three-day growth of beard on his
face, and he put on the tattered costume of a veteran Union soldier
and stood in the line of jeering veterans for a retake of the scene
Schary had objected to. He delivered his line – 'Hang your clothes
on a hickory limb and don't go near the battle!' – in a callous
manner, showing contempt for the Youth and the other raw
recruits. Playing the bit galvanized him into tremendous activity.
He went about his work still wearing the costume. As the day neared
its end, the air became cold, and he put on the bedraggled coat of a
Confederate officer and sat on the running board of a sound truck,
and listened carefully, through earphones, to the recording of
Confederate and Union soldiers calling to each other across what
would eventually appear to be a river. Without any lessening of
energy, he invited Reinhardt and his crew up to his ranchhouse for
a drink, and there showed them a present the leading members of

the cast had given him. It was a saddle, to which was affixed a silver plate engraved, 'To John Huston with affection from his damn Yankees'. He put his arms around it and said it was just about the greatest saddle he had ever seen. The forward pitch was beautiful, like the fenders on a Rolls-Royce. 'It follows the shape of the horse,' he said, running a caressing hand over it. 'This is as beautiful underneath as it is on top. It's abstract sculpture, that's what it is.'

Reinhardt adjusted a beret he was wearing and yawned.

'No saddle has ever compared with it,' Huston said to him.

'Beautiful!' Reinhardt said, suddenly enthusiastic, and then urged him to change his clothes so they could drive to the studio in Culver City. 'We must talk about the music for the picture,' he said.

'I've thought about that, Gottfried,' Huston said. He spoke about the death scenes. 'The music should have the feeling of death,' he said. 'The way it is when you're going under anaesthesia. Circular. Coming closer and closer and closer.'

'Great,' Reinhardt said. 'That will be great.'

For the next two days, The Red Badge of Courage company worked at the studio, on a set representing the Youth's camp. They did some scenes of the camp at night-time. In another part of the studio, a lot known as Joe Cohn Park, Huston did a retake of the shot of the dead soldier the Youth comes upon in the woods. The new shot, he said, was more satisfying – just as gruesome but not as stagy as the one he had taken in Chico.

Schary had been seeing the rushes of The Red Badge of Courage every night. 'I'm really crazy about the picture,' he said to Reinhardt. 'It's got a great feeling about it. Audie is swell. Much better than I thought he would be. It's going to be a great picture. It won't be brought in early but it'll be a great picture.'

On the last day of shooting their picture – they had gone three days over the allotment – Reinhardt and Huston sat in the latter's office and talked as if they had trouble thinking of things to say.

'God, it feels kind of funny, doesn't it?' Reinhardt said.

Huston was sketching nightmare faces on a pad, and he frowned as he sketched. 'To be finished,' he said, not lifting his eyes from the paper.

'Jesus!' said Reinhardt.

'Did you see the last shot in the picture, where they march away from the battlefield?' Huston asked.

'Yes,' said Reinhardt.

'That ought to run and run and run,' Huston said, sketching.

'Yes,' said Reinhardt. 'And you even got Audie to smile once.'

There was a long silence. Huston crumpled the sheet he had been sketching on and threw it across the room.

'It's funny,' Reinhardt said. 'I feel funny. Now we deliver the picture into the hands of the octopus.'

'I'm going away for a couple of days' rest,' said Huston.

Reinhardt wanted to know where he was going. Up north, with Terry Wilson, the stunt man, Huston said. They were going to shoot ducks.

'I shouldn't say this,' Reinhardt said, and he knocked wood three times. 'But we've got something solid.'

Huston laughed. 'This is like seeing your sweetheart off,' he said. 'You've taken her to the airport. Her plane has taken off. You stand there. We'll never make *The Red Badge of Courage* again.'

Reinhardt said, 'I think we've got something great. Very seldom have great novels become great pictures.'

'*David Copperfield* came the closest,' Huston said.

Reinhardt said. 'If *Red Badge* turns out to be great, it will give you and me terrific inhibitions about what we do next.'

Huston said he knew what he was going to do. He was going to direct and collaborate on the screenplay for *The African Queen* for his own company, and he wanted the picture to make money. 'I don't have any inhibitions about making a pile of dough, Gottfried,' he added, and laughed.

The company assembled in Joe Cohn Park and shot what they thought would be the last scene – a night scene showing the Cheery Soldier coming upon the Youth lying unconscious in a field. The Cheery Soldier was sprung on the company as a surprise; he was the well-known actor Andy Devine. (Because of the shortness of the part, Devine did not want to be given a screen credit.) With a good deal of bounce and zest, Huston urged Devine, who carried a lantern (lit by a system of wiring wrapped around Devine under his uniform) in one hand and supported Murphy with the other, as he guided the Youth back through the woods to his regiment.

'Anyway – dyin's only dyin'. S'posin' you don't hear th' birds sing tomorrow – or see the sun come out from behind a cloud. It'll happen jest th' same!' the Cheery Soldier said to the Youth.

'Dyin's only dyin',' Huston said in a singsong to Devine. 'Pep it up, kid. Make it fast and funny.'

'Dyin's only dyin',' Devine began, immediately catching Huston's rhythm. It was a fast and cheery scene.

After it had been taken, Callow brought a microphone over to Huston, and everyone gathered around. Callow said that, as the loudest voice in the company, he had been chosen to present Huston with a token of appreciation from the crew. The token was a pair of binoculars.

'Oh, God, isn't this something!' Huston said. 'My God, these are just marvellous.' Many of the crew looked almost tearful. Huston said he knew how hard they had worked for him. 'This has been the easiest picture for me to direct, entirely thanks to you, and despite all the hardship I'd be willing to start all over again tomorrow,' he said.

'I feel so sad,' Reinhardt said to Huston.

'I never had a crew like this,' Huston said.

'I feel so sad,' said Reinhardt. He looked almost tearful, too.

Huston said, 'I once told you we would never make this picture.'

'And I said, "It depends on us,"' said Reinhardt. 'I'll never forget it.'

Huston and Reinhardt shook hands and said they would get together in a few days, when Huston returned from his duck shooting.

Reinhardt had written a long letter about promoting the picture to Howard Dietz, vice-president in charge of advertising, publicity, and exploitation for Loew's, in New York. Dietz had written back that it was dangerous to ballyhoo a picture without stars far in advance. Now Dietz was making his bi-monthly visit to the studio, and Reinhardt had persuaded him to come along to the Beverly Hills Hotel for a drink with Huston, who had just come back from his shooting trip. Dietz and Reinhardt waited for Huston in the hotel bar. A bland man with a bored air, Dietz had collaborated on several Broadway musicals before he became a publicity director. He had worked for Samuel Goldwyn before M-G-M was founded, and it was he who devised the trade mark of the lion and, with the advent of talking pictures, suggested endowing it with the celebrated roar. His boredom seemed to increase as Reinhardt tried to steer the conversation toward the promotion of *The Red Badge of Courage*.

'We have terrific stuff in the picture,' Reinhardt said. 'We must sell it as one of M-G-M's great pictures.'

Wearily, Dietz lifted his eyebrows.

'Wait till you talk to John,' Reinhardt said, looking anxiously in the direction of the door. 'I want you to talk to John.'

Dietz sighed, and said he wished he were back home, playing bridge. 'Why don't people out here play bridge?' he asked.

'You don't like it here?' Reinhardt said.

'I don't like it because I have to live in a hotel and I don't like hotels,' Dietz said.

At this point, Huston and his wife walked in. Huston shook hands with Dietz and told him he had been shooting ducks.

'My icebox is packed with wild ducks,' Mrs Huston said.

'I hate chicken, but I just love the taste of wild duck,' Huston said.

Dietz gave a bored half smile.

'I've been telling Howard about the picture, John,' said Reinhardt.

'Oh, how are things going with it?' Huston asked offhandedly.

'We have terrific –' Reinhardt began.

Huston did not seem to hear him. He was greeting Sam Spiegel, who had just come into the bar. Spiegel said that it was a great surprise to find everybody right here. 'Maybe you can tell me when you will start to write *The African Queen*,' he said to Huston. 'So, how about dinner tomorrow night to talk about it?'

Huston nodded vaguely.

'What are we going to do about all the ducks, John?' Mrs Huston asked in alarm.

'You just clean the ducks, honey, and hang on to them,' Huston said, carefully enunciating each syllable. Suddenly, against an out-of-focus bar background, Huston, his beautiful wife, and the un-answered question about the ducks turned into a Huston scene that was full of mysterious, even sinister, possibilities.

Thirty-eight days had been devoted to shooting *The Red Badge of Courage* – more than the number allotted. Of the estimated total cost of $1,434,789, $1,362,426 had already been spent and the latest estimated cost of the movie was $1,548,755. The first rough cut of *The Red Badge of Courage* was ready to be shown to Huston. Its seven thousand feet of film would take one hour and eighteen minutes to run off. The close-up of the old man with the lined face had been cut out, but when Huston, accompanied by Reinhardt and me, saw the film, he did not give any indication that he had even noticed it. The close-up of Huston as a ragged veteran had also been eliminated, but he said nothing about it. He made a few suggestions to Reinhardt for trimming one scene and for varying a long scene of the Youth's regiment on the march with close-ups of soldiers and horses, but he said that for the most part it was a remarkable job of cutting. He seemed satisfied and ready to drop the picture as his concern, but Reinhardt held him to it. The picture was too short, Reinhardt said, and the story was not clear. 'I wrote out my thoughts about this,' he added, handing Huston a typewritten memorandum, single-spaced and three and a half pages long.

Huston looked at it impatiently.

'This is very serious, John,' Reinhardt said, with the air of a man who takes pleasure in the seriousness of things. 'Please read it.'

Huston read:

Aside from its spectacular appeal, the subconscious satisfaction of reliving a glorious and vital chapter of American history, and the nobility, beauty, and deeply moving tragedy of its scenes, The Red Badge of Courage must meet one basic requirement to become a success, artistic as well as commercial: the story of the Youth must be convincing. Its development must be organic, consistent, and unbroken. The Youth must inspire measureless sympathy; we must feel for him, go with him all the time. We must understand him, 'root' for him, and, finally, admire him.

While I think the first-mentioned requirements have been admirably fulfilled by the film — and I mean 'film', for now the footage must speak for itself, all good intentions, all arguments about faithfulness to Stephen Crane, all promises of the script, all preconceived notions that might easily be read into the film, must now be brutally disregarded as irrelevant — while I believe we have a spectacular, stirring, pure, and beautiful, and at times deeply moving picture, I submit this question to all who are helping to make The Red Badge of Courage, and I submit it at the eleventh hour: have we done right by the Youth? For if we have failed to do that, we will have failed altogether.

What is the story of the Youth? (Let us not delude ourselves, however attractive the wrapping may be. The content is what matters. The picture must have a story.) One day, on a drill field on a Civil War front, we meet a young fellow. Unlike his comrades, he is in desperate fear of battle . . .

The memo went on to trace the sequence of the picture and declared that there was nothing in it to indicate why the Youth suddenly stops being a coward and becomes a hero. 'A beat is missing,' the memo ended. 'The Youth's story becomes somewhat lost. The line is broken. Such a beat would also bring the picture to its proper length.'

'You're right, Gottfried,' Huston said when he finished.

Reinhardt looked pleased. He said he had run into Mayer a couple of hours before and had told him that The Red Badge of Courage had turned out to be a great picture.

'What did he say, Gottfried?' Huston asked patiently.

'He said only one thing – "Does it have a story?"' said Reinhardt.

The two men stayed at the studio late that night, working out scenes that they hoped would give the picture a story.

The following evening, Huston and Reinhardt showed their picture to Dore Schary at the latter's house. A couple of hours earlier, Reinhardt went to a party Mike Romanoff was giving to celebrate the laying of the cornerstone of his new restaurant. Albert Band drove him and me from the studio to the party in Reinhardt's car. 'I am so worried about Mocha,' Reinhardt said, on the way. Mrs Reinhardt was in New York, and there was no one at home to feed their French poodle. 'Poor Mocha,' Reinhardt said.

'Let's go on to the party,' Band said. 'Mocha will be all right.'

'Mocha will go hungry while you stuff yourself at the party,' said Reinhardt.

'Mocha will be all right,' Band said peevishly.

'Albert,' Reinhardt said reproachfully, 'someday you will be head of the studio, but right now I think someone should go home and feed Mocha. Then he will be all right.'

The site of the party was a large lot in Beverly Hills a few blocks from the old Romanoff's. A canopy had been set up, and under it were tables covered with food and drink. A crowd was already in an advanced stage of celebrating the new cornerstone when we arrived.

'Everybody is here,' Band said, looking over the party. 'Clark Gable. Everybody.' He was about to join the party when Reinhardt told him that first he had to go feed Mocha.

'And stand over Mocha while he eats,' Reinhardt said as Band started off. 'Mocha is very nervous.'

Band left, and Romanoff asked Reinhardt why he was late. 'You missed the ceremonies,' he said haughtily. 'You missed Ethel Barrymore's address.' He touched his fingers to his lips in a gesture of acclaim. 'She was better than Franklin D. Roosevelt.'

'All that mortar and pestle,' a lady standing nearby was saying. 'Like it was for the cornerstone of a museum.'

'No place else in the world will you find all this,' a gentleman with her said, sweeping his arm at the party. 'We've got everything in Hollywood. Where else will you find Picassos in the bathroom?'

Reinhardt, watching Ronald Colman and Clark Gable laughing and talking to Louella Parsons, took a Martini from a passing tray. 'What are they laughing at?' he asked a writer named Charles Lederer, who was standing by.

'Don't ask questions. Laugh,' Lederer said.

Reinhardt laughed.

Band returned to the party, Huston showed up, and the three of us drove off with Reinhardt to Schary's house. We found Schary in his living room, wearing grey slacks, a navy-blue blazer, a baby-blue sports shirt, and loafers, and looking relaxed and happy. With him were Mrs Schary and Benny Lewis.

'Hello, baby,' Schary said, grinning at Huston.

Huston gave Schary an affectionate slap on the back. 'How *are* you, kid?' he said. Everybody sat down.

'Where ya been, doll?' Schary asked Huston.

Huston said he had been hunting, and started talking about ducks, but already the wall panel was sliding up, disclosing a white screen, and he fell silent.

The changes suggested by Huston at the previous showing had been made. Now it was Schary's turn to offer suggestions. 'Benny, make a note about that scene,' he said as the soldiers began drilling on the screen.

'Yes, sir,' said Lewis.

'Make a note about the river crossing,' Schary said.

Lewis made a note.

'Catch the guy saying "Oh, no!" after the digging. It's too modern,' Schary said.

When Tim Durant had his horse do a circus dance and shouted 'Yippee' several times, Reinhardt gave a loud laugh.

'Got to do better with those "yippees",' Schary said.

'We have some new "yippees" we haven't put in yet, Dore,' Huston told him.

The scene of the Cheery Soldier finding the Youth in the woods was too dark, Schary said, and the men all agreed that it would be best to reshoot it.

The lights went on. The panel returned and the white screen disappeared. There was a momentary silence.

'Sweetie, that line "gone coon",' Schary said to Huston. 'We had a line just like it in *Crossfire*. About being busier than a coon. We got two cards at the preview with objections. I don't think we ought to take a chance on this one.'

'Possum,' Mrs Schary said. 'There's a good little animal.'

Schary immediately pointed at Band. 'Say "possum", say "coon",' he commanded.

Band said quickly, 'Possum, coon. Possum, coon. Pos – '

'"Goose,"' said Huston.

'"Gone goose,"' Schary said. 'That's it.'

Schary then said that there was no fighting in the picture after the Youth's regiment met the enemy at the wall. Huston said he wanted to avoid hand-to-hand fighting, and anything else that would come under the heading of 'North v. South'.

Schary said, 'The main thing is I feel a lack of climax and culmination in the charge. You don't feel that grabbing and lifting up. What we had in Battleground, for instance.'

'Well,' Huston said, 'we've got one more criticism, and it's more serious than this.' He stood up and, putting his hands in his pockets, said that the complaint was that the picture didn't show what the Youth's state of mind was after he ran away from the battle and before he returned and distinguished himself. 'It's an emotional thing, rather than a logical thing,' Huston said. 'If there could be a quiet scene after the boy returns to camp. The Lieutenant with his back to a tree sleeping. Another writing a letter. And the Youth restless in his sleep. A kind of stillness. To show that the boy is not as he was before.'

'The more we show of the Youth in camp, before he becomes a hero, the more of a story we have,' Reinhardt said.

Schary said, 'Dissolve to the boy lying there wide-awake and wide-eyed. Then dawn comes, and a bugle call.'

Reinhardt and Huston agreed with Schary that such a scene would give the picture more of a story, and Huston said he would dictate it the next day.

The death scenes of Dano and Dierkes were great, Schary said – great scenes.

'It's good battle stuff, isn't it?' Huston said.

'Gorgeous,' said Schary. 'Gorgeous shots.'

There was a pause, and Mrs Schary told Huston that she had almost finished a painting and wished he would look at it. Huston said he'd love to. Schary suggested a change in the sequence of some minor scenes at the end of the film. Huston said that the suggestions were excellent, just swell, then turned back to Mrs Schary. 'Show me your painting, honey,' he said.

'Dore,' Reinhardt said, as Huston and Mrs Schary left the room, 'you think anybody will come to see this picture?'

Schary said yes.

Reinhardt asked him how he liked Audie Murphy.

Murphy was very good, Schary replied, 'And Mauldin is good,' he said. 'He looks like Howard Hughes.'

Reinhardt sighed with relief.

When Mrs Schary and Huston came back, she told Reinhardt that she loved *The Red Badge of Courage*, and to Huston she said, 'You've got a good picture.'

'Thank you, honey,' Huston said, with dramatic earnestness.

'The picture has a great feeling of the period,' Schary said as we were about to go. 'It has real validity.'

'It will be a great picture,' Reinhardt said.

'Good night, sweeties,' said Schary.

As we drove away, Reinhardt said, 'Every night he does this. My God, the junk he must look at!'

The next morning, Reinhardt found an advertisement in a motion-picture trade paper for *The Red Badge of Courage*. It was illustrated with a photograph showing Audie Murphy chatting across a fence with the farm girl whose pig was stolen in the picture. In this photograph, the farm girl was looking worshipfully at Murphy across the fence. There was no such scene in the picture. The promotion on *The Red Badge of Courage* had begun.

Huston had his final session with Reinhardt and his key crewmen in a projection room, where they viewed the revised cut of the picture, including the retakes and the additional scenes in the Youth's camp that had been taken and that Reinhardt and Huston hoped would give the picture more of a story. The showing lasted an hour and twenty-eight minutes – ten minutes longer than the version they had decided was too short. Huston said that the picture looked padded. He was for clarity and direct, brief statement, and wanted no more film than was absolutely necessary. Reinhardt and Huston rearranged the sequence of several scenes and shortened some shots, and by such legerdemain they were able to move the

Youth around on the battlefield so that he fought in the battle on film in a more satisfying manner than he had fought in the battle on the ground. Now Benny Lewis, working under the combined direction of Reinhardt and Margaret Booth, began to piece together the shots so as to imprint the Youth's revised movements on the film for what they thought was forever.

M-G-M had given Huston permission to suspend his contract while he made an independent picture, and he moved his belongings from his corner office in the Thalberg Building to a small cottage in the California Studios, in Hollywood, where Horizon Pictures, and his partner in it, Sam Spiegel, had their headquarters.

When Huston left, he left his picture, and his four-thousand-dollar-a-week salary, behind. He would now be getting twenty-five hundred dollars a week at Horizon, on his job of converting C. S. Forester's novel *The African Queen* into a screenplay. He left Albert Band behind at M-G-M, too. Before he went, he promised to arrange to give Band credit for adapting *The Red Badge of Courage* to rough screenplay form, and he told Band that he would talk with Dore Schary about giving him a new job. At Horizon, Huston seemed to have forgotten all about Schary, about Albert Band, about Gottfried Reinhardt, Audie Murphy, Stephen Crane, and *The Red Badge of Courage*. Reinhardt was philosophic about Huston's exit from the scene after they had been together constantly for ten months. 'You see a lot of your colleagues when you make a picture,' Reinhardt said. 'You see them, be they friends or enemies, and then the picture is finished and you don't see anything of them. Neither closeness nor distance affects the basic relationship.' However, Reinhardt's work on *The Red Badge of Courage* would not be over until the picture was ready for release, and his work continually reminded him of John Huston. Also, he said, he was disturbed by the uncertainty about the future of Albert Band. Band missed Huston. He did not know what he was supposed to be doing for M-G-M, and he sat in his office reading. Like Reinhardt, he was on the first floor of the Thalberg Building, but, unlike Reinhardt, he had only a small office with a battered leather chair, a worn carpet, a desk, a typewriter, and an old couch. His name was not engraved on a brass plate on his door; it was typed on a white card placed in a slot, from which it could easily be removed. There were several photographs of Huston on the walls, and from time to time Band stared at them glumly. Finally, Reinhardt took the matter of Band's career in his own hands. He sent Dore Schary a memorandum saying that Band had rendered a most valuable service to *The Red Badge of Courage*, not only during the production and the cutting but also during the preparation of the script. Reinhardt wrote, 'I believe that, if given a chance, he would prove to be a great asset to the Studio as a writer, as well as, perhaps, one day, a director. In any event, I should like to put in a good word for him and ask you to keep him on the payroll and give him an assignment.' Schary responded by offering Band to Reinhardt, and Band now became Reinhardt's assistant.

A Sunday-night party at David Selznick's is a kind of institution among motion-picture notables, and Huston occasionally dropped in on them. The parties were held in an elaborate Beverly Hills house that once belonged to John Gilbert. Late in the festivities one night when Huston was there, Selznick, who has been an independent producer for many years, drew him aside. 'So you finished the picture,' he said. 'I'm really surprised.'

'Yeah,' Huston said, looking uncomfortable.

'I'm surprised they made it,' said Selznick. 'I'm really surprised.'

'They made it,' Huston said. 'Dore was for it all the time.'

'I'm really surprised,' said Selznick. 'How much did it cost? One five?'

'About that, David,' Huston said.

'I'm really surprised,' said Selznick.

They talked for a while about Schary's support of the making of the picture and Mayer's opposition to it. 'I'd like to know what L. B. thinks of your picture,' Selznick said to Huston.

'I wouldn't,' Huston said.

Bronislau Kaper, who, Reinhardt told me, was a serious and talented musician, was now composing the musical score for *The Red Badge of Courage*, and members of the sound department were adding sound effects to the film track. Production No. 1512 was the sixty-fifth picture Kaper had written music for in sixteen years of working for Metro-Goldwyn-Mayer. He is a voluble man, in his late forties, who was born in Poland, and as a young man had a career as a composer in Germany and France. In the early thirties, L. B. Mayer heard him play some of his compositions in Paris and signed him to an M-G-M contract. He numbers among his talents the ability to beat two-four time with one hand while beating three-eight time with the other, and the ability to make remarks that will get laughs. While composing for *The Red Badge of Courage*, he seemed to be constantly working hard at making remarks that would get laughs, depending for his wit on a mild and oblique insult. He always smiled whenever he delivered one, and, for some reason, the recipient usually smiled back. Kaper seems eternally cheerful, but he has a persistent look of dissatisfaction, together with a tremendous enthusiasm for composing music for pictures.

'Every picture is sick,' Kaper told me. 'That is my premise. We must take the picture and find out what it needs to make it well and healthy.' He had seen *The Red Badge of Courage* three times. He knew every foot of it, he said, and what the picture needed would have to be supplied by the music – a strengthening of the continuity, and a definite viewpoint toward the major characters, and he gave me a brief lecture on how he planned to do all this. 'After the Youth's regiment wins the first battle, the soldiers act happy,' he said. 'But I come along, and I tell the audience, with sad music, what is so good about this? I make a little ridiculous the whole idea of one American killing another American. Sometimes I bring phony emotions into the picture to wake the audience up. Other times, on a close-up, I stop the music. Some of the scenes are too punchy. I must bring them down. The music provides the sustained mood that will give the picture continuity and smoothness. The important contribution of the music is to tell the story of the boy. It must be told musically. This is a boy who is a coward, and then he becomes a hero. Why? The music will tell it. The boy sees two men dying. The two death scenes are the most overwhelming ever seen in pictures. This does something to the boy. The power of the death scenes eliminates the boy, so you've got to play the effect of the deaths on the boy. Which is the most important thing in the picture. I play the Tall Soldier's death by letting his breathing be the soloist. The music is the background to the breathing. When he dies, there is a sudden silence. No music. No comment. I give the audience a chance to make its own comment. The second death, as the Tattered Man wanders down the hill to die, with the Youth following him, I play with two instruments only. A trumpet, for the military death, and a harmonica – a gay tune – to show the irony of it. In the letter-writing scene, I said to John Huston, "It is important not to get sentimental. The Youth is writing a letter home." "The boy is afraid," John said, "and it is funny." I said, "I don't know how to score him as funny." John said, "He shouldn't be treated tragically. He is a little ridiculous." Then he said, "Banjo!" A stroke of genius! We have a funny sound coming from outside while the Youth sits in his tent and writes. A funny sound to a sad situation. In this way, we give a story to the picture. It is musically interesting when the boy runs away from the battle. I play the fears inside the boy. The music is spasmodic. Like a heartbeat. The entire prologue of the picture, a short scene showing the Youth on sentry duty, will be silent. No music can be as loud as silence.'

In the meantime, Reinhardt was working with a writer named Jan Lustig and with Albert Band on the story for a picture called *The Burning Secret*. During conferences with Lustig and Band on the general plan for the screenplay, Reinhardt digressed frequently to talk about other matters. One day, he told them that his mother, Else Heims, at the age of seventy-two, was starring in a play in Berlin. He then talked to them about their work and told them not to worry about problems like length when they were writing. 'You can always cut later,' he said. He told them he had taken up golf, because he wanted to have something he could talk about, the way other people talked about tennis or horses. He talked about Hollywood and said that he would never buy a house there, because deep down he had the feeling that he did not want to stay there. He said that Hollywood people were unsure of themselves as soon as they got away from Hollywood. 'As Sam Hoffenstein used to say, we are the croupiers in a crooked gambling house,' he said. He talked about what was wrong with the motion-picture business. 'Dividends are still being paid,' he told them, 'but the assets are whether Gable is a star. Whether we can cook up a good story.'

Reinhardt gave a sad sigh and went on to talk about The Burning Secret. One of the problems they had to work out, he said, was whether to include an implication of adultery and, if so, how to do it and still leave plenty of room for doubt in the minds of the audience. Another was whether the eleven-year-old boy hero should be shown wearing a Hopalong Cassidy suit. While Reinhardt was deep in this problem, his secretary came and and handed him an inter-office communication from Dore Schary:

Dear Gottfried:

I hate to burden you with bad news just before I go away for a holiday, but our film supply is to be cut exactly 50 per cent. In view of this, we must establish a rule that there is to be only one print of each take during any of your pictures in production and that any additional prints must by O.K.'d by Joe Cohn. We must make every effort to cut down the amount of film used on tests and also wherever possible cut down on the number of tests. Costume tests will be made by the new method of slides.

Will you please advise your directors of this circumstance; and during the shooting of pictures an effort must be made to make certain of values in a scene before shooting it. In other words, we will have to dispense with the 'Let's try one just to see what happens' point of view.

I'm sorry, Gottfried, I couldn't get to see you before I left but I've been literally swamped. I'm anxious to see the preview of Red Badge of Courage and that will be the first thing to look at when I get back.

My best,

D. S.

Reinhardt put the communication down and turned back to Band and Lustig, and with what appeared to be considerable effort he again took up the problems of adultery and the Hopalong Cassidy suit.

One day in the middle of December, Huston and James Agee, the novelist and former Time writer who had been hired to collaborate with Huston on the script for The African Queen, were working in the Horizon cottage, trying to finish the script in time for Huston's and

Spiegel's departure for Africa, where the picture was to be filmed. In the front room of the cottage was a false fireplace containing a gas log. Huston's Academy Award statuettes stood on the mantel. Agee was saying, as Huston paced in small circles, that the trip the river captain, Humphrey Bogart, and the missionary's sister, Katharine Hepburn, would make together down the river on the captain's boat in *The African Queen* could symbolize the act of love.

'Oh, Christ, Jim,' Huston said. 'Tell me something I can understand. This isn't like a novel. This is a screenplay. You've got to demonstrate everything, Jim. People on the screen are gods and goddesses. We know all about them. Their habits. Their caprices. But we can't touch them. They're not real. They stand for something, rather than being something. They're symbols. You can't have symbolism within symbolism, Jim.' He paced the floor and said he was going crazy. 'I really hate the city,' he said. 'I've got to get out to the country and get on a horse. I get all mixed up in the city. You know where I'd like to be this very minute, Jim?' He spread his long arms along the mantel of the fireplace. 'I'd like to be in Mexico. God!' He gave a stifled laugh, and said he guessed one of the best periods of his entire life had been spent, in his eighteenth year, in the Mexican cavalry. 'What a time that was!' he said. 'Always going places in Packards. You'd go the rounds of the cafés. Then you'd go to somebody's *finca*. Then you'd play the next thing to Russian roulette. You'd cock a pistol and throw it up and hit the ceiling with it. It was great. Just great. I was their top jumping rider. God, those were wonderful days!'

Spiegel put his head in the door. Huston stared at him for a moment without saying anything. Then he pretended to be shocked. 'Christ, Sam'l, for a minute there you looked just like an act Dad used to do in vaudeville,' he said in a menacing tone. Spiegel came into the room and looked from Huston to Agee with a hesitant smile. 'I was six when I first saw Dad do this act!' Huston went on in his special tone of amazement at his own words. 'Dad played a house painter, come to paint this lady's house. There was a picture of her husband inside the front door. The husband's face would begin to make faces, and then this big head would shove through the door with electric lights for eyes. And I'd roar. And Dad would sing,

"I Haven't Got the Do-Re-Mi". It was just wonderful. Ho! Ho! Ho!'

'So,' said Spiegel. 'How are things on the script?'

Huston said things were fine. 'Only trouble is, Sam, we just demolished two weeks' work. Threw out every bit of it,' he added lightly.

Spiegel swallowed hard, 'When?' he asked.

'Just now,' Huston said, with a forced grin.

'My ulcers are being formed,' Spiegel said, and gave Agee an appealing look.

Agee seemed bewildered.

'We leave in four weeks,' Spiegel said to Huston. 'We must have the script before we leave.'

'Don't worry, Sam'l,' Huston said, in the reassuring tone he had used in talking with Reinhardt about the script for *The Red Badge of Courage*.

Spiegel said, 'Beneath this façade of worry is worry. Did you get anything done today?'

'Don't worry,' said Huston. 'There's nothing to worry about.'

'I like to know what I'm worrying about,' said Spiegel. 'Now it's that I worry and I don't know why.'

'John,' Agee said, 'when are you going to do the retakes for David Selznick?'

Spiegel wet his lips. 'You expect to do retakes for Selznick?'

Huston nodded. 'David is in a jam,' he said.

'You can't. You have no time,' Spiegel said. 'Why? Is he offering you a fortune?'

'I'm doing it for nothing,' Huston said.

Spiegel shook his head. 'You can't do it,' he said.

'When a pal of mine is in a jam, I do what I can to help,' Huston said.

'You can't do it,' said Spiegel.

'Like hell I can't,' Huston said.

'No,' Spiegel said. .

Huston gave a choked laugh. 'Your ulcers, Sam'l,' he said softly.

Humphrey Bogart, who had made a number of pictures with

Huston, was enthusiastic about making another. He and his wife, Lauren Bacall, were getting ready to go to Africa. At the same time, Bogart was finishing *Sirocco* for his own company, Santana, a chore he did not especially care for. 'Too many business worries,' he told me one day in his living room, while his wife, with the aid of a writer named Richard Brooks and Mrs Brooks, trimmed a Christmas tree. 'The role is a cinch. The role doesn't bother me. I've been doing the role for years. I've worn that trench coat of mine in half the pictures I've been in. What I don't like is business worries. I like to work with John. The monster is stimulating. Offbeat kind of mind. Off centre. He's brilliant and unpredictable. Never dull. When I work with John, I think about acting, I don't worry about business. With Santana, I'm bowed down with business worries.'

'You and me both, Bogie,' said Brooks.

'You know what my director, Curt Bernhardt, said to me today?' Bogart said to Brooks. 'He was shooting the ending of a Bette Davis picture over at R.K.O. He said to me, "When we made the picture, we couldn't decide on an ending. It had an unhappy honest ending, but it was not honest. The dishonest happy ending was honest. The ending now – it's not dishonest and not honest. It'll be something new." At least they've got an ending. Santana has had eleven writers on *Sirocco*, and none of them goons has come across with an ending yet.'

'This you call a worry?' Brooks said. 'Everybody I know is trying to lick an ending.'

'Humphrey,' Mrs Bogart said, 'how about giving us a hand with this tree?'

'I like to wait till the end,' Bogart said. 'Then I throw the snow on it.'

'I have news for you,' Mrs Bogart said. 'There's no snow this year.'

'What's the matter? No guts?' Bogart asked.

'Don't pay any attention to him,' Mrs Bogart said to Mrs Brooks.

'My shoulders are heavy with business troubles,' Bogart said. 'I've got to talk to the monster and get some comfort.' He picked up the telephone and called Huston. A moment later, his face glowed. 'Hello, you son of a bitch,' he said. 'When we going to Africa?'

In January 1951, Huston and Agee went to stay at a ranch near Santa Barbara, to continue their work on the script of The African Queen. Reinhardt was worrying again about The Red Badge of Courage, and he went up to Santa Barbara for a weekend to see Huston. When he returned, he was downhearted. Huston had been very busy. He had had to go foxhunting, he had had to see David Selznick, and he had had to work on the script with Agee. He did not seem interested in talking to Reinhardt about The Red Badge of Courage.

'We do not have a great picture,' Reinhardt said to me when he came back. 'There is no story, because we do not show what the Youth is thinking. It is not in the script. John said he would put it on the screen. It is not on the screen. One day in my office, John and I acted out the scene where Audie grabs the flag and leads the charge. It was great. John was Audie, and he was crying. I was the Loud Soldier, and I was loud. The next morning, I went right up to see L. B. He usually does the acting. This time, I did the acting. I acted the scene out for him. Then I asked him, "Isn't it great?" He said yes, it was great. But we still don't have it. Audie does not cry. The Loud Soldier is not loud. It isn't on the screen.'

Dore Schary was vacationing in Florida when the trade papers carried lead stories reporting that his contract with Metro-Goldwyn-Mayer had been supplemented by an option to buy a hundred thousand shares of Loew's stock within a period of six years at the then current market value, which gave Schary a chance of making substantial capital gains if the stock went up. The papers also reported that Nicholas Schenck and William Rodgers were with Schary in Miami Beach, where they were to attend a special showing of Go for Broke!', a picture personally produced by Schary. There was no mention of L. B. Mayer in any of the reports.

While looking around for new pictures to do, Reinhardt often said that he missed working with Huston. He wired Schary in Florida suggesting that he and Huston do a picture together about Colonel Paul W. Tibbets, Jr, who dropped the atomic bomb on Hiroshima. 'WERE IT NOT FOR NUCLEAR INGREDIENTS SHOULD CALL IT DYNAMITE,' he wired. 'IDEAL VEHICLE FOR HUSTON.

SCRIPT COULD BE READY UPON HIS RETURN FROM SPIEGEL
ADVENTURE WHICH SHOULD MAKE HIM EVEN MORE EXPERT
IN DANGEROUS LIVING. URGE YOU TO CONSIDER THIS
MOST SERIOUSLY AND TO MAKE COMMAND DECISION.
HOPE YOU GRASP HEAVY IMPLICATION. HEARTIEST CON-
GRATULATIONS ON NEW CONTRACT. FINANCIAL SECURITY
OF BOSS ALWAYS SOURCE OF PEACE IN EMPLOYEES.'
Schary's reply was a memo saying, 'I will discuss the TIBBETS
story with you on my return. Everybody wants to do the story, so
if we do close the deal I will not make any decisions until my arrival
home. Meanwhile, get RED BADGE OF COURAGE ready for what
I hope will be a wonderful preview.'

Metro's promotion department got up an idea for a trailer
advertising *The Red Badge of Courage* – when the title appeared the
'Red' would fade out and 'White and Blue' would fade in.

Bronislau Kaper played the score for *The Red Badge of Courage* on the
piano for Reinhardt, and afterwards Reinhardt told me that the
picture might turn out to be great, after all. 'The music says what
Crane says in the novel,' he said. 'That was what was missing – what
goes on inside the boy. I called John and sang practically the whole
score to him over the telephone. He was delighted.' Reinhardt
looked delighted, too, and said he was going to talk to Schary about
the possibility of M-G-M's issuing the score in an album called
The Red Badge of Courage Suite. He asked me to go along with him to
watch the recording of the score for the picture.

The music was recorded on a large sound stage, off which was a
glass-enclosed monitor room. Reinhardt and Kaper and I sat in the
room with a man called the mixer, Mike McLaughlin, whose job it
was to regulate the volume of each section of the orchestra and
blend the sounds correctly. The studio's fifty-piece orchestra sat
facing the monitor room. (The orchestra included some of the
finest musicians in the world, Reinhardt said, and M-G-M paid its
musicians better than most symphony orchestras. The first violinist's
salary was $25,000 a year, and all the others had a year's contract
guaranteeing a minimum of $15,000.) The conductor wore ear-

phones, through which he could hear the dialogue of the picture, which was projected on a screen in back of the orchestra. A wide vertical line, called the cue line, moved across the screen, super-imposed on the picture, to indicate to the conductor exactly when the music was to start or stop.

The main musical theme was a triad, three notes of the tonic scale in C major – G, C, and E – to express the Youth's fear. 'The triad is great,' Kaper said. 'It is simple and tragic.'

'We're going to have a big fight with Dore,' said Reinhardt. 'He likes music in pictures to be conventional, discreet, and unobtru-sive. We, come right out and say it.'

'Dore should like this theme,' Kaper said. 'There is destiny in the theme. It is anticipation of something bad that becomes something beautiful.'

One of the first sections of the score to be recorded was the accom-paniment for the scene in which the Youth and the Loud Soldier, overhearing the General giving orders to attack, rush off to tell their comrades. Most of the instruments played a simple two-note theme for the attack, with a steady, exciting pulsation from the violins and short calls from the woodwinds.

'Not enough trumpet, Mac,' Kaper said to the mixer. McLaughlin turned a dial and brought up the sound of trumpets.

'As soon as the audience hears the music, it's no good,' Reinhardt said to Kaper. 'We have to be careful.'

As Kaper had worked out the plan for the score, the picture would open with the M-G-M lion's roar, accompanied by the sound of drums, which would be dissolved in gunfire, and then there would be the silent prologue, showing the Youth on sentry duty; that would be followed by a harmonica playing the familiar gay folk tune called 'Kingdom Coming' for the main title – as the name of the pictures and all the credits combined are called. Just as Kaper finished explaining this, the words 'Produced by Gottfried Rein-hardt' came on the screen without music. 'Directed by John Huston' was accompanied by piccolos. 'Music by Bronislau Kaper' had trumpets. Reinhardt said jokingly that if Kaper had trumpets, the least he should have under his name was strings. Kaper conferred with the conductor about putting strings under Reinhardt. Margaret

Booth came into the monitor room at that moment, and Reinhardt told her that the music for the main title was wonderful. The orchestra started rehearsing the music for the letter-writing scene.

'I've been seeing so many pictures,' said Miss Booth. 'I just finished cutting Show Boat. I cut two thousand feet out of it.'

Kaper said he did not like the way the orchestra was playing.

'I think you're overdramatizing this little piece of music,' Miss Booth said to him, and left.

'She walks in right in the middle of the recording!' Kaper cried. 'This is impossible! It must stop!'

'Margaret likes me,' Reinhardt said. 'She wants to see that everything goes all right with my picture.'

Reinhardt and I went back to his office, where we found Band waiting.

'Albert, fix me a drink,' Reinhardt said.

Band went into the next room and returned in a moment with a highball.

Reinhardt sighed and sat down behind his desk. Doubts about the chances of the picture's being a hit were again assailing him. 'I should have listened to Mayer,' he said. 'He begged me not to do it. He was like a father to me. He said, "This is thoughts. How are you going to show the boy's thoughts?" I promised him we would show them. He told me about John's picture The Asphalt Jungle. "Pavement", he called it. He said, "I loved the picture, but nobody is going in."' Reinhardt sighed again. 'I never should have made this picture,' he said. 'I did it because I love the book and because I love John. And I thought that John would be able to show what goes on inside the boy. If we had narration for the picture – maybe with that we could show what goes on inside. But John kept saying, "No narration." Billy Wilder in Sunset Boulevard had the nerve; after the man is dead, he has him do the narration. Joe Mankiewicz uses narration. Narration is good enough for them but not for John.'

He sipped his drink in gloomy silence. Then he said that in the past he had always been able to sense impending catastrophe. 'When I was making The Great Sinner,' he said, 'I had a wonderful cast – Gregory Peck, Ava Gardner, Melvyn Douglas, Ethel Barrymore,

Frank Morgan, Agnes Moorehead, Walter Huston. L. B. Mayer visited my set. Anything I wanted, I got. Then, one day, I looked at the picture. And I tied a terrific drunk on. "The characters are not alive," I said. I had wanted John to direct the picture. The studio wanted him. He agreed to do it and then Sam Spiegel pre-empted him. I got someone else. So both John and I made bad pictures. Before the reviews, even, people would not go to the theatre. It was a catastrophe. I felt it coming. I feel it coming now.'

Twenty days after the date Sam Spiegel had set for his and Huston's departure for England, where they were going to stop over en route to Africa, Huston was still in Santa Barbara working on the script for *The African Queen.* Reinhardt telephoned him there from his office. 'Stranger!' Reinhardt said. 'You never call me any more! You missed the recording. It was wonderful. It has the purity, the honesty, the tragedy, and the nobility of the novel. I am really crazy about it. I expect not too good a reaction from Dore, but you'll be just insane about it. In the first battle, in the lull in the fighting, they're carrying in the hurt Rebs. Very slowly the music starts. Very strange and eerie it is, and then we cut to the bird singing. It is just glorious. I am just crazy about it. Wait. I'll put Albert on.'
Band took the telephone, 'John,' he said, 'you're going to faint when you hear the music.'
'Sing him the tune!' Reinhardt commanded.
Band sang 'Kingdom Coming' over the telephone, and then Reinhardt took over again. 'The title is just marvellous,' he said, and laughed. 'Piccolos under your name, strings under mine. You will go out of your mind.'

Dubbing for sound is the process whereby all sound for a picture is put on a single sound track and synchronized with the picture film. 'It is really simple,' Reinhardt told me. 'We combine the sound tracks made while we shot the picture with all the sound tracks we made here – the additional spoken lines, the gunfire effects, close shellbursts, far shellbursts, birds singing, murmuring voices, dragging feet, wind, water, crickets, music. We have three music tracks, including the orchestra, the trumpet calls, and the drum rolls.

We run all the tracks through together and put them on a tape recording. This saves sound film. If anything is wrong, we can correct it before the sound on the tape is recorded on film for the final sound track. For the preview, we will have two tracks, one for the picture and one for sound. If the picture is O.K.'d by Mayer, Schary, and the other executives, we make a composite called Movietone. This is what is used in the theatres. Hollywood's technical superiority is one of the things that make American pictures more popular all over the world than European ones. The sound men look at a picture as though they were looking at an automobile engine. Chi-chi does not impress them at all. They are all, somehow, scientists.'

The Red Badge of Courage was dubbed for sound in a dark, close projection room that had what is known as a dubbing console at the rear of the room. Three men were seated at the controls. They were called Bob, Jimmy, and Sparky, and they all looked as though chi-chi would not impress them. They dubbed one reel of film at a time. For guidance, in addition to the picture itself and the counsel of Reinhardt, Kaper, and Band, the dubbers had charts showing at what point in the footage of each reel they were to dub in such effects as 'soldiers yelling', 'wounded men shuffling along the road', 'bodies thumping in falls', and 'horses milling'. Reinhardt would hear too much caisson-rolling and not enough music, or Band would hear too much of the Youth's flight from battle and not enough artillery, or Kaper would hear gunfire overwhelming his drums. When Reinhardt said he did not hear enough birds, Sparky and Jimmy and Bob pushed buttons and turned dials on their console or phoned the sound library for more bird calls. The sound men recorded and re-recorded and re-re-recorded until each one of the critics heard what he wanted to hear.

The process took five days. Reinhardt and Band and Kaper sat with Sparky and Jimmy and Bob hour after hour in the room, seeing the reels over and over, and working for perfection of sound – one more shellburst here, one less rifleshot there, the substitution of a bugle call recorded on Huston's ranch for a stock bugle call from the sound library. One of the most difficult reels to dub had four dialogue tracks, three music tracks, and ten sound-effect tracks, which included, for one scene, a set of sounds labelled 'Chickens, calm' and a set labelled 'Chickens, excited'. They worked for a couple of hours on this particular scene. Band finally suggested eliminating the calm chickens, and then the sound was just right. When the dubbing was complete, Reinhardt thanked Jimmy, Sparky, and Bob, and told them they had done a wonderful job. Automatically, the sound men told Reinhardt he had a wonderful picture.

'The sound department is like granite,' Reinhardt said to me. 'The music department is hysterical, the sound department never.'

The first showing of The Red Badge of Courage to an outside audience was given in a large projection room at the studio. Huston came down from Santa Barbara for the big night. Reinhardt had invited the cast of the picture, along with Sam Spiegel; William Wyler, the director, a close friend of both Huston and Reinhardt; an M-G-M producer named Sidney Franklin; Paul Kohner, Huston's agent; and Pablo, Huston's fifteen-year-old adopted son. Schary, who had returned from Miami Beach, couldn't come because he was home with a cold. The official preview of the picture was to be two nights later. Reinhardt told Huston that he had talked to Schary on the telephone, and that Schary had asked him how the picture was. 'I told him that Bronny Kaper made the actors act,' Reinhardt said. 'When are you leaving, John?' Huston said he was leaving right after the preview. It was too bad, because he hadn't had the time to do the retakes he'd promised Selznick, he said, but then Selznick had persuaded him to forget the whole thing, and, besides, Huston had already given Selznick – and Arthur Fellows, an employee of Selznick's and a friend of Huston's – some help on the cutting of the picture.

Reinhardt and Huston turned up at the projection room a few minutes early.

'Is anybody here?' Reinhardt asked a projectionist, shakily.

'Did anybody come?' Huston asked.

'Pablo is here,' Reinhardt said.

'Well!' Huston said, with his peculiar way of making the word expand.

Reinhardt and Huston looked at each arrival with the solemnity of people watching for relatives at a funeral. Mrs Spiegel. Mrs Huston. Mrs Reinhardt. Audie Murphy. Tim Durant. John Dierkes. Reggie Callow. Hal Rosson. Paul Kohner. Andrew Marton. Lee Katz. Bronislau Kaper. Benny Lewis. Albert Band. Reinhardt sat down at the rear of the room. Huston sat up front. Reinhardt called him back. 'I want all the family together,' he said.

The lights dimmed. The showing began with a Fitz-Patrick travelogue about Holland, in Technicolor.

'I didn't think the picture was in colour,' Huston said, and forced a laugh.

The audience shuffled their feet, whispered, and looked around. William Wyler arrived late and sat next to Huston. 'Is this it?' Wyler said.

'I didn't know it was in colour,' Huston said to him, and laughed nervously again.

Drums sounded and the M-G-M lion roared. Immediately, there was an awful silence in the room. *The Red Badge of Courage* started, with the prologue showing the Youth on sentry duty on the screen. Huston watched the picture with his mouth open. Reinhardt laughed unconvincingly at the first amusing scene and stared at his neighbours, as if to encourage them to laugh. He stopped in surprise when he saw that they were already laughing.

The audience appeared to be moved by the scenes of Dierkes, the Tall Soldier, running up to the hilltop to die and Dano, the Tattered Man, wandering downhill to his death. 'Jesus, Johnny!' Wyler said to Huston as the Tattered Man died on the screen. 'Jesus!'

When the lights went up, the audience sat very still for a moment. Then Kohner turned around to Huston and broke the silence. 'Damn good, John,' he said.

'Wonderful, Johnny,' said Wyler.

'My congratulations, John,' Band said.

'Johnny, wonderful, wonderful,' said Mrs Kohner.

'Well!' Huston said.

'It's a gem,' Sidney Franklin said to Reinhardt.

'Gottfried, I wish I had brought my jelly beans!' Mrs Reinhardt said. 'I am starving.'

Spiegel looked at Huston, obviously impressed.

'Terrific, Gottfried. Terrific, John,' said Kohner.

'Well!' Mrs Huston said, looking very happy.

'Boy, Dad!' said Pablo Huston.

There was a sudden surge of excitement in the room. Everybody was shaking hands with everybody else.

'He's the guy!' Huston said, his arm around Bronislau Kaper. 'He wrote the music. I just made the picture.'

'A beautiful score,' Spiegel said. 'I discovered Bronny. I brought him to Hollywood.'

'I put my heart into it,' Kaper said. 'I worked harder on this score than on any other ever. I wrote my heart out for this score.'

'Jesus!' Wyler said to Reinhardt. 'That fella who goes down the hill and dies.'

'Royal Dano,' Reinhardt said proudly. 'He is magnificent.'

'Terrific dolly shot,' Wyler said.

'Four hundred and fifty feet,' said Reinhardt.

'Makes you realize that a war eighty-five years ago was tougher than a war today,' said Wyler.

'We've got incredible stuff,' Reinhardt said.

'It was the bloodiest war,' said Wyler. 'No Red Cross. Nothing.'

'Incredible. The two sides murdered each other. We've got incredible stuff,' said Reinhardt. 'How is your new picture, Willie?'

Wyler shrugged. 'It's all a gamble,' he said. 'The only way is to lose big or win big. You can have the biggest success or the biggest flop in the world – initially, it's the same gamble.'

Mrs. Kohner came over and said, 'Isn't it wonderful?'

'Great,' said Wyler.

Murphy looked bewildered. 'Seems I didn't do all that,' he said softly.

'You sure looked good,' Dierkes told him.

Everybody was now telling everybody else that it was a great picture. Huston hugged Reinhardt and said, 'It's the best picture I ever made.'

'You've got a picture there,' Spiegel said, and pursed his lips.

Wyler and Spiegel wandered out together. 'The worst that can happen, it will break even,' Wyler was saying. 'How much did it cost?'

'A million five, Willie,' said Spiegel, with satisfaction. 'So, it's M-G-M's money.'

'M-G-M can afford to make this picture for prestige,' Wyler said. 'If they get the American Legion behind it – basically, it's that kind of story.'

'The music was great,' Spiegel said.

'M-G-M has nothing to lose making this,' Wyler said thoughtfully.

Reinhardt joined them and stood beaming with delight as they told him that he had made a *great* picture. He lowered his head modestly. 'John embraced me and said it is the best picture he ever made,' he said. 'John is in the clouds.'

What's Wrong with Mocha's Opinion?

ONE afternoon in February 1951, six months after Metro-Goldwyn-Mayer put *The Red Badge of Courage* into production, Huston and Reinhardt set out together for its first preview. From the beginning, the picture had stirred up an extraordinary amount of debate at M-G-M. Reinhardt and Huston wanted to make what Reinhardt, over and over again, referred to as 'a *great* picture', and the debate was about whether it would, in fact, turn out to be a great picture, and if it did, whether it would also make money. Everybody involved in producing the film felt that what happened at the preview would probably answer the question. The New York office, in the person of Schenck, Loew's president, stood by waiting to hear the results; with Schenck were other top executives, including William F. Rodgers, Loew's general manager in charge of sales, who five months before had said to Reinhardt, 'Its greatness depends on how it is received by the public.' In Hollywood, Mayer, Loew's second in command, who at first had opposed producing the picture but had finally, for reasons of his own, given in, and had been watching the picture's progress closely ever since, was still watching. In Hollywood too, Schary, who, possibly with Schenck's support, had backed Huston and Reinhardt from the first, and had insisted ever since that he had confidence in the picture's commercial as well as artistic prospects, was still insisting. The latest estimate that Loew's executives had on the cost of *The Red Badge of Courage* – Production No. 1512 – now stood at $1,548,755, or about $50,000 over the maximum that Huston and Reinhardt had promised Dore Schary the picture would cost.

Before the preview, Reinhardt and Huston were going to stop off at Schary's home to show him the picture there, because he had a cold and couldn't get to the theatre. I drove with Reinhardt to Santa Monica, where we were to pick up Huston. Reinhardt was wearing a blue beret, and he was smoking a long cigar. On the way, he said that the studio publicity department had shown the picture to Hedda Hopper and that she had telephoned him to say it was the best war picture she had ever seen. 'She is absolutely giddy,' said Reinhardt. 'Tonight, Mayer will be at the preview. Afterwards he might talk to us. He might not. You can never tell. People say, "Did you see L. B.'s face?" And they think they have a flop. The next morning they say, "It's O.K. He liked the picture."' Reinhardt drove recklessly. 'Everybody says we have a brilliant picture,' he said, as we sped along. 'John is in seventh heaven.'

We met Huston in the cocktail lounge of a hotel overlooking the Pacific Ocean. His exuberance matched Reinhardt's. He immediately said. 'Hopper's man, Spec McClure, called me. Hedda says it's the greatest war picture ever made.' He and Reinhardt exchanged significant looks, and both burst out laughing.

'We have a great picture,' Reinhardt said. He turned to the waiter and said, 'Martinis.'

'Well,' Huston said and, tilting back in his chair, he put a brown cigarette in the corner of his mouth and slowly looked around the cocktail lounge. It was early in the afternoon, and we were the only patrons there. A cleaning woman was swabbing the floor near the entrance with a mop.

'When are you leaving for Africa?' Reinhardt asked, as the waiter brought the drinks.

'In two days, Gottfried,' Huston said, lighting his cigarette and, over the flame, intently watching the cleaning woman mop the floor.

'You finished the script for *The African Queen*?' Reinhardt asked.

'Almost, Gottfried,' Huston said absently. 'I'll do the last of it on the plane going over.'

Reinhardt took a long sip of his drink. 'We will have to do the retakes for *The Red Badge of Courage* in Africa,' he said, and laughed with considerable satisfaction.

'Yeah,' Huston said.

'When I think of all we went through,' Reinhardt said.

'Christ. Gottfried, wasn't it worth it?' Huston said.

Reinhardt gave a nod of happy agreement. 'Now, if anything goes wrong tonight, we will have to do everything over in Africa,' he said, laughing again.

'Yeah, we'll have to do it all over in Africa,' Huston said. 'Ho! Ho! Ho!'

Reinhardt choked on his laughter. He stood up, and, as he was paying for the drinks, Huston put on a Burberry and matching cap. He pulled the cap down over his eyes and strode quickly over to the cleaning woman who was mopping the floor. He bowed to her and took the mop from her hands. Then he put his arms around the mop and, hugging it, he did a rakish waltz around the deserted cocktail lounge. Reinhardt beamed at him, and Huston, laughing quietly, danced back to the cleaning woman, returned her mop, and then danced out of the lounge alone to the street. 'Cut!' cried Reinhardt.

As we drove toward Schary's house, Huston and Reinhardt talked about the private showing they had held two nights before for a couple of dozen friends and colleagues in the motion-picture industry, including William Wyler, Paul Kohner, and Sam Spiegel. They discussed the enthusiastic response The Red Badge of Courage had got at the showing.

'You know, Gottfried,' said Huston, 'I never had such a reaction to a picture before. I never heard Sam and Paul talk that way about a picture. And Willie Wyler called me and said it's one of the greatest pictures he's ever seen. This is Willie's picture. I never made a picture before that Willie didn't have some criticism to make of it. He kept grabbing my arm that night and saying, "Jesus, this is wonderful!"' Huston laughed. 'Willie said that the Tattered Man's death scene was the most amazing he ever watched.'

'We have a great picture,' Reinhardt said.

'Well, boys,' Dore Schary said when he received us, 'I've got bad news for you. Hopper likes the picture.'

'Christ, kid!' Huston said. He and Reinhardt both laughed.

'You're happy, huh?' Schary said.

'Christ!' said Huston.

'You're leaving for Africa,' Schary said.

'Yeah,' Huston said.

'I'll show you a couple of things when you get back,' Schary said.

'Christ, kid,' Huston said. 'I've never had a reaction like this to a picture. Willie Wyler says it's the greatest picture he's ever seen.'

'You had Willie there?' Schary said.

'Yeah, and – ' Huston paused, as though his mind had gone blank. 'Who else was there, Gottfried?'

'You look sort of gay in that cap,' Schary said, not giving Reinhardt a chance to answer.

'Well, I'm kind of a sport,' Huston said, taking off his cap and coat.

Schary ushered us into the living room. Huston said, 'Dore, before you see any of this, I just want to tell you it's the best picture I ever made. I never, never had such a reaction before.'

'Let's run it and we'll talk later,' said Schary.

'You want to close the blind?' Reinhardt asked. The sun was streaming in.

'Pull it down, Gottfried,' Schary said, and Reinhardt pulled down the blind.

The wide panel in the wall at one end of the room slid up, exposing the white screen, and the M-G-M lion appeared on the screen, and its roar dissolved in the sound of gunfire. The prologue of the picture started, showing the Youth on sentry duty near a river. Two of Schary's children bounded into the room and sat down facing the screen.

Schary got up and led them out of the room. 'I told you to stay out. I want you to stay out,' he said.

Nobody said anything during the showing, and except for some subdued laughter from Huston and Reinhardt at an early comic scene in the movie, there was no sound in the room at all except what came from the sound track. At the end of the picture, the lights came on. Schary turned slowly to Reinhardt and Huston and said, 'I think you ought to reprise these guys at the end.'

'The faces,' Huston said, nodding emphatically.

'Yeah,' said Schary. 'By the way, I'm glad to see you dubbed in "gone goose" for "gone coon".' He was apparently taking his time about giving his opinion. After another long pause, he said, 'Well, it's a wonderful picture.'

Huston leaped to his feet and went over to Schary. Reinhardt shakily held a match to his cigar, which had gone out.

'I have two suggestions,' Schary said, as the heads of his children peered around the door. 'I think some of the picture will be swallowed by the music. If it were my picture, I would yank the music out of the scene where the boy writes the letter. Close the door, kids!' The heads vanished. 'Each time the music has the sense of warmth and nostalgia, it creates a mood that is helpful to the picture,' Schary went on. 'As soon as the music gets highly inventive, it hurts the picture. I think it'll hurt your picture, John. This picture is gonna stand up for years to come. It's a great, great picture.'

Reinhardt and Huston did not interrupt. They were tense, and they were giving Schary their full attention. 'A great picture,' Schary repeated. He glanced at some notes he had made. 'The only scene I don't like – I still don't understand it, it destroys the mood – is the scene where the recruits are marchin' past the veterans and the veterans are laughin' at the guys.' He had lapsed into an even more homespun and chatty manner than usual. 'That irony at the end, when the guys think they're winnin' a battle and then it turns out they're not – that's accurate and real. I don't accept it in the other scene. It confuses me. I have to reorient myself. I think that scene should come out. I think it hurts you.'

Huston started walking in small circles. 'Uh-huh,' he said. 'Uh-huh. I'm just trying to orient the thought, Dore.'

Reinhardt said nothing. He seemed to be making an effort to keep his face blank.

After a while, Huston said haltingly, 'The only value the scene has, it's an interruption of that slam-bang of battle.'

'That's not a valid argument,' Schary said. 'The mood of battle is sustained. You don't have to break it.'

'You're right,' Huston said. 'It doesn't need to be there.'

Schary looked pleased. 'It just confuses you,' he said. 'The scene always bothered me.'

Huston said, 'You think it's an error, Dore, to take the view that the sole purpose of the scene is to give you a lift?'

'You don't need the scene,' said Schary. 'Boys, I think this picture is a great document. It's gonna be in the files. It's gonna be in the history books. It's a great picture.'

'Then it comes off,' Huston said.

'It must be sold as a great battle story,' Schary said. 'If we make it too special, you know – a great novel and all that – we'll drive away the kids who come to see a war story.'

'The danger is it might be slapped into the big theatres for short runs,' Reinhardt said.

'It won't be,' said Schary.

'It ought to go to a big theatre that will give it time to build to a long run,' said Reinhardt.

'You mean, Gottfried, like the Astor?' Huston asked.

'Yes. Show that the makers of the picture have faith in the picture,' Reinhardt answered.

Huston said that reprising the faces at the end of the picture was a great idea.

'Just goes to prove the value of reading your mail,' Schary said warmly. 'A letter comes from a fella, he says, "I run a theatre. Why don't you put the name of the picture at the end? All it ever says at the end is 'The End'. This is a great idea and it costs you nothing." So I'm puttin' in this new thing at the studio.' Schary seemed to be in especially high spirits. 'I think this is the best picture you ever made, John.'

'So do I,' said Huston, laughing.

'So glad we made it,' Schary said, and chuckled.

'Yeah, we finally made it,' Huston said.

'It's a great picture, and it'll get great notices,' said Schary. 'I told you what your notices would be on *The Asphalt Jungle*, didn't I?'

'You did,' said Huston. There was a moment of silence.

'You fellas call me right after the preview,' said Schary.

'Jesus, I'd love to see this be a big success,' Huston said. 'You know why, Dore. After everything we've been through with L. B. on this picture.'

'Don't worry about it, kiddy,' Schary said, grinning.

'Dore, you like the picture?' Reinhardt asked.

'I told you – this picture is gonna be remembered,' Schary said. 'It's a great picture.'

'It ought to run in a theatre like the Astor or the Music Hall,' Reinhardt said.

'Not the Music Hall,' Schary said. 'It should go into a house where

people will come to enjoy seeing it, not a place where it will be the
object of concern about whether it will gross this much or that
much.'

'The thing is it's got to have time to grow,' Huston said. 'I'd go to
towns where *Asphalt* had just opened and the managers would tell
me business was picking up, but they couldn't take the chance of
keeping it on for five more days.'

Schary said that this was the kind of picture that should have
special showings, to special groups, who would promote it. Also, it
should have a special, and dignified, kind of publicity campaign.
'Too bad you're leaving,' he said to Huston. 'You could handle
some special showings yourself.'

Huston said it was imperative that he be in England in four days,
on his way to Africa.

'I could send the picture to New York with you,' Schary said.

'I'll be in New York only one day – Sunday,' Huston said.

'Too bad,' said Schary. 'The press will go crazy about this picture.
This is a magnificent picture. It has intelligence and it has art. It
fulfils the purpose of the cinema as a medium of entertainment
and education. Nothing is wrong except that one scene. And a few
tiny places where you go out too quick or hold too long.' His
telephone rang. The call was from Benny Thau, one of the company's
vice-presidents. 'I feel pretty good, Benny,' Schary said. 'No, I can't
be at the preview. I don't know whether you'll like it or not, but
you're gonna see one of the greatest pictures ever made.'

When Schary had hung up, Huston said, 'Can he afford not to like
it now?'

Schary chuckled.

'I saw L. B. today,' Reinhardt said slowly. 'Mayer said to me,
"Maybe the picture is a good picture, but it can't possibly be a
success at the box office." I told him, "I don't know if it is commercial, but it is a great picture."'

Schary said dryly, 'You played that scene wrong, Gottfried. If I
had been playing that scene, I would have said, "If I were starting all
over again, I would now enter upon the making of this picture with
greater confidence than ever before, with complete and unmiti-
gated confidence."'

'Too many people say that,' Reinhardt said in a low voice.

'L. B. thinks a picture's no good if you don't say it,' Huston said.

'I don't agree with you on the music,' Reinhardt said suddenly to Schary.

Huston and Schary looked startled. Schary said, 'I have no conviction. It's just my personal reaction.'

'Audie is twice as good with the music under him, I tell you,' said Reinhardt.

Schary replied coolly, 'I think all music in pictures has to be cliché to be effective. Let's not debate it. I'll prove it to you. In Marine pictures, you play "Halls of Montezuma". In Navy pictures, you play "Anchors Aweigh". In this picture, the music that's effective is the sentimental-cliché music. It's a fact. Let's not debate it.'

Schary quickly asked Huston whether he intended to sell his father's country house in the San Bernardino Mountains, and told him he'd be interested in it if Huston ever set a price on it.

'So you're going to have your Berchtesgaden,' said Reinhardt.

Schary did not seem to hear him. 'I'm getting to the point where I want a place of my own. A *place*,' he said. 'With *things* on it.' He stood up, and congratulated Huston and Reinhardt again. 'Call me after the preview, kiddies,' he said.

The preview was at the Picwood Theatre, a fifteen-minute drive from Schary's house. M-G-M often previewed pictures there. It was a modern, comfortable theatre, and on preview nights the lights on the marquee always read, 'MAJOR STUDIO PREVIEW TO-NIGHT'. The purpose of a preview – usually called a sneak preview – is supposedly to spring a picture on an audience without warning, in order to get an uninfluenced reaction. Many previews are advertised on marquees, in newspapers, and by word of mouth, but even these are known in the trade as sneak previews, or sneaks.

The marquee of the Picwood said 'HARVEY' as well as 'MAJOR STUDIO PREVIEW TONIGHT'.

'I hate previews,' Reinhardt said to me as he and Huston and I got out of the car. 'The smelly house. Popcorn. Babies crying. Ugh! I hate it.'

Bronislau Kaper buttonholed Reinhardt in the lobby. 'Tell me. What did he say? Tell me everything.' Reinhardt led him aside to tell him what Schary had said.

Johnny Green, head of M-G-M's music department, and Margaret Booth came up to Huston and asked him what Schary had said.

'Who's got a nickel?' Huston said. 'Albert! Get me some popcorn.' Albert Band, who was now working as Reinhardt's assistant, made his way through the crowd to a gleaming popcorn machine, as streamlined as the Picwood Theatre itself.

A man asked Huston whether he had ever heard Tallulah Bankhead's radio show. 'If I could find the right thing in the picture, I might get a spot for it on Tallulah's show,' he said.

One of the company's vice-presidents, L. K. Sidney, came over to Huston, took a handful of his popcorn, and said, 'Good luck, John.'

A short man with a cherubic face came over to Huston and pumped his hand. 'Remember me? Swifty,' he said.

'How are you, Swifty?' said Huston.

'I know you're thinking of other important matters tonight, but this I gotta tell you,' said Swifty.

'Of course, Swifty,' Huston said, looking very interested.

'The latest about Jack Warner!' Swifty announced. 'One of Jack's producers suggests he do a picture about Mexico. So Jack says, "I don't like Mexican pictures. All the actors in them look too goddam Mexican."' Swifty let out a wild guffaw.

'A great story, Swifty,' Huston said.

'I knew you'd appreciate it,' said Swifty.

Huston tossed pieces of popcorn into his mouth. 'Eddie Mannix!' he said, moving to greet a square-faced, hulking man who looked like a football coach – another of M-G-M's vice-presidents.

'Good luck, fella,' said Mannix.

Mrs Huston arrived breathlessly, having driven in from Malibu Beach with Pablo, Huston's adopted son.

Mrs Reinhardt turned up and said that she had reluctantly left her French poodle, Mocha, at home. 'Gottfried!' she cried. 'Mocha wanted to come to the preview.'

'Silvia, please!' Reinhardt said.

'What's wrong with Mocha's opinion?' Mrs Reinhardt asked.

'L. B. Mayer is here,' someone said to Huston. 'He just scooted inside.'

'How are you? Glad to see you,' Huston was saying, shaking hands with still another M-G-M vice-president, as Reinhardt took a stand at Huston's side.

I went in and sat down in the rear. When *The Red Badge of Courage* flashed on the screen, there was a gasp from the audience and a scattering of applause. As the showing went along, some of the preview-goers laughed at the right times, and some laughed at the wrong times, and some did not laugh at all. When John Dierkes, in the part of the Tall Soldier, and Royal Dano, in the part of the Tattered Man, played their death scenes, which had been much admired before, some people laughed and some murmured in horror. The audience at the private showing had been deeply and unanimously moved by the death scenes. There was no unanimity in the audience now. Several elderly ladies walked out. Now and then, there were irrelevant calls from the balcony; one masculine voice, obviously in the process of changing, called out, 'Hooray for Red Skelton!' Two or three babies cried. Men posted at the exits counted all departures. I could not see where Huston and Reinhardt were sitting. Across the aisle from me I could see L. B. Mayer, white-haired and bespectacled, sitting with his arms folded, looking fiercely blank-faced. Several M-G-M people nearby were watching him instead of the movie. During a particularly violent battle scene, Mayer turned to a lady sitting on his right and said, 'That's Huston for you.' There was a slight stir in his vicinity, but Mayer said nothing more.

In the lobby, the Picwood manager, assisted by several M-G-M men, stood ready to hand out what are known as preview cards – questionnaires for the audience to fill out. The first question was: 'How would you rate this picture?' Five alternatives were offered: 'Outstanding', 'Excellent', 'Very Good', 'Good', and 'Fair'. Other questions were: 'Whom did you like best in the picture?' 'Which scenes did you like most?' 'Which scenes, if any, did you dislike?' 'Would you recommend this picture to your friends?' Below the questions there was this additional request:

We don't need to know your name, but we would like to
know the following facts about you:

(A)   Male.
      Female.

(B)   Please check your age group:

      Between 12 and 17.
      Between 18 and 30.
      Between 31 and 45.
      Over 45.

When the showing ended, the preview-goers milled about in the
lobby, filling out the cards under the resentful surveillance of the
men who had made the movie. Mayer walked out of the theatre and
stood at the kerb out front, looking as thought he would like to have
somebody talk to him. Reinhardt and Huston went into the manager's office, off the lobby, and sat down to await the verdict. Johnny
Green, Margaret Booth, Bronislau Kaper, and Albert Band alternately
watched the people filling out cards and Mayer. Most of the other
executives had already departed. Benny Thau joined Mayer at the
kerb. Mayer got into his town-and-country Chrysler, and his
chauffeur drove him off. Benny Thau got into a black limousine and
his chauffeur drove him off. Band went into the manager's office.
Huston and Reinhardt sat looking glumly at each other.

   'Did Mayer talk to anybody?' Reinhardt asked.

   Band reported that Mayer had talked to Benny Thau.

   The manager came in and handed Reinhardt and Huston a batch
of preview cards he had collected from the audience. Reinhardt
read through them rapidly. Huston read some of the comments
aloud. '"This would be a wonderful picture on television,"' he
read. '"With all the money in Hollywood, why can't you make
some good pictures?"'

   'Fair. Fair. Good. Fair,' Band read. Here's one with Fair crossed
out and Stinks substituted.'

   'Here's an Excellent,' Huston said.

   'No Outstandings yet,' said Reinhardt. He was perspiring, and he
looked grim. 'Here's a Lousy,' he said.

'The audience hated the picture,' Band said.

Huston seemed dazed. 'Call Dore, Gottfried,' he said.

Reinhardt dialled the number. After getting Schary, he said, 'Dore,' in a low, shaking voice, and after listening for a moment he said, 'You know?... Who told you?... Well, then you know.... Well, a lot of people walked out.... Well, a new batch of cards is coming in.... We've counted twenty-two Outstandings so far, fourteen Excellents, thirty Very Goods, fourteen Goods, and forty-three Fairs.... Well, Margaret Booth said the reaction was terrible.... No, I didn't talk to L. B. I didn't talk to Mannix.... Well, I think we should take it out again tomorrow, with a serious picture. Not with *Harvey*. Maybe with *The Steel Helmet*.... He is right here.'

Reinhardt handed the telephone to Huston, who said, 'Well.... Well, Jesus Christ. Dore, I had the feeling they'd rather be anywhere than in this theatre. Must have been a dozen people walked out on the scenes I think are the best – the two death scenes. Wait till you see the cards. They're extraordinary. They're either raves or they say it's the worst picture they've ever seen. They just hate it. It's extraordinary.'

An M-G-M man put his head in at the door. 'Thirty-two walk-outs,' he said. The capacity of the Picwood was sixteen hundred, and it had been filled at the start of the showing.

The manager said sympathetically to Reinhardt. 'How much did it cost? A million five?'

After Huston hung up, he said to Reinhardt, 'Christ, Gottfried! I never saw one like this before, did you?'

'You can't force an audience to like a picture,' Reinhardt said bleakly. 'God! Tomorrow morning at the studio! How I hate to walk in there! They'll all be my enemies.'

'Well, good night, Gottfried,' Huston said. He was driving home with Mrs Huston and Pablo.

Reinhardt walked to his car with his wife and me. 'It's a cruel business,' he said. 'It isn't worth it. Almost a whole year.' He looked at his half-smoked cigar with distaste. 'M-G-M doesn't know what to do with a picture like this.' He put the cigar in his mouth. 'Did you see John? John was demolished tonight.'

The next morning, Reinhardt telephoned me, sounding serious and tense, and said that the studio was going to have another preview that night, in Pasadena. He had not slept a wink all night, he said. He had not heard from Schary. He had not heard from Mayer. He had called Huston, who was going to meet him at the studio to go to the Pasadena preview, and he invited me to go along with them.

When I arrived at the Thalberg Building, Reinhardt was in conference with a writer about a possible new picture. I waited in the room at the rear of his office. Preview cards were scattered about. The Goods, Very Goods, Excellents, and Outstandings occupied the armchairs. ('Huston is to be congratulated. To those who can take grim reality, it's in the class of *All Quiet on the Western Front*.') Everything below Good was spread out on a couch. ('The worst I have ever seen. The Tall Soldier's death scene is tripe.' 'Very poor. I fell asleep. Most monotonous picture I have ever seen.' 'Audie Murphy is too good of an actor to be stuck in such a stinker as this.') Albert Band came in and said that Reinhardt wanted to put narration — passages from the Crane novel — into the picture and to add a scene at the beginning that would show the Stephen Crane novel being opened and its pages being turned, so that the audience would know the picture was based on a great book. 'Gottfried wants to move the prologue, that wonderful scene with the Youth on sentry duty at the river, and put it in later on,' Band said indignantly. 'I don't approve.'

In Reinhardt's inner office, a while later, Huston sat rocking back and forth in a chair across the desk from Reinhardt. Band was pacing up and down behind him.

'Mayer has written it off,' Reinhardt said. 'Dore will back it. It's a good thing this is not a cheap picture. If it were, they would forget it entirely.'

'Did you speak to L. B.?' Huston asked.

'He wouldn't talk to me,' said Reinhardt. 'Margaret Booth told me to call him. I said, "Why should I? He should call me." But then I called him. He didn't call me back. L. B. told Dore. "There are flops and there are successes. There are good pictures and bad pictures. Let's go on making pictures."'

Huston gave a low, muffled laugh.

'I always felt you must put over this picture the shadow of Stephen Crane,' Reinhardt went on. 'We must come right out and say, "Here is a great American novel about the Civil War." With your blessing, John, I would like to try a preview where we have narration. And at the end the narrator will say' – he picked up a copy of the novel, opened it, and read – '"So it came to pass that as he trudged from the place of blood and wrath his soul changed. He came from hot ploughshares to prospects of clover tranquilly, and it was as if hot ploughshares were not. He had rid himself of the red sickness of battle. He had been an animal blistered and sweating in the heat and pain of war. He turned now with a lover's thirst to images of tranquil skies, fresh meadows, cool brooks – an existence of soft and eternal peace."' He clapped the book shut. 'Spencer Tracy should do it,' he said.

'How many passages?' Huston asked wearily.

Band, who had talked the matter over with Reinhardt, said five passages.

Reinhardt said, 'John, you have to tell people what the picture is. We should start the narration at the beginning, before the scene at the river. That scene is puzzling. You pay for clever openings. We must tell them, "Here is a masterpiece." You've got to tell it to them.'

Huston got to his feet and began pacing around the office.

'It might make the difference between life and death,' Reinhardt said.

'It might very well,' Huston said, without conviction. 'Let's try it, by all means.'

'The people must know this is a classic,' Reinhardt said.

The second preview was held at the Pasadena Theatre, in Pasadena. It was a Friday night, and a long line of teenagers in bobby socks and blue jeans stood at the box office. The feature attraction was a picture starring Ginger Rogers. The scene of the veterans jeering at the recruits, which Schary had disliked, had been cut for this showing. It was the only change that had been made so far. The audience showed absolutely no appreciation of the improvement. Emerging from the darkened temple, they joyfully got to work on the preview cards. The character several of them liked the best was, they wrote, 'the pig', and one, in apparent reference to the farm girl whose pig was stolen, wrote 'the sister'. Which scenes did they like most? Answer: 'Where the guy went crazy.' Reinhardt hovered anxiously around the audience as they gave him their considered opinion of his picture. 'Look, they're grinning,' he said, staring hopelessly at a pack of youngsters in blue jeans giggling over their preview cards. 'Take a good look at your movie audience.'

'Well,' Huston said.

'Terrible,' Reinhardt said, leafing through a batch of the cards. 'Worse than last night.'

'Christ!' Huston said. 'Listen, Gottfried. I want to tell you a story about Dad. The morning after he opened in *Othello*, in New York, I went around to see him at his hotel. The reviews were just terrible. Through the door, I heard Dad laughing, "Ho! Ho! Ho!" I went in, and there stood Dad, the tears running down his face, and he was laughing, "Ho! Ho! Ho!"'

'I'm in a humorous mood,' Reinhardt said.

'That's apparent,' said Huston. 'Is Norman Corwin in town? We ought to get him to do the narration.'

'Spencer Tracy,' said Reinhardt.

Too down-to-earth, Huston said. The narration should be read as if it were poetry, he said, and suggested Gregory Peck.

'Spencer Tracy should do it,' Reinhardt said.

'Get "the sister" to do it,' said Albert Band and started to laugh. Huston and Reinhardt silenced him with their glances.

'Albert,' Huston said, 'someday you will be head of the studio.' He spoke mechanically, sounding flat and sad, and there was nothing at all of the former theatrical emphasis in his manner. He seemed tired. He walked away from Reinhardt and then turned around and faced him silently, his face drained of all expression.

'We'd better call Dore,' Reinhardt said.

On the way back to town, Reinhardt had some violent things to say about the audience, about all movie audiences. He denounced bobby-soxers. He denounced everybody under the age of twenty-one. He denounced reviewers of motion pictures and said that they were responsible for all this. Then he subsided and was quiet for a long while. When he spoke again, he sounded puzzled. 'It never happened to me like this before,' he said.

The next day, Huston left Hollywood. He telephoned me in the morning to say good-bye. He did not say anything at all about *The Red Badge of Courage*. 'Well, now I'm off to Africa, kid,' he said. 'We're going to have a lot of fun making *The African Queen*.' There was nothing in his tone to indicate he believed it.

At noon, about the time Huston's plane was taking off, Reinhardt, standing outside the M-G-M barbershop at the studio, was confronted by L. B. Mayer. Some producers and several directors and actors were standing nearby, watching the two men. Mayer shook a finger in Reinhardt's face. 'You don't want to make money!' Mayer said. 'You want to be an artist! Would you work as an artist for one hundred dollars a week? You want to make money. Why don't you want the studio to make money? Are you willing to *starve* for your art? You want to be the artist, but you want *other* people to starve for your art!'

Reinhardt reported the details of the scene to his wife. 'Mayer hated the picture,' he said. 'I knew it would be like this. It was terrible, going to the studio. They are all my enemies now.'

His wife suggested that the two of them go out of town for a day's rest. Reinhardt welcomed the idea. He telephoned Albert Band, who had taken care of Mocha in the past, and asked him if he would keep an eye on Mocha. Band refused. Reinhardt took the refusal stoically.

Reinhardt felt it was now up to him to figure out changes that might be made in *The Red Badge of Courage* that would bring the reactions of audiences closer to what might be considered favourable. 'In the projection-room, this picture is great,' he said, pacing fitfully in his office after his day's rest, while Band lounged in an armchair, taking notes on a memo pad. 'In the theatre, the audience is looking for a story and there is no story. The Breen Office loved the picture. They O.K.'d the whole thing. I keep trying to tell the studios they must *sell* the picture. Suddenly, nobody on the lot understands Stephen Crane. And John is gallivanting in Europe and Africa.' He sat down behind his desk and took a cigar from a large mahogany box. 'I wish I were rid of the red sickness of battle.' He cut off the end of the cigar with a small gold knife. 'I'd like to go far away.'

'To Africa?' Band asked, with a short laugh.

'Albert, you are the most insensitive sensitive man I have ever known,' Reinhardt said morosely.

Band batted his eyes. 'The audience hated Tim Durant's high-pitched voice for the General,' he said.

'John loves Tim's voice,' Reinhardt said. 'John thinks it is wonderful to have a general who does not boom.'

Reinhardt and I left his office for the commissary, to have lunch. 'John doesn't care any more about the picture,' he said as we walked along. 'John doesn't care about anything, and I am left here to listen to Louis B. Mayer.' When we arrived at the commissary, Reinhardt ordered the M-G-M special cold plate, Fresh Shrimp à la Louie, and ate it in gloomy silence.

A couple of days later, Reinhardt wrote a memorandum to Schary:

Dear Dore:

I know you are busy, and as it is hard to reach you, I shall make a written report.

(1) We are dubbing the General's voice. I have interviewed several actors and found a very good one.

(2) We will have a less confusing opening. We start with a dignified period cover of the novel, underlining the classical value and illustrating the style and subject matter of the piece. As we leaf through the pages the credits appear. The last page we show brings what was previously the foreword. Narration fades in as if it were being read from the book and, as the printed words dissolve to the drilling, the rest of the foreword is spoken, setting the pattern for the rest of the film.

(3) The sentry scene, in this case, comes, I believe very effectively, after the letter scene. He [the Youth] is already scared, we know him already a little when he has his first contact with the enemy.

(4) We take out the dead soldier in the woods. I think, without the slightest sacrifice, we can thereby eliminate excessive grimness.

(5) At various moments in the picture, we will hear Stephen Crane's words sketching, in short and poignant and beautiful sentences, the psychological development of the Youth. (I have always maintained that what makes the book outstanding are the thoughts and feelings of the Youth, not his actions. How can they possibly be dramatized? John thought they would be inherent in the scenes, in the expressions of the Youth's face.)

(6) I have tried out the passages in question with the film, and am convinced that this technique, legitimate as it is when filming a great novel, will do wonders to the picture. It will not make some of the people who basically dislike the picture like it. But it will immensely clarify it for those who are now confused. It will prepare them for what is coming and tell them what it is about; namely, the inner evolution of a man. It will also demand the necessary respect from the average audience, so that we can at least expect a true and more dignified reaction. I, personally, believe that, in addition, it will make the picture actually better and more dramatic.

(7) Especially the last passage of the book read over the last shot — 'So it came to pass that as he trudged from the place of blood and wrath his soul changed. He had been to touch the great death and found that, after all, it was but the great death. Scars faded as flowers and the Youth saw that the world was a world for him. He had rid himself of the red sickness of battle. He turned with a lover's thirst to images of tranquil skies, fresh meadows, cool brooks — an existence of soft and eternal peace' — should make our end one of real beauty and filled with emotion.

(8) As you will have heard, the Breen Office approved the picture in toto and loved it. Could we perhaps release it exclusively to them? Seriously, I was quite baffled by the violent reactions pro and con; the accolades of the Wylers, Schary's, Hoppers, and numerous unsolicited admirers on the lot and, on the other hand, the brutal reception by so large a part of the audience, especially those terrible kids at the last preview. However, taking a leaf from our hero, I have since regained, yes, increased my courage. Have you?

(9) I have several ideas as to the presentation and selling of Red Badge. Would you, and perhaps Howard [Dietz], like to discuss them with me? (One is to run, prior to the release, tantalizing pictures of our actors in the papers without mentioning their names — only the names of the characters.)

(10) Incidentally, we are going ahead with your idea of reprising pictures of the cast at the end.

(11) Second veterans' scene has been cut out.

(12) I am at your disposal.

At Dore Schary's invitation, I dropped into his office in the Thalberg Building at eleven-thirty one morning a week or so after the Pasadena preview. Schary's name, on the plate nailed to his door, was engraved in letters twice the size of Reinhardt's. Hanging on the wall in the outer reception room was a bronze plaque reading:

There is hardly anything in the world that some man cannot make a little worse and sell a little cheaper, and the people who consider price only are this man's lawful prey.
                                                                          Ruskin

I found Schary's two women secretaries and his executive assistant, Walter Reilly, in the secretaries' room, busily discussing how busy their boss was.

'He got in early, before me, and cleaned up his desk,' one of the secretaries was saying.

'At four o'clock, he has Garbo,' the other secretary said. Her telephone rang. 'Will let you know. Will call you,' she said. 'It's murder today.'

'Wow! Some day!' said Reilly. 'And tomorrow San Francisco.'

Through an open door, I could see Reinhardt sitting, alone and dejected, in an adjoining conference room, at the head of a long table, staring at a bright-red leather couch. He had at last succeeded in getting a fifteen-minute appointment with Schary to talk about his memorandum. When he left Schary, he was going to work on the problem of dubbing in narration for *The Red Badge of Courage*. He had not obtained Spencer Tracy as narrator, and was trying out various actors he thought had a narrator's kind of voice.

The door to Schary's office swung open and Schary came out, his face composed and smooth, and his eyes innocent behind rimless spectacles. 'Gottfried!' he called.

Reinhardt followed Schary into the office and closed the door.

'Wow!' Reilly said again, looking at a secretary's calendar. 'How's he going to get through in time to go home and pack?'

'You going to San Francisco with him?' one of the secretaries asked.

Reilly nodded. 'Got to get him there first thing in the morning,' he said. Turning to me, he added, 'He's speaking on the Drama Festival at the College of the Pacific, at Stockton. You want to read his speech?' He handed me a mimeographed copy. Hollywood, Schary was going to say, was the intellectual whipping boy for all the other communities – 'maybe because we are more critical of what we love most'. I read on:

I might say that there appears to be a slight change going on, and we in the motion-picture industry look on this change with a little bit of hope and, at the same time, with enormous sympathy for the medium which is about to inherit the abuse that normally and consistently is pinned upon us. That medium is television. Television, because of its time strictures and enormous demands, is beginning to deflect some of the criticism from the motion-picture industry. Some of us look upon this with mixed feelings. We listen to the critics belabour TV. Every once in a while, of course, we pick up a small stone and toss it ourselves, just to keep the pot boiling. . . . There have been florid, fluent, and flatulent explanations about the art of the cinema and its differences in Germany, France, Italy, England, and America. I have studied these differences, I have noted them, I am aware of them. I respect them, but I still maintain that the American motion-picture industry, which is best identified by its generic term 'Hollywood', has accomplished more, has entertained, enlightened, and informed more people over a longer period of time, than any other motion-picture community in the world.

Schary went on to say that movies were criticized for their sentimentality, but that he thought sentimentality was a good thing, because it was the answer to cynicism. He would tell the students, 'Keep your sentimentality fresh, abundant, sweet-smelling. To do so is to believe in humanity.' He concluded his speech by saying, 'Sentimentality should be worn boldly, like Cyrano's white plume, and if anyone detects a trace of that plume in my hatband, I am not ashamed but proud.'

Reinhardt came out of Schary's office and, with a sad, tired smile, said to me, 'Dore is giving careful study to everything I wrote him. Now Dore wants to see what happens with the narration.'

In his inner office, Schary told me, 'I like a busy room. I don't like a bare room. I concentrate better in a busy room.' His room was busy, not only with visitors, secretaries, and assistants but with hundreds of small, medium-size, and large gadgets. From where he sat, he looked out on several lions, made of iron, paper, or plastic;

autographed baseballs; a bowling trophy won by a team known as the Schary Hunky-Dorys; an ancient typewriter in a glass case; an antique lamp with a red glass shade; lead soldiers, in the uniforms of various ages and nations; and a large china pitcher embossed with a portrait of George Washington and the words 'Peace, Plenty, and Independence'. On a shelf at his side, near his head, was a photograph of his mother. On his walls were paintings by his wife, including one of the Schary family in their back yard.

Schary sat at an L-shaped table with a glass top. 'I like air underneath.' he said. 'I concentrate better with air underneath.' He was pleased at having been given an option on a hundred thousand shares of Loew's, Inc., stock at the current market value of $16.50 a share. He explained to me that if within the next six years he bought the stock and its value went up to twenty-one dollars, for example, he could sell it and make a profit of a half million dollars.

'Mayer used to own a lot of stock, but he's sold most of it. He's still my boss, though. Mayer and Mr Schenck are my bosses,' Schary said. He went on to say that he liked his job and got along fine with his top boss, Mr Schenck, and that he enjoyed tussling with the problems that came along and working them out. 'I love problems,' he said. 'I love the problems inherent in show business. I love the risks, the excitement in the work, and all the people who are problems. The only thing I miss is the time to study. I love to read a lot. In about ten years, I want to get out of the industry. I've been in show business for eighteen years, and when I retire, I want to write books about it and teach and lecture. I love to teach the youngsters who are just coming up in show business.'

For the time being, Schary said, he was content to just go along in charge of production at Metro-Goldwyn-Mayer. He knew where he stood with Mr Schenck. Mr Schenck, in New York, decided on general policy – the number of pictures to make each year, and which ones, and at what cost. 'The how he leaves completely to me,' Schary said. 'Of course, I'm in close touch with him all the time. There's not a thing that goes on in this studio that he doesn't know about. He knows the place inside out.' Exactly what Mayer did at the studio was not so clearly defined. 'He calls me and tells me what he thinks of the pictures,' Schary said. Mayer had told him that *The Red*

Badge of Courage was grim and had no story and would not make money.

'I still think *The Red Badge of Courage* is a beautiful picture,' Schary said confidently. 'It's ahead of its time and behind its time.' He paused, then continued, 'To me, the picture is a moving, completely honest, perfect translation of the book. It's imaginative and it has good performances. It's a wonderful picture. A normal business risk. Of course' – he unwrapped a stick of chewing-gum – 'Mayer says, "If they're so goddam artistic, why don't they spend their own money?"' Schary chuckled tolerantly and put the chewing-gum in his mouth. 'And there is some validity to what he says. So you have to find reasonable ground to stand on. There are big gambles worth taking, but you can't go crazy. The discipline of art is important.'

Schary said he was tired of listening to people rant and rave about the limitations put on the creative artist in the movie business. There were limitations, he agreed, but they were not peculiar to the industry. 'It's the age-old problem of any individualist,' he said. 'When it comes to subjecting the artist to pressure, the history of art shows that art flourished under pressure. Titian's art flourished under pressure. The pressures in our business or in radio or in television only serve to create better programmes. Art in motion pictures improves whenever the heat is on. During the war years, when anything went, pictures were worse. With the heat on us now, better pictures are being made and more individuals are asserting themselves. Pressure is not necessarily a bad thing. It enables us to compete on a much higher level.'

Reinhardt was on a sound stage with a young actor, working on a test recording of the narration that was expected to make audiences aware that *The Red Badge of Courage* was a classic.

'"He now wished he was *dead*,"' the actor said into a microphone.

'"He now wished *he* was dead. He now wished *he* was dead,"' Reinhardt said. His eyes looked bloodshot.

'"He now wished *he* was dead,"' the actor said.

'Right. "He now wished *he* was dead,"' Reinhardt said passionately. Then he sighed heavily. 'You know, my father didn't want me to go into this business,' he said to me. 'My father always said, "Only on the stage is it good. Everything behind the stage, in back of the scenes, and everything that goes on before, all of it is no good."'

The actor said. 'Mr Reinhardt, how's this? "He wished that he, too, had a wound, a red badge of courage. He now thought that he wished he was *dead*."'

'All right,' Reinhardt said listlessly. 'God, I wish I was dead!' He gave a cynical laugh.

A week later, Schary had a new lamp on his desk. Its base was a three-foot brass figure of a bearded, helmeted Viking. Schary had found the figure in a small shop in Los Angeles. 'The boys on the lot made the lamp for me,' he said. 'I love it. When I left R.K.O., I wanted to form an independent company, and I planned to use the Viking as my symbol. It stands for everything I like – courage and initiative and everything.' He gave the Viking a look of approbation and then he told me that *The Red Badge of Courage* was going to be all right now that narration was being added. He had not yet decided definitely on who would do the narration. 'The voice of the narrator must be warm, intimate, and dignified,' he said. 'I may have to do it myself.'

Schary said he might make some other changes. 'I want to get more of the text of the book into the picture,' he said. 'I want to tell the audience the narration is from the book. A lot of people don't know this is a book. I want to be blunt with them. Put them in a more receptive mood. I want to tell them they're gonna see a *classic, a great novel*.' Apparently he now agreed with what Reinhardt had said in his memorandum, and had forgotten the idea he had when he saw the picture with Huston and Reinhardt, of selling the picture as a great battle story instead of making it special – a great novel and all that, which would drive away the kids who would come to see a war story.

I asked Schary about an item I had come across in the New York *Times* saying that the picture would be released in small art theatres, rather than big theatres. 'Another unfounded rumour,' he said. 'Your first impulse with these rumours is you want to run them down. I was reading Sandburg's life of Lincoln the other night. The part where Lincoln said you can't run down all rumours. So I suddenly decided the hell with it. Everything is so close in this town you're bound to get rumours no matter what you do. Lincoln would have said, "The hell with it."'

'Chaplin never got it. Garbo never got it. Lubitsch never got it,' Reinhardt was saying. 'Luise Rainer got it twice.' He was referring to the annual Motion Picture Academy Award. Clad in a dinner jacket, he was driving to the R.K.O. Pantages Theatre, where the presentations for pictures released in 1950 were to be made. A large sticker, bearing a picture of the statuette, was pasted on the windshield of his car, to get it past police lines. His wife and I were with him. 'The best ones never got it,' Reinhardt said.

The stage of the Pantages Theatre was dominated by a giant copy of the statuette, and rows of smaller copies were arrayed on each side of it. This time, Joseph L. Mankiewicz got it, Darryl Zanuck got it, and L. B. Mayer got it – Mayer in a 'special presentation' honouring him as the founding father of the Academy and the inaugurator of the star system. He received a big hand. 'This is truly an experience,' he said, holding the statuette to his chest. 'This fills me with humility and great responsibility in the years to come.'

M-G-M gave a party at the Beverly Hills Hotel after everybody who was going to get it had got it. Huston had been one of the nominees for his direction of The Asphalt Jungle, but Mankiewicz had beaten him with All About Eve. Almost all the top executives, stars, producers, and directors of M-G-M had accepted invitations for what they had hoped would be more of a celebration. At the party, Schary stayed on one side of the room and Mayer stayed on the other. Both had a good deal to say about who had got it and who had not got it, and they both concluded that things weren't too bad, because Paramount had done worse.

It was the privilege of Arthur Freed, producer of most of M-G-M's successful musicals, to use L. B. Mayer's private dining room at the M-G-M studio with or without Mayer. The day after the presentation of the Academy Awards, he invited me to lunch there. The room opened off the main dining room, where most of the M-G-M people lunch at small tables with paper doilies bearing the figure of a lion. Mayer's room had one table, a round one with a white tablecloth, on which places were set for six. Among the room's appointments were mirrors, fluorescent lights, a telephone, and a menu headed 'Mr Mayer's Dining Room', from which Freed ordered M-G-M Special Chicken Broth and Fresh Crab Legs à la Louie. Freed had not attended the presentation ceremony; he had listened to the speeches over the radio. 'I'm glad L. B. got it,' he said. 'He's a great picture-maker.'

Freed is a stocky, unsmiling man of fifty-six who has worked for M-G-M for twenty-three years. He said that Mayer had started the producer system in Hollywood when he made Irving Thalberg his first producer, and that Thalberg, a brilliant man, had had sense enough never to put his name on the screen. 'Irving always said credit is great when it's given to you, not when you take it,' Freed explained. Mayer had chosen Thalberg because he had recognized his capabilities. 'L. B. always believes in getting somebody smarter than himself,' said Freed. 'The average fellow wants somebody not as smart. L. B. thinks in terms of an attraction. He is known as an extravagant man. That's what built this studio – his extravagance. He isn't cut out for the small picture. He has a great inspirational quality at this studio. I've spent twenty years with Louie Mayer at the studio and I used to have dinner with him every night, and I have a real understanding with him on a real basis. He's the only man who never got panicky in a crisis, of which this business faced many, and the only executive who thought always in big terms. Every musical I made, there wasn't one I didn't find Louie Mayer a help in. He's nuts about my latest musical, Show Boat. He came to the preview and cried.'

Freed exudes an extraordinary kind of confidence in his musicals, and he usually carries with him reports showing the receipts of his current releases. The reports indicate that Freed's pictures are making money. A successful songwriter before becoming a producer, Freed wrote the lyrics for Pagan Love Song, Singin' in the Rain, Broadway Melody, and You Are My Lucky Star, among others, and he had since incorporated most of the songs into musicals, some of which he named after the songs. The first musical he produced was *Babes in Arms*, in 1939, starring Mickey Rooney and Judy Garland, which netted the studio more money than any musical in the past ten years. 'It was the biggest moneymaker M-G-M had that year,' Freed went on. 'Everybody said I was nuts when I said that Judy would be a star. Everybody said I was nuts when I picked Gene Kelly. I gave Gene his first break. I brought him out here. I'm not interested in the Arrow Collar type. I'm interested in *talent*. Same with Judy. As a kid, she had talent. I gave Judy her first break. I ran *Babes in Arms* the other day, and I swear I had *real* tears in my eyes. I bought *Annie Get Your Gun* for Judy. Just because I thought she would like it. When she left the picture it cost the studio a million dollars to get somebody else. Not that money matters. L. B. was so concerned he himself said he personally would foot her doctor bills. He didn't have to. The studio paid. The studio *cared* about what happened to Judy. After all, we practically brought her up. She meant something to us. After all, musicals have been the backbone of M-G-M for years.'

The biggest money-making star at M-G-M, Freed told me, was Esther Williams, and he told me why. 'She's not only good-looking, she's *cheerful*,' he said. 'You can sell cheerfulness. You can't sell futility. Take John Huston. A great talent. I'd like to make a picture with him myself. He makes a picture, *Treasure of Sierra Madre*, and it's a success with the critics, but it'll take years to get its cost back from the public. Why? It's futile. Even the *gold* disappears in the end. It's not television that is our competition. No more than night baseball. Television can't run the movies out of business. Fundamentally, a picture is not complete unless an audience is out there. Without an audience, you don't know where the laughs are. This is show business. You need laughs. You need cheerfulness. That's the whole reason for show business in the first place.'

A waitress brought the chicken broth and Freed bent his head to it. After he finished it, he said, 'L. B. knows how to bring up the stars. L. B. is a great baseball man. He has always believed in that second team coming up. He learned it from watching Connie Mack build up the minor leagues in baseball. One thing about L. B. He never makes any pretension about pictures as anything but enter-tainment. If a writer complains about his stuff being changed, he always says, "The Number One book of the ages was written by a committee, and it was called the Bible."'

After lunch, we went to Freed's office. Vincente Minnelli, the director, was there waiting for him. Freed asked his secretary to let him know when L. B. was free. He then started a discussion with Minnelli of plans to make a musical based on *Huckleberry Finn*. Freed said that he wanted to make *Huckleberry Finn* the kind of picture that Mark Twain would love. 'I want to find a new kid to play Huck,' he said. 'I want to find a *real* kid. You find a *real* kid, they're real like Lassie or Rin-Tin-Tin. Say, Vince, I meant to tell you the latest about Joe Pasternak. He's talking about this new girl he's got and he says, "You should hear her sing. She's a female Lena Horne."'

The dictograph buzzed, and Freed switched it on. 'You there?' a voice said.

'Yeah. How ya fixed, L. B.?' Freed said. 'Yeah. Right away.' He switched off the machine and asked me to go along to Mayer's office with him.

'I'm leaving,' Minnelli said.

'Yeah, so long,' Freed said, and hustled me upstairs.

Fred and I came to a door that was guarded by a dapper young man with a small moustache, who whispered to us to go right in, Mayer, seated at his cream-coloured desk, was talking into one of his four cream-coloured telephones, thanking someone for congratulating him on getting the Academy Award. On a couch sat the actor George Murphy, who nodded to us.

'I'd rather be loved than get ten million dollars,' Mayer was saying emotionally.

Freed motioned me to a cream-coloured leather chair, and he sat down in another.

When Mayer had finished with his call, Freed stood up, took a paper from a pocket, and showed Mayer the receipts on his latest musicals.

'Great! I knew. I knew before it opened!' Mayer said, sweeping Freed back into his chair. He turned to Murphy. 'Did you go to the Republican dinner last night?' he asked.

'I couldn't,' Murphy said. 'I was with you.'

'That's right,' Mayer said. There was a soft buzz, and he picked up his telephone. 'Thanks,' he said. 'I couldn't hear anything. I couldn't see anything. My eyes were blinded with tears. They're giving me a record of the whole ceremony, so I can know what I said and what happened. So I can hear it.' He hung up and turned to Freed. '*Show Boat*!' he said. 'I saw *Show Boat* and the tears were in my eyes. I'm not ashamed of tears. I cried. I'll see it thirteen times. Thirteen times! Tears! Emotion!'

'It's great entertainment,' Freed said. 'It's show business.'

Mayer stared across the top of Freed's head.

'There's a singer in the picture,' he went on. 'Black. He has one song. He' – Mayer jabbed a finger in Freed's direction – 'got the man to come all the way from Australia to sing this one song. The way he sings, it goes straight to the heart.' Suddenly, Mayer lowered his voice to a basso profundo and began a shattering rendition of 'Ol' Man River'. Tears came to his eyes. He stopped in the middle of a line. 'It's worth more than a million dollars,' he said. 'Talent!' Again he jabbed a finger at Freed. 'He found the singer. All the way from Australia.'

'There's no business like show business, all right,' Freed said.

'It takes work to find talent. These days, all the smart-alecks know is cocktail parties,' Mayer said.

'I hate parties,' Freed said. 'I go to a party, I always get sat next to somebody I have to talk to. Some people in this town, they'll book eleven parties a week if they can.'

'Money!' Mayer went on, as though he had not heard Freed. 'Do I personally need any more money? I have a job at the studio. Do I stay here for money?' He paused.

Freed said quickly, 'If you make seventy-five thousand dollars a year, you can say, "I make more money than a Supreme Court Justice." That's all money is good for any more. You can't keep it any more.'

'I need money the way you need a headache,' Mayer said. 'I want to give the public entertainment, and, thank God, it pays off. Clean, American entertainment. Opera! Mr Schenck tells me they don't like opera. We make a picture, *The Great Caruso*. Look at the receipts! My wife broke down and cried when she saw the picture. But Mr Schenck says they don't like opera!' He glared at Freed.

Murphy cleared his throat. He stood up and asked if it was all right to leave.

'Hold yourself in readiness!' Mayer said.

'Yes, sir!' said Murphy, and left.

'Sentimental,' Mayer went on. 'Yes! Sentiment is the heart of America. I like Grandma Moses. I have her paintings in every room of my house. I'm not ashamed of it. This is America. I know. I used to chase turkeys myself on a farm. Her pictures are life.'

The dapper young man came tiptoeing in. 'Mr Zimbalist is waiting,' he whispered, and tiptoed out.

This elicited no sign from Mayer. He was talking about people he thought were trying to harm the motion-picture business, the allies of the people who wanted to make pictures showing mothers being socked on the jaw; namely, the movie critics, who praised all kinds of sordid pictures made in foreign countries and discounted the heart-warming pictures made in Hollywood. 'As soon as it says the picture was made in Italy, some eighty-dollar-a-week critic writes a big rave review calling it art,' Mayer said. 'Art. *The Red Badge of Courage*? All that violence? No story? Dore Schary wanted it. Is it good entertainment? I didn't think so. Maybe I'm wrong. But I don't think I'm wrong. I know what the audience wants. Andy Hardy. Sentimentality! What's wrong with it? Love! Good old-fashioned romance!' He put his hand on his chest and looked at the ceiling. 'Is it bad? It entertains. It brings the audience to the box office. No! These critics. They're too tony for you and I. They don't like it. I'll tell you a story. A girl used to knock our movies. Not a bad-looking girl. A little heavy back here. All of a sudden, the girl disappears. Then I hear she went to Warner's, writing scripts for a thousand dollars a week. I'm on the golf links. I see Howard Strickling running across the green. You know Howard.' Mayer huffed and puffed to demonstrate how Strickling ran across the green. '"Why are you running?" I ask Howard. He tells me the girl tried to commit suicide. I go with him, just as I am, in my golf clothes. In the hospital, the doctors are pushing her, trying to make her walk. "Walk! Walk!" She don't want to walk.' Mayer got up and acted out the part of the girl. 'Suddenly, she sees me, and she gives a cry! "Oh!" And she walks. And this is what she says: "Oh, Mr

Mayer, I am so ashamed of myself. When I think of how I used to knock the movies, I am *ashamed*."'

That was the end of Mayer's story. Freed looked puzzled.

'You knock the movies, you're knocking your best friend,' Mayer said.

Looks Like We're Still in Business

SUDDENLY, late in the spring of 1951, the big word around the M-G-M studio was 'narration'. Having reached the conclusion that his friends and colleagues had loved *The Red Badge of Courage* because they understood it, and that the public (or at least that very odd sampling of the public that comprises preview-goers) had hated the picture because the public was unable to understand it, Reinhardt, with Huston's and Schary's consent, had begun to dub in narration. Only Mayer didn't think that narration ('Jabber, jabber, jabber. Who wants to listen?') or anything else would help. 'We are using the words of Stephen Crane himself to tell the audience what is happening,' Reinhardt said to his wife one night, 'and the picture will start with an introduction that tells the audience that they are going to see a *great classic*. Dore is writing the introduction himself. L. B. says to me the picture is no good because there is no story. I tell him we are adding narration to the picture, but he says narration won't help what isn't there. L. B. is a dangerous man. If you're his enemy, he destroys you. If you're his friend, he eats you. John is gone, and now I have to face L. B. alone. I don't know why it is; every time I go to lunch, I have to run into L. B. Today, on my way to lunch, he came at me like a battleship: "Mr Reinhardt!" Then he told me the same things all over again. "Why don't you want to make a hit? Why don't you want to make money for the studio?" Today I said to him, "When John Huston comes to me and says he wants to make a picture, I am honoured. You hired him. I didn't." He didn't hear me. He talks about the picture as though it were refrigerators.'

'Gottfried!' Mrs Reinhardt said. 'I think everybody is demented.'

'You know, I like Dore,' Reinhardt went on. 'Dore still speaks well of the picture. He backed the picture in the beginning and he does not change because of the previews. Dore is a lucky man and a nice man. Dore says to me, "The jury is still out."' Reinhardt laughed. 'Dore is really lucky. He is on the telephone every day now with Nick Schenck. Dore is a nice man. Nick Schenck thinks the picture might be a bust. But Dore doesn't want it to happen.'

'Gottfried!' Mrs Reinhardt said. 'Now I know everybody is demented.'

The next morning, Reinhardt made his daily visit to the studio barber shop, to be shaved. The chief barber, whose name is Mano, lathered Reinhardt's face and whispered the latest gossip in his ear. At the studio, Mano had the reputation of being an M-G-M authority, having served as L. B. Mayer's barber for ten years and having seen every M-G-M picture produced in that period. 'Did you see the list of the ten worst pictures of the year?' he asked Reinhardt.

Reinhardt shook his head.

'Dore's personally produced picture is on it,' Mano said. 'The Next Voice You Hear . . . Best. Worst. So many lists. How's your picture?'

'Great,' Reinhardt mumbled.

'L. B. cried at the preview of The Great Caruso,' Mano whispered, shaving Reinhardt's chin. 'Six hundred tears they counted.'

A man sitting in the next chair – Edgar J. Mannix, one of the M-G-M vice-presidents – looked over at Mano and said, 'You mean six million dollars.'

Reinhardt closed his eyes and sighed.

'L. B. and Dore,' Mano whispered soothingly. 'It's going to be a knock-down, drag-out fight.'

A week later, another picture personally produced by Dore Schary, Go For Broke!, which was based on the activities of the Japanese-American troops in the European campaigns of the last war, was having what is called an invitational première at the Egyptian Theatre, in Hollywood. I attended it with the Reinhardts. On the way to the theatre, Mrs Reinhardt kept up a steady chatter about her French poodle Mocha and Mocha's resistance to taking pills for his hay fever, but Reinhardt acted as though his mind were on some faraway subject. Mrs Reinhardt asked him several times what was the matter, and each time he replied that nothing was the matter.

Schary's picture got a big hand. As the Reinhardts and I were driving home, a limousine carrying Schary and his family drew up alongside us. Schary, looking elated, rolled down a window and shouted, 'Did you have a good time?'

'Wonderful!' Reinhardt shouted back, and let the Schary car cut in ahead of him in the heavy traffic.

Ten days after the opening of Go for Broke!, I joined Mayer as he sat in his private dining room at the studio talking about the picture to Arthur Freed, the M-G-M producer of musicals. Mayer had not approved of Go for Broke! 'I don't like Japs!' Mayer said. 'I remember Pearl Harbour!' He looked grim. Picking up his private menu, he said he wanted some lamb chops, and Freed said, 'Likewise.' Freed remarked that lamb chops were easy to digest. Mayer told Freed about a friend of his who had dropped dead that morning. Heart attack. No warning.

When his chops arrived, Mayer fell to with what seemed to be a hearty appetite. When he had finished, he pushed his plate away. 'Dore wants to make pictures about Japs,' he said. 'All right. I'm through trying to tell him.' Mayer said that he'd had plenty of disagreements with other M-G-M production heads working under him – especially Irving Thelberg and David Selznick – but they'd always admitted in the end that he was right. 'Do you know how many times Irving would have seen Quo Vadis?' he said. 'He'd have worn out the prints! Or David. That boy could have been one of the outstanding men of our time. Why, he even wrote poetry, and it was beautiful. I told him, "You have an opportunity to be the greatest, and you're just frittering it away." He didn't listen.'

The waitress brought Mayer's dessert – a bowl of fresh strawberries. 'I'll tell you Irving's words to me,' he went on, mashing up the strawberries. 'He was with Laemmle. Making three hundred and fifty dollars a week. Laemmle didn't like him – a young fella, getting all the attention. I hired him for five hundred dollars a week, and then I asked him, "Why did you leave Laemmle?" He said, "I watched you in New York when you were a distributor of pictures.

You were different. I would rather be first violin under your direction than conductor of the orchestra." Those were Irving's words to me. After six months, I wanted to make him a partner. Irving knew the business, and what he didn't know he was willing to learn through work. And he listened to me. Stars. Garbo. I was over in Europe making Ben Hur. They tell me about this girl and the man – '

'Mauritz Stiller,' Freed said.

'"Tell him I want him and I want the girl," I said. Her arms were like that,' Mayer continued, spreading the fingers of his hands around an imaginary watermelon. 'She had legs! Fat! But the face! I make a deal. Four hundred a week for her, and a thousand for him to bring her over. I told her American men don't like fat girls. "Ja, ja, ja, ja." That's all she could say. When she got here, she had taken off tremendous weight. "Ja, ja, ja, ja."' Mayer fluttered his lashes like Garbo. 'No professional I ever handled was as honourable as her. I offered her a hundred and fifty thousand dollars once to hold her in case we made a picture. "Suppose I took the money,"' Mayer said, again pretending to be Garbo, '"and then the studio did not do the picture." Imagine! A few weeks ago, Benny Thau brought her in my office. She wanted to do a story that would never be a hit in this country. In Europe, yes. Here, no. She always said, "I want to play opposite an artist." Gable? No, she didn't want Gable. But, you know, I never got mad with her. Turning down a hundred and fifty thousand dollars! Can you question a woman like that?'

'Talk of art grows and the audience diminishes,' Freed said.

'I'll never forget the way Irving used to swing his watch when he was thinking,' Mayer said. 'He was in my office, telling me a story. I say, "A man as able as you, you've got an inferiority complex." He goes ahead and tells his story, and I don't like it. I say, "Irving, I don't like it." He starts acting out the story. It's The Red Headed Woman. For Jean Harlow. I say, "Irving, you're going to jail. Tell the truth. It's a wonderful thing to tell the truth. Jean Harlow, she's a platinum blonde – that's the truth." Irving says the hair won't show. That was Irving and I working together. He'd get mad. He'd come back. Then he'd start again. He'd always come back. That I like. Stand up!' he cried abruptly, looking at me and standing up. 'I stand up for you. Why? I stand up for a lady.' He sat down. 'Nowadays, there's no

manners. He's making pictures about the Japs. Last week, who went
to see the picture? All the Japs! This week, the bottom fell out of his
box office.'

Sam Spiegel flew in to Hollywood from London for a few days to
take care of some business matters. He telephoned me to say that he
had left Huston, sick in bed with the flu, twenty-four hours before
in a hotel in London, where Huston had gone on his way to Africa.
'I have never seen John so depressed. He is so shocked and disappointed because of the bad reaction to *The Red Badge of Courage*,'
Spiegel said. 'I have never been so rushed. I just had my smallpox for
Africa. In New York, I get the tetanus. The typhus I'll get when I go
back to London. I have a million things to do. I can't be bothered
worrying about M-G-M's pictures; otherwise I would call Dore and
tell him not to touch John's picture. Too bad. I guess the picture is a
bust.'

'You know, I really like Dore Schary,' Reinhardt said as we drove
from the Reinhardts' house in the hills above Sunset Boulevard to a
theatre in the town of Pacific Palisades for the third preview of *The
Red Badge of Courage*. The picture was being shown for the first time
with narration, with a booming voice dubbed in for Tim Durant's
thin, high-pitched one, with the scene of the dead soldier in the
woods cut, and with some other slight changes that Reinhardt
thought would increase the audience's understanding of what the
picture was about. 'Dore is one of the few sympathetic executives I
know,' Reinhardt went on. 'He called me today and he said, "Don't
worry. Don't be disturbed. I am coming with a baseball bat, and
anybody who doesn't like the picture I will hit over the head."'
All the leading M-G-M executives attended this preview, with the
exception of L. B. Mayer, whose absence was puzzling to some
people. The picture in its new form opened with a shot of the cover
of the Stephen Crane novel. James Whitmore, the actor, had been
chosen for the role of the narrator, and as the book was opened,
Whitmore was heard delivering the introduction written by Dore
Schary, in which it was explained that the picture was based on a
classic written in 1894, and it was pointed out emphatically that the

novel had been 'accepted' by critics and public alike as a classic story of war'. 'Stephen Crane wrote this book when he was a boy of twenty-two. Its publication made him a man,' Whitmore said. A portrait of Stephen Crane was flashed on the screen. The introduction explained, further, that Stephen Crane's book had a story. 'His story is of a boy [the Youth] who, frightened, went into a battle and came out of it a man with courage,' Whitmore said, in Schary's words (Huston's idea of the theme of the movie, which was simply that courage is as unreasoning as cowardice, was not alluded to in the introduction), and then Whitmore said that the remainder of the narration was taken from the classic itself.

The third preview audience was no more and no less respectful than the first two had been. People did not seem impressed by the fact that they were seeing a classic. Many people laughed at the tragic scenes, exactly as people in the other audiences had laughed; just as many others seemed shaken or moved by the same scenes. A shot of a crazed soldier marching in a line of wounded and singing 'John Brown's Body' while keeping time with a tree branch for a baton had been received at the previous showings with some laughter as well as horror. This audience laughed or acted horrified, too. The death scenes of the Tall Soldier, played by John Dierkes, and the Tattered Man, played by Royal Dano, had been hooted and jeered at by the audiences at the earlier previews, and they were similarly received now. Some young patrons had giggled and elderly patrons had walked out on an especially noisy scene showing the Youth, in his flight from battle, coming upon an artillery battery, and some young patrons giggled and elderly patrons walked out on the scene now. On the other hand, some patrons previously had given the movie their quiet attention, and there were patrons now who did the same.

After the showing, the executives and Reinhardt gathered around Schary in the lobby. He seemed to have a new attitude towards the picture. There was no baseball bat in his hand. He looked angry.

'Gottfried, the way this picture plays now, it's got no story,' Schary said.

Reinhardt glanced quickly at Margaret Booth, at Johnny Green, and at Bronislau Kaper, who nodded in agreement as Schary said that he thought the pattern of the battle scenes was wrong. He suggested changing the order of certain scenes and eliminating others.

Reinhardt looked puzzled and hurt and was silent.

'We make these changes, we'll bring the picture into its proper focus,' Schary said.

Reinhardt looked surprised, and still said nothing.

Schary said that he wanted to cut out the death scene of the Tattered Man. Huston and Reinhardt had often said that it was not only the best scene in *The Red Badge of Courage* but the best scene of its kind ever made, and that it brought out some of the essence of the novel.

Reinhardt seemed too distraught to reply.

'The construction of the sequence in which the troops are withdrawn is bad,' Schary went on in an indignant tone. 'You can't have 'em going back and forth, back and forth. You've got to get the audience worked up, and then you've got to deliver. Like you do with a dame. The way you have it now, Gottfried, you get the dame interested and then the guy leaves her.'

Reinhardt stared at him mutely.

'Get 'em ready and charge!' Schary said, raising a clenched fist. 'Charge, Gottfried! Build to a climax, and bam!'

'Yes! Yes!' Johnny Green said.

'Maybe what we need is more of the kind of effect we had in *Go for Broke*!' Schary said.

'Yes, make it add up,' Margaret Booth said.

'The Tattered Man makes the audience seasick,' said Schary.

'Correct!' said Bronislau Kaper, who six months before had called the scene 'overwhelming' and had been so proud of the combination of sharp trumpet (for the military effect) and gay harmonica (for the ironic effect) he had worked out for the scene.

'He's absolutely right!' said Margaret Booth, who had sent Huston a memo eight months before saying that the scene was 'simply wonderful'.

'They'll cheer!' Schary said.

Reinhardt's face turned red. He stared at Schary in silence and then said slowly, 'No, Dore. I don't see it that way.'

'Get 'em ready, Gottfried, and it'll be a good picture,' Schary said.

'It'll play like a doll.' He did not seem to have noticed Reinhardt's objection. 'They'll cheer.' He clapped a hand on Reinhardt's shoulder. 'I'm leaving. See ya at the factory, kid.' He walked off.

Albert Band came up to Reinhardt. 'Best preview cards so far,' he said. 'We got several Outstandings.'

'Now, on top of everything, I have a fight with Dore,' Reinhardt said, as I walked with him and Mrs Reinhardt to their car. 'I told John till I was blue in the face we should have only one battle. John is lost in the jungles of Africa and I have to fight with Dore.'

On our way back to the Reinhardts' house, Reinhardt kept on complaining that now he would have to argue with Schary, particularly about saving the Tattered Man's death scene.

'I must tell you, Gottfried,' said Mrs Reinhardt, 'you are the only man I know who will make himself a martyr. For what? For a scene that irritates everybody? I tell you, everybody hates that scene.'

'They loved it until now,' said Reinhardt. 'The greatest thing in the picture.'

'Gottfried! Look!' Mrs Reinhardt cried suddenly, as Reinhardt slowed the car for a traffic light on Wilshire Boulevard. She pointed out the window. Louis B. Mayer was walking, with great energy, along the street; he was taking his nightly constitutional.

Reinhardt gave a sigh and nodded his head knowingly. 'He wasn't there tonight,' he said. 'I was so happy to think I no longer had to fight with him. Now I find out I have to fight anyway. I have to fight with Dore.'

'Gottfried, you are so cryptic!' Mrs Reinhardt said.

'All right,' Reinhardt said grimly, as he drove past Mayer. 'Mayer is leaving the studio. Eddie Mannix told me the day of the *Go for Broke!* preview. L. B. Mayer is leaving M-G-M.'

The next day Reinhardt found several preview cards on the desk in his office. They ranged from one marked by a 'Male – Over 45' that said, 'It all stinks. Talk, talk, and bum-bum boring,' to one marked by 'Female – 31–45' that said, 'I will tell everyone I know not to miss it. Pictures of quality, poetically conceived and executed

with originality, are rare. This is one of the greatest ever made.'
Reinhardt sent the cards to Schary, along with a memo:

Dear Dore:
   *These cards came in today and I happened to find them on my desk. I wish you
would read them. Not that they make a special point, or one we don't know ourselves – not that they can teach us much (in fact, one of them attacks something we
know has helped the picture enormously, if only because it killed every single bad
laugh – the narration) – but I do think they bear out what I was trying to articulate
this morning: those who don't like the picture will never like it. I doubt that with the
material at hand we can make them. Those who like it – well, they just like it. They
may object to this or that detail, but they will like the quality. And that is the only
thing we've got to sell, and that is the only reason why you and I wanted to make
the picture.*

                                                            Gottfried

A couple of days later, Schary personally took over the supervision
of changing The Red Badge of Courage. I found him sitting at his table in
his office, with his sleeves rolled up. 'While the narration helped,
the big trick was setting up an outside voice saying, "Look, this is a
classic",' he told me. (The big trick had been achieved by his
introduction.) 'It set up the proper frame of reference. It identified
the picture, and now the first third of the picture plays like a doll.
Now' – he put his feet up on a stack of M-G-M manuscripts on his
desk – 'the trick is to make the points of the story clear without
disturbing the integrity of the picture. I'm reconciled to one thing.
There's a group of people who, no matter what we do, won't like the
picture, so we've got to play to those who will. This is what I'm
gonna do with the picture: The way Gottfried and John had the
picture, the regiment begins to charge and then withdraws and then
charges again. The audience anticipates a climax that does not come,
because the regiment does not go through with the first charge. I'm
gonna take the two charges and make them one. That'll help the
audience. The audience feels the picture is diminishing. "Is the
Youth gonna have the courage to charge again?" is too subtle a
concept for the audience. They want that mental relief. They want
the satisfaction. Then when the charge comes, we'll stay with it. And

the audience goes along! And *bam*!' Schary pounded a fist into the palm of his other hand.

'I've been giving a lot of thought to *Red Badge*,' Schary continued. 'I'm gonna see the picture with the changes tonight. I'm doing an experiment. I'm cutting out the Tattered Man's death scene. I think it won't work, but I want to look at it that way. One thing keeps circulating in my head. The audience loses sympathy for the boy when he runs away from this hurt and bleeding man. I wrote to Gottfried about it. He sent me some of the preview cards and I told him you have to approach these things with firm conviction but with an open mind, with passion and yet reasonableness, with experience and yet the desire to be bold and new. I told him there was no easy way to make pictures. They all pull at your guts and at your mind. I told Gottfried to keep his heart brave, and that I wouldn't hurt his picture ever.'

Schary was silent for a moment, and then went on, 'The trouble with this job is if you're a fella who never wavers, they say you're an obstinate son of a bitch. If you change your mind, then they say, "You can talk him into anything." I know that there's a lot of criticism of me – of how I want to like people and how I want them to like me. If I'm honest, I have to say it's something deeper, but it is also a weakness.' Schary paused, as though embarrassed at admitting a weakness. 'I don't want to hurt anybody, and I don't like to be hurt myself. You try desperately to work out a relationship with people. Whatever way you do it, it doesn't seem to matter one way or the other. Zanuck doesn't care about whether he's gonna hurt someone. But it doesn't help him. It wouldn't make my job any easier if I did it his way.'

As I was leaving Schary's office, I met Albert Band, who was going in. He said he had an appointment with Schary to talk about an original story he had written. 'I prefer direct contact with Dore to going through Gottfried,' he said.

'I don't understand it,' Reinhardt said to his wife at their house that evening. He was going over to Schary's to see what had been done to his picture. 'This morning, I told Dore I understand his problem but he must not get panicky. He's going ahead without me.

I don't understand. So many of them loved the picture. John isn't here, and it's terribly unfair. It puts me in a bad position.'

Reinhardt said he had to be at Schary's house at a quarter to ten and left. Mrs Reinhardt asked me to stay with her while he was gone, and, as we sat around, with Mocha lying at her feet munching contentedly on pistachio nuts, she talked at some length about problems of life in southern California, including dresses ('Nobody in this entire city knows how to fit the bosom'); coats ('You don't have to go to I. Magnin or to Teitelbaum for a mink coat any more. They are selling them now in the Thrifty Drug-stores'); hairdressers ('They never give you anything to read. Every time I pick up a movie magazine, all I find is "The Happy Home Life of June Allyson"'); history of the cinema ('I wish Gottfried were Baby LeRoy. Baby LeRoy retired at the age of four and a half with four million dollars in the bank'); and literature ('Gottfried's latest writer has been out here for ten weeks on a fifteen-hundred-dollar-a-week, week-to-week basis. Now he tells Gottfried, "I need more time. I've got to live with the characters awhile. I don't hear the drums yet." He is like a writer I know who is doing a screenplay for Sam Goldwyn and says, "Sam Goldwyn is to pictures what Aristotle was to the drama"').

Three hours passed before Reinhardt came back. 'I need a stiff drink,' he said. He poured a stiff drink and drank it at one gulp. He poured another and sat down. He shook his head sadly. 'Love's labour's lost,' he said. 'Love's labour's lost. They took out the cavalry charge, which Margaret Booth calls the roughriders. They took out the wounded man singing "John Brown's Body", and another wounded man who complains about generals. They took out the veterans, and Dore turned to me and said, "Do you miss it? I don't miss it at all." They took out the Tattered Man's death scene. Again Dore turned to me and asked did I miss it. It reminds me of my good friend Bernie Hyman, who wanted to put Mozart in The Great Waltz. I said, "You cannot put Mozart in a picture about Strauss." He said, "Who's gonna stop me?" Same thing. I don't know what to say when Dore says, "Do you miss it?" Sure I miss it, but how can you argue about it with Dore?'

They had changed the battle scenes around, he said, to fit Dore's pattern of battle. 'Dore doesn't see the difference,' Reinhardt said. 'It's silly to work on finesse. Nobody appreciates it. Because some people in the audience laughed, they took out the artillery scene John wrote to show what Crane meant when the Youth is running away from the battle and sees the artillerymen still fighting and calls them fools. They took out the key scenes that built the picture up to the feeling Crane had in the novel. I'd like to know what John would have said. It is grotesque. The narration put the audience in the right mood for the picture, and it kept them in the right mood. But suddenly Dore wants to change the picture. It is now like a different picture.' He spoke in a low monotone, with a good deal of puzzlement. 'I am stymied,' he said. 'I don't know how to combat it. I don't understand any of them. They *loved* the picture. And now this is what they are doing to it.'

John Huston's wife was living at Malibu Beach with their year-old-son, awaiting the birth of their second child. When I went over to see her, she told me she had not heard too much from Huston since he had gone abroad to make *The African Queen*, but in that week she had received two letters. She sat on the beach, in the balmy sunshine, reading about her husband's adventures in the Belgian Congo:

Last year there were some man-eating lions about, and they seized the natives out of their huts and dined on them. Every morning and evening we go after elephant. I'd like to get one with really big tusks. In fact, we've got him all picked out. But so far something has always happened so that I couldn't get a shot. Stalking elephant is most exciting. They don't see at all well and if one stays down wind of them one can get very close. Yesterday morning we were after them in some forest and we weren't more than six or eight yards away from them finally. Just a little wall of vines between us and them. I tell you it gave me a very funny feeling.

The second letter started:

To begin with, I didn't get my elephant. Never saw the big tusker again. . . . The company, including Katie and Bogie, will arrive tonight. They've been in Stanleyville for several days. Naturally, I haven't seen any of them yet. Sam is with them. I'm anxious to get him here, what with mosquitoes and leopards and snakes and all.

On 23 June 1951, the local newspapers carried front-page stories announcing that L. B. Mayer was quitting M-G-M, the studio he had helped establish twenty-six years before. One story said, 'The sixty-five-year-old production chief, one of the giants of the film industry, started more rumours brewing by adding that he is not retiring. "I am going to remain in motion-picture production, God willing," he said. "I am going to be more active than at any time during the last fifteen years. It will be at a studio and under conditions where I shall have the right to make the right kind of pictures – decent, wholesome pictures for Americans and for people throughout the world who want and need this type of entertainment."' Another story pointed out that Mayer had been dissatisfied with M-G-M policies since the appointment of Dore Schary as chief of production three years before; that he had been in disagreement for a long time with Nicholas M. Schenck, president of Loew's; and that for seven consecutive years he had received the highest salary in the United States.

Now that the news was official, people in the industry seemed rather shocked by it. Many who had formerly spoken harshly of Mayer now spoke sympathetically.

'After all those years on the throne!' an M-G-M vice-president said to Reinhardt. 'What's going to happen to him now in this lousy, fake town?'

Reinhardt gave a short, cynical laugh. 'I am rather proud that I have never, during my eighteen-year relationship with M-G-M, kowtowed to L. B.,' he said. 'I marvelled at him. I was amused by him. I was afraid of him, and sometimes I hated him. I never flattered him. I never flattered myself that he liked me. And I never believed that Mayer would really leave the studio.'

The two men reminisced about Mayer's hey-day. The vice-president knew a man in New York who had once mentioned the size of Mayer's salary to Schenck. Schenck, who, though president of the company, took a smaller salary himself, had waved a disparaging hand and said, 'Oh, Louie likes that sort of thing.'

Two days after the news about Mayer was out, The Red Badge of Courage was previewed again, at the Encino Theatre, in Encino. Nobody looked for Mayer this time. When I arrived, I found Dore

Schary beaming at a placard that announced the next attraction, Go for Broke! 'It's gonna play here all next week,' he said.

Before The Red Badge of Courage started, a newsreel came on.

'The picture looks better already,' Mrs Reinhardt said in a loud voice.

Reinhardt laughed uneasily.

The Tattered Man's death scene had definitely been cut out, and most of the other changes that Reinhardt had seen at Schary's house had now been made permanent. The battle sequences added up to an entirely different war from the one that had been fought and photographed at Huston's ranch in the San Fernando Valley. The elimination of scenes accounted for part of the difference. The old man with the lined face who was digging was gone, the ragged veterans gibing at the recruits both before and after a battle were gone. Many small touches – brief glimpses of the men at war – had been trimmed, including a close-up of a wounded man berating an officer for 'small wounds and big talk'. The last shot in the picture – of the Youth's regiment marching away from the battlefield – which Huston had wanted to run long, had been cut to run short. (Reinhardt had succeeded in getting Schary to restore the wounded man singing 'John Brown's Body' and part of the scene of the Youth shouting at the artillerymen.) The revision had some odd results. Audie Murphy, who played the Youth, started to lead a charge with his head wrapped in a bandanna, rushed forward without the bandanna, and then knelt to fire with the bandanna again around his head.

The audience reaction seemed to be friendlier, although there still were walk-outs and laughter at tragic scenes. Schary emerged from the theatre and, as Reinhardt came over to him, Schary grinned and said confidently that the picture was now a doll. 'Everything is better now, sweetie,' he said to Reinhardt. 'The audience understands this boy now.'

'The Tattered Man scene was the greatest in the picture,' Reinhardt said.

The picture was better without it, said Lawrence Weingarten, an M.G.M. executive. 'Now Dierkes stands out as a single vignette,' he said.

'If you would just put back the Tattered Man –' Reinhardt began.

'You're wrong, Gottfried,' said Schary. He turned to Weingarten. 'Did you miss the scene?' he asked.

'Not a bit,' said Weingarten.

'It's one of the greatest scenes,' said Reinhardt.

'Did *you* miss it?' Schary asked Kaper.

'No!' Kaper said. 'No! No!'

'You haven't disturbed your picture at all, Gottfried,' said Schary.

Reinhardt drew a deep breath. 'Missing it or not missing it is not the point,' he said.

'You're wrong,' said Schary.

Schary left, and Reinhardt began to read some preview cards Albert Band had put in his hands.

'Not a bad preview,' Band said.

'"A war picture about the Civil War is ridiculous at this time,"' Reinhardt read aloud. He shrugged and gave the cards back to Band. 'The funny thing is that tonight John would have sided with Dore.'

'John doesn't care,' Kaper said. 'Call me Metro-Goldwyn-Kaper, but I tell you the purpose of a motion picture is to be successful.'

'This picture will not make money,' said Reinhardt. 'I knew it the day I saw the first rushes.'

'I knew it when I first read the script,' Mrs Reinhardt said.

'She hated it,' said Reinhardt. 'She wouldn't talk to me when I told her I was going to make it.' He looked blankly at his wife, at Kaper, at Band, and at me. 'So now I do not have a great picture *and* it will be a flop.'

Two days later, Reinhardt told me that he had made a study of the latest preview cards. The percentage of members of the audience who said they would recommend the picture to their friends was much higher. 'That is the important thing,' he said. 'I had a very serious talk with Dore. He will accept the responsibility for the picture as it is now, and he will write this to John. He is going to release the picture as it now is. He said he would be a bad executive if he let the picture out any other way.' Reinhardt did not sound happy, but he sounded happier than he had two nights before.

Huston was now concerned with other things. To his wife, he wrote:

We're in a place called Biondo that's on the Ruiki River about thirty miles from Pontiaville and the Lualaba. But what a long thirty miles it is. Once a week provisions are brought in and the exposed film is taken out. There hasn't been very much rain (for the Congo) and the river has fallen several feet so that now it's just barely navigable. . . .

At about the time Huston was writing this, Reinhardt, who had not heard anything at all from him since the first preview of their picture, sat down alone at home one evening after dinner and typed out a letter to him by the one-finger method:

Mr John Huston
  Darkest Africa
Dear John:
  This is not an official letter. This is not the producer writing the director, but rather the Tall Soldier addressing the Youth. For despite the physical incongruities implied in this statement, that is exactly how I feel: like the Tall Soldier, having 'in his ignorance' held the line, now giving up his soul, telling the Youth who ran away what happened. 'Laws, what a circus!'
  Lacking all signs of life from you, I find it difficult to carry the analogy much further. I am too unfamiliar with your present circumstances, although I presume that on a Spiegel location you will have had a brush with a Tattered Man, a very short one, to be sure, for the Tattered Man turned out to be one of the first casualties, in more ways than one, and is one of the main reasons for this accusatory confession.
  However, whatever these transitory episodes, one development is inevitable, one happening is sure to be in store for you: you will one day return to your regiment, and that will be painful. True, your desertion will not have been noticed. People will say you have been fighting somewhere 'on the right'. And you will say we have seen nothing of the real fighting. But it will be painful just the same. For, no matter what anybody says, you will find your regiment decimated. Irretrievable casualties will stare in your face, and the survivors are bruised and battered and bitter.
  The Tall Soldier will be gone, or at least his soul. The real adversary of all of us, Louis, the Captain — he will be gone. The minor executives, the Lieutenants, will be, as usual, asleep. But in Dore you will find again your Friend. For that he is.
  He did have his moments of wavering, and serious moments, too. When, in the

heat of battle, he parted with his watch, when he cut out the death of the Tattered Man, when he wanted to cut out 'John Brown's Body' (or shall I say: 'John's Body'?), a surgical operation which I was able to prevent him from performing, when he shortened the last shot of the picture, when he eliminated the first veterans as well, maybe, deep in his heart, sometimes he, too, felt tempted to run away. And the only reason he stuck it out in the end was that he was more afraid of the Captain than of the public. Be that as it may, he did stick it out. And he is a Friend. And, whatever his mistakes (and who knows, maybe they aren't even mistakes; maybe he is right?), if this war of ours should by a miracle, in spite of all the confusion, the intramural disagreements, the unpopularity of the cause, the abundance in casualties, be crowned by victory, he will in his way be as responsible for it as the Tall Soldier or even the Youth.

But even if you should disagree with him completely, your position will be a weak one. Just as the Youth's triumph, when he returns the watch to the Friend, is a hollow one, no arguments of yours can retroactively make up for your absence. Right or wrong, the decisions in battle must be made by those who take part in the fighting. As you know, it doesn't matter how beautiful the strategy may be. The test of battle is what counts. So, all that remains for you upon your return is to 'get mad' and, even if somewhat belatedly, to become a hero, and to fight bigger and better battles, make better, if not necessarily bigger, pictures, and stay with them.

This, in short, is what happened: after you left us, there was a long lull in the fighting. The picture was taken off the release schedule and all decisions were postponed until, as we discussed doing the day before your departure, we had another preview with narration. Only four weeks ago did we have this preview. The reason for this delay was that we couldn't get into the dubbing rooms. A lot of other products had to be rushed through first. Unfortunately, it leaked out what kind of an audience reaction we had had at the first two previews and there were some damaging items in the press to that effect. Especially, a New York Times story did word of mouth a good deal of harm. Professional circles in New York and locally were whispering that M-G-M had a dud on its hands and didn't know what to do with it. Some went so far as to assert that The Red Badge was so bad it couldn't be released. There were those who conceded that the picture may very well be an artistic achievement but would surely be a commercial disaster. There was very little I could do to stem this tide of unfavourable and often vicious comment, especially as some of it unquestionably emanated from the studio itself. The New York Times man, for instance, told me that his information came directly from one of our executives. Naturally, the whole Mayer situation, which, thank God, has since come to its dénouement, did not help matters any.

Reinhardt told Huston about the picture's new opening, which involved the shots of the book and the portrait of Crane, about Schary's introduction and about the narration, which 'seemed to succeed in keeping the audience concentrated on the Youth's inner development'. 'Fewer people walked out,' he said, 'and while I did not kid myself and still felt that a large part of the audience did not care for the picture at all, I was quite satisfied with our effort. I felt we had a very distinguished, immensely beautiful, and, to those who appreciated it, very moving and even great picture.' He then said that Schary, seeing the picture for the first time with an audience, had become worried:

Dore had secretly higher hopes for the picture box-officewise than I. I was long resigned to the limited appeal I believed we could count on. And all I tried to do was to put the picture in its best possible shape to further this appeal, recognizing fully its limitations. Dore was not quite in the same mood. He wanted to conquer the resistance of the audience, which he clearly – and we both – felt. I, frankly, believed that was futile. And dangerous to boot. Because I seriously questioned our ability to win the hearts of those who objected to the picture basically; those who hated it. On the other hand, we might easily, in trying to win them, lose those who were already our friends, those who loved the very things the others hated. Actually, there wasn't much of a fight. I was in a very bad position to fight. Dore had behaved wonderfully all along in the face of violent opposition, bordering on sabotage. I had to be – and am – very grateful to him for that. In acting so courageously, he assumed a definite and heavy responsibility for the picture. How could I deny him the privilege to salvage a million-and-three-quarter-dollar investment?

It took Reinhardt several more hours to outline the changes that had been made in the picture. And then he wrote:

Well, John, I felt very bad. Except for the time when I finally gave in to you on Audie, I hadn't been that miserable. You see, I had been able to fight all studio opposition, because I always had the deep conviction that I was helping make a work of art. Not these two times. The fact that I could have never won my fight without Dore's blessing made this last situation only more difficult and painful. I never harboured much hope for a commercial success. I know you did. I reminded Dore of his letter to Mayer where he explained that this kind of picture should be made by a studio like M-G-M regardless of commercial considerations. It was to be a 'classic'. Mayer and all the other executives loathed the idea. To go ahead with the project under the circumstances was a fateful decision for a producer. More than for a director. A producer is not supposed to divorce his judgement, from commercial considerations. Even the head of a studio can sometimes with impunity think in purely artistic terms. He makes forty pictures a year. The producer makes one or two. If those are flops – that's his product. He is a flop. He may be an 'artist' but a flop. I knew and weighed all that. I didn't care. I was delighted to make this picture with you. Up to these two moments, when I suddenly saw before me the spectre of the unartistic flop.

I sincerely hope that all this is terribly exaggerated. In any event, my dwelling on it seems highly superfluous. The fourth and last preview with these changes (all except the cavalry charge, which I made Dore put back before) went unquestionably much better. The cards too for the first time showed an astonishing improvement. Only thirty per cent would not recommend the picture this time. The picture had lost some of its complexities and colours. It was now a straighter, simpler picture. The consensus was, 'You can follow it now. You can understand it now.' Whether that is desirable I shall leave to posterity's judgement. Anyway, Dore was happy. He felt – and, in a way, was – vindicated. He was sure. Everybody agreed with him. Weingarten, Kaper, the cutters, the assembled studio personnel, even Silvia. It is probably a very fine picture. Everybody tells me it is.

But I would have to lie if I said it was the picture that I had hoped for (even in my 'limited' way) or that I wanted to make. I cannot speak for you, of course. For you are not here. But I tried to. In fact, I did. I did try especially to persuade Dore to put back the Tattered Man scene. He was adamant. And, I admit, there is a lot of sense in what he says. And I believe that the audience, or a large part of it, agrees with him. Certainly very few will miss the death of the Tattered Man, since they haven't seen it. But I have seen it.

I would never have made this picture without you, John. I wanted it to be a John Huston picture. For it to be anything else now seems to me senseless. I told Dore that. Dore thinks it still is. Maybe he is right. Everybody tells me so. Maybe I have a special idea of a John Huston picture. Maybe even more special than John Huston has.

Dore told me that he would write you, that he accepts the whole responsibility for the present cuts, that he knows he is right, that this is one of those times when an executive has to step in and make the final decision – if he wants to be an executive.

I sincerely hope that he is right. I pray that he is right. I know that I have done everything I could to make this what it should be. I pray that the discrepancy between what it should be and what it is is not too great. I wish nobody ill. I believe in sincerity and friendship and talent. Yet I realize that these three priceless qualities can be easily defeated by geography and power. I bow smilingly and, as I said before, without ill will. And with humility. Because I can be terribly wrong.

Good luck, John.

Yours always,
Gottfried Reinhardt

Huston's reply, a cable from darkest Africa, was briefer. He said, 'DEAR GOTTFRIED. JUST GOT YOUR LETTER. KNOW YOU FOUGHT GOOD FIGHT. HOPE YOU NOT TOO BLOODY MY ACCOUNT. LET'S MAKE NEXT ONE REINHARDT NOT A HUSTON PICTURE. JOHN.' Reinhardt read the cable, then went upstairs to Schary's office to ask the man who now had the authority of vice-president in charge of production and of the studio to give him an assignment, in addition to the two he had as a producer, as a director of a motion picture.

Schary was talking to me one afternoon a week later about the future of motion pictures. His photograph had appeared in the Los Angeles papers that morning, along with the news that he had been chosen judge for the Downtown Business Men's Association talent show, open to boys and girls between the ages of five and eighteen. In the photograph, he had a slight, bemused smile, and his eyes were good-natured. He looked exactly the same now. People in the motion-picture industry, he told me, had to be constantly prepared for change. 'People who make predictions about change are those who are afraid of it or don't know about it,' he said. 'You say, "Let's try this" or "Let's try that". You watch and see what happens. The pontifical statements about change in our industry amuse me. A certain progression of changes was inevitable in this business even before the advent of TV. Of course, with TV there's a certain kind of picture we won't be making. We'll say, "Let TV make it." We'll make fewer pictures and bigger ones – bigger in the sense that we will aim higher.' He cited *Quo Vadis* as an example of the kind of picture that TV would never be able to make, an eight-and-a-half-million-dollar picture dealing with the history of Christianity. 'They sat here with *Quo Vadis* for years,' he added, 'but I activated it. They'd still be stalling around with it if I hadn't been here.'

Schary was inclined to be gracious about his predecessor, L. B. Mayer. He had heard that Mayer had not liked *Go for Broke!*, but he thought that Mayer had a right to his opinion. 'Mayer was surrounded by enormous prestige and enormous power,' he said. 'He undoubtedly left his studio with bitterness. Why? What do people tell me? *Good* things about myself, not *bad* things. What did they use to tell *him*? Good things, not *bad* things. He had no way of knowing. I have to be careful now not to be put in the same position Mayer was in. I understand Mayer. He's an old man. He's rich. He's healthy. Let him enjoy himself now. I don't know what the hell he got mad about. He could have been so happy here. Mayer once said to me, "Wouldn't it be better if you had men with years of experience to sit down with you and help you make decisions? Wouldn't you like it better?" I said no. This job has to be a one-man operation. There has to be *one* boss. He listened to everybody and he came up with a piece of junk. Before I arrived at the studio, he made the basic decisions. The committee would tell him stories. They had a story board and two storytellers to help him pick the stories. That was the first thing I felt was all wrong. I wanted the authority to pick the stories. I said I would discuss controversial stories with him and we would come to a decision. I got the authority. And the only difference of opinion I ever had with him was on *The Red Badge of Courage*. And that was settled amicably. After we decided to make the picture, he said, "We're in this now and we're in it together." Maybe the reason he got mad was because he had a disagreement with Nick Schenck six months ago. Mayer was annoyed with Schenck because Schenck did not tell him the details of the deal in which I was given the option to buy a hundred thousand shares of Loew's stock. The deal was a New York decision. Maybe Schenck didn't *want* to tell anybody.'

It was Mayer who, in 1948, had invited Schary to come over to M-G-M. Schary was head of production at R.K.O., which Howard Hughes had bought a few months earlier. Hughes had told Schary he did not want to make *Battleground*, a picture Schary had been preparing to produce himself. 'That's why I left,' Schary said. 'Hughes didn't think the picture was a commercial picture. I came over here and bought the story from R.K.O. for a hundred thousand dollars. And we made it. The rest is history. It cost a million six, took forty-five days to shoot, and will probably clear a profit of three million.' When Schary left R.K.O., Mayer immediately sent word to him that he'd like to see him. 'I went to see him at his house, and he told me he'd like me to come and run production at M-G-M. I said I wanted him to know that if he thought of me as the executive who would get out the scripts, I wasn't interested. I said if I took the job, I wanted to be head of production. He said then that he planned to leave the studio and retire in one year, two years, or, at the most, three years. We signed a three-year deal. And we agreed on what I said I meant by "head of production". I would pick the stories, I said, and be responsible for the cast, for who directs, and for who produces. I said, "If that's what you mean, fine." I said, "I'd be challenged by the idea, if you want me to do the job." And that's the way we signed it.'

Schary grinned and leaned forward. 'Let me tell you about Nick Schenck,' he said. 'Schenck is a man near seventy. He's a wonderful fella. He's shrewd. Smart. Hard. You always know exactly how you stand with him. Because he tells you. You know exactly what he's thinking. Because he tells you. He says, "You fellas make the pictures!" He only wants to be consulted on high policy. From there on in, you know exactly where you stand. He's a great businessman.'

Schary was to take the train to New York the next day for a conference with Schenck.

Things were going to be different from now on, Reinhardt told me on 3 September 1951, the day he started his first job as a director. His picture, *Invitation*, was about a wealthy girl (Dorothy McGuire) who has only a year to live and whose wealthy father (Louis Calhern) hires a handsome, penniless young man (Van Johnson) to marry her. 'I have stars and I have a story in this picture,' Reinhardt said. 'I will try to make this picture a little gem.'

T - G

In addition to stars and a story, Reinhardt had expressions of good wishes from his wife (a solid-gold watchchain charm engraved *Forti Nihil Difficile*) and from his brother, Wolfgang (a forty-franc gold coin their father, Max Reinhardt, had carried as a good-luck piece), a memo from Margaret Booth ('I know you are going to have a wonderful picture and needless to say you will be a fine director, so all my best wishes and thoughts are with you. With love'), and a letter from Schary ('My every good wish today on the start of INVITATION. You're a versatile fellow, and I'm sure we'll have a good picture with this one. Good luck and my best wishes').

Reinhardt felt so pleased about the picture he was going to direct that he began to feel more pleased about the picture he had recently produced. *The Red Badge of Courage* was now ready to be released. Schary told Reinhardt that he would order 'the boys in New York' to give the movie the special promotion a classic film derived from a literary classic deserved. 'It is up to New York from here on,' Reinhardt said to me. For the past year, he said, he had been trying to make a picture that was both an artistic and commercial success; now he was going to simplify matters. 'I will give them just what the doctor ordered,' he said. He had a new job, a new outlook, and a new contract with M-G-M. To celebrate, he bought a new Cadillac convertible. 'Money is good for bribing yourself through the inconveniences of life,' he said. Reinhardt rapidly gained the reputation of being pleasant to work with, patient, quiet, modest, and a good director, and several people on the set eventually paid him one of the highest compliments the industry knows. 'Gottfried is a real person,' they said.

Band tagged after Reinhardt around the lot, and the slightly rebellious manner he had developed right after the disastrous first preview of *The Red Badge of Courage* faded completely away. Now, when he was asked to look after Mocha, he was extremely solicitous of Mocha's ailments, and he listened with a respectful manner whenever Reinhardt was talking.

After a week of shooting, Reinhardt had a visitor on the set – his friend Joe Cohn, M-G-M vice-president and head of the Production Office. Cohn is a cheerful, white-haired man with white rings around the pupils of his eyes, which gives him a bird-like look. He had told Mayer that the studio shouldn't make The Red Badge of Courage. 'How you doing, Gottfried?' he asked. 'How's the picture? On schedule?'

'We'll bring this one in early,' Reinhardt said.

Cohn said he had heard that The Red Badge of Courage would open in New York in a few weeks.

'The Astor?' Reinhardt asked quickly.

'I have news for you,' Cohn said cheerily. 'The Trans-Lux, a little place on Lexington Avenue in the Fifties. Don't worry, Gottfried. It'll get brilliant reviews, and it won't make a nickel.'

Four days before The Red Badge of Courage opened in New York, for its first regular run – at the Fifty-second Street Trans-Lux, a house with a seating capacity of five hundred and seventy-eight, only half that of the Astor – the first advertisement appeared in the New York newspapers: 'M-G-M, the company that released Gone with the Wind, presents a new drama of the War Between the States – Stephen Crane's immortal classic, The Red Badge of Courage.' The ad announced 'A John Huston Production', 'Screenplay by John Huston', 'Adaptation by Albert Band', 'Directed by John Huston' (letters three times as large as those in the other credits), and 'Produced by Gottfried Reinhardt' (letters the same size as Albert Band's).

The day after the opening, I saw Reinhardt at the studio, and he said he had not had time to read the reviews. Two days after the opening he ran into Eddie Mannix at lunch. Mannix told him that the first day's business had been weak.

A week later, Reinhardt showed me the reviews that had been relayed to him from the New York office. The Tribune said:

Stephen Crane's The Red Badge of Courage has been transformed by John Huston into a striking screen close-up of a young man's introduction to battle. With war hero Audie Murphy as a raw recruit in Union blue, this seventy-minute vignette is a study of one man's emotional adjustment to an environment chokingly filled with powder smoke and animal terror. The dialogue is sparing but acute, and the camera work is a procession of visual effects detailing most vividly the progress of a Civil War battle. Except for a redundant narration that clutters up the sound track from time to time explaining facts already clear in the images, there are no concessions made to movie conventions in this film.

The Times critic wrote, 'Now, thanks to Metro and John Huston, The Red Badge of Courage has been transferred to the screen with almost literal fidelity.' He felt, however, that the picture could not convey the reactions of Crane's hero to war, for Crane had conveyed them 'in almost stream-of-consciousness descriptions, which is a technique that works best with words'. He continued:

This is a technical problem Mr Huston has not been able to lick, even with his sensitive direction, in view of his sticking to the book. Audie Murphy, who plays the Young Soldier, does as well as anyone could expect as a virtual photographer's model upon whom the camera is mostly turned.

The Mirror's reviewer called the picture 'a brilliant emotional drama, a memorable war saga', added that 'the carnage between the states forms a grim backdrop for the personal story of a young raw recruit', and wound up by saying that the picture 'comes aptly as the industry celebrates its silver jubilee. It's a wonderful example of modern film art.' The Daily News critic gave the picture a three-star rating. The Morning Telegraph called it 'fine' and 'thought-provoking', and said it 'has been brought to the screen by the brilliant John Huston as an offbeat motion picture, not to be compared or contrasted with anything else you've seen lately, a strange and strangely exciting work that stands unique in the recent history of the movies'. The reviewer went on to say that the picture 'may not fit very neatly into the idea that motion pictures represent entertainment for the whole family, but it comes very close to a true work of art for all that'.

The World-Telegram & Sun reviewer said, 'John Huston has written and directed a stirring film in an understanding and close reproduction of the novel'.

'If someone other than John Huston had made Stephen Crane's The Red Badge of Courage, there would have been little cause for disappointment,' the Post critic began, and then praised Huston, saying that he 'studies his men in intimate close-ups, he lays out his battles in long vistas with climaxes mounting as attackers climb the screen like the Teutonic knights coming across the ice of Lake Peipus in Eisenstein's *Alexander Nevsky*'. He continued:

The picture does not become a fully realized experience, nor is it deeply moving. It is as if, somewhere between shooting and final version, the light of inspiration had died. Huston got tired of it, or became discouraged, or decided that it wasn't going to come off. Perhaps the story itself stood revealed, too late, as a thin and old one, and there wasn't enough time to go back and do it over. So they cut losses and cut footage, thereby reducing a large failure to the proportions of a modest, almost ordinary picture. . . . Mr Huston's product is that of a splendid director who had lost interest, who was no longer striving for that final touch of perfection, who had missed the cumulative passion and commentary on human beings that mark his best pictures.

Time said that Huston had avoided 'the customary Hollywood clichés of battle' and that 'both the camera and the spoken commentary (taken word for word from Crane's novel) are filled with human understanding as they follow Murphy's wanderings through the rear areas'. *Newsweek* said that '*The Red Badge of Courage* bids fair to become one of the classic American motion pictures', and the *Saturday Review of Literature* remarked that 'If Stephen Crane's *The Red Badge of Courage* is considered a classic of American nineteenth-century literature, John Huston's adaptation of it for the screen may well become a classic of American twentieth-century film-making. Adhering to Crane's characters, his structure, and his theme, Huston has discovered for all time how to make a printed page come alive on the screen.'

Not one of the reviews made any mention at all of Gottfried Reinhardt, Dore Schary, Louis B. Mayer, or Nicholas M. Schenck.

A couple of days later Reinhardt received a cable from Huston: 'REVIEWS RECEIVED. THINK EXCELLENT ON WHOLE ONLY THEY DON'T KNOW HOW MUCH OF WHAT IS GOOD IN FILM YOU ARE RESPONSIBLE FOR. BUT I DO. JOHN.'

By the time *The Red Badge of Courage* was in its second week at the Trans-Lux, I was back in New York. I dropped in at the theatre late one afternoon and found the manager standing in front of the box

office gossiping with the cashier. The marquee said, 'JOHN HUS-
TON'S THE RED BADGE OF COURAGE. A MAJOR ACHIEVEMENT
– N.Y. TIMES. MASTERFUL – CUE.' I asked the manager how
business was. 'Not socko,' he said.

Schary came to New York the next week, and I went over to the
Sherry-Netherland to see him. Walter Reilly, Schary's executive
assistant, invited me in to the sitting room of Schary's suite. 'The
boss'll be right with you,' he said. 'We just got back from Washington. He saw the President.'

Schary, when he appeared, looked full of health and energy. 'Just
got back from Washington,' he said, giving me a cordial handshake.
'Saw the President. Had a fifteen-minute appointment. He stretched
it to twenty-five. Nice guy, the President. Boy, I'll be glad to get on
a train and get the hell out of New York. I never liked living in the
East anyway. The pressures! I'm running around all the time.
How's my schedule, kiddy?' he asked Reilly.

Elizabeth Taylor would be up to see him in twenty minutes,
Reilly said, and the next day there would be Winthrop Rockefeller,
who wanted to talk about making a short subject.

'You ever met a Rockefeller?' Schary asked me.

I said no.

'Hah! Some people lead such a sheltered life,' said Schary. 'My,
but I keep busy! Reviewing the studio policies with the New York
boys can exhaust a fella. Today I had an all-day session with Nick
Schenck. At the end of an all-day session, he looks as though he
just got out of a shower, and you're punchy. The way his mind
works! He asks for a complete picture of a situation and asks what
you think, and you tell him, and then he makes his decision, and
that's it.' Schary said he had also been working with Howard Dietz on
the advertising campaign for Quo Vadis. It was going to open simul-
taneously at the Astor and the Capitol in a week. 'If you make a
picture with enough vitality, you do very well with it,' he said.

The Red Badge of Courage had vitality now, he said, but it was too
early to tell how it would do. 'Great notices,' he said. 'That picture
is a credit to the studio. By the way, Reinhardt is gonna be a hell
of a director. I saw his picture Invitation. It's a good little picture.

Reinhardt is a great raconteur. Like John, he knows how to tell a story. He is gonna be a very stylish director, a very terrific director.'

Schary said he had been having a hell of a lot of fun working with Schenck. 'I'm very crazy about that man,' he said. 'You know exactly where you stand with him. A very reasonable man. He thinks fast. He's agile. He doesn't waste a lot of time going around through Dixie. He's the most respected man in the whole picture business. He's smart and he's shrewd. He has tact and he has wisdom. He's got wonderful balance. There's not a thing going on at the studio he doesn't know about. He knows how to manage the business.'

There was a buzz. Reilly admitted Elizabeth Taylor and her agent, Jules Goldstone.

Schary asked Miss Taylor if she wanted a drink. She asked for a gin-and-tonic.

'Take sherry,' said Goldstone.

'Gin-and-tonic,' said Miss Taylor.

'Give the girl anything she wants!' Schary said exuberantly.

Reinhardt received a letter from John Huston:

Dear Gottfried:

A fine thing! What gets me is the sneaky, underhand way you went about it. I can see now that you had it all planned out way back there: 'When Huston's deep in the African forest, stricken with malaria, his consciousness dimmed by bites of the tsetse and his limbs swollen with elephantiasis — then I shall become a director.' No doubt your hands tremble as you are holding this letter. I, Huston, have returned. I am among the living, and I know well how to deal with your treachery. I shall strike without warning. Silvia may find you sprawled on your wide veranda, transfixed by one of those same arrows from a pygmy's blow-gun. Or it may happen in your office, late of an evening, when you and Albert are working over your next script. The cleaning women will discover the two of you at your desk, inclined a little forward, grinning at each other as though in delight at having finished a perfectly splendid scene. I take it for granted that Albert will be sitting in the big chair behind the desk; he is the producer now, of course. Now that the cat's out of the bag, you might tell me some of the details. As a matter of fact, I heard about it only day before yesterday. I don't know the name of the picture or who's in it or anything, except that your leading lady thinks you're the best director she ever had. I expect I'll be in New York in a week or two. Your letter, if one is forthcoming, may not reach me before I leave. I'll call you in any case.

The Monster

Huston arrived in New York from London just as Reinhardt arrived to work on a screenplay with a writer here. Neither Huston nor Reinhardt went to the Trans-Lux, where The Red Badge of Courage was in its sixth, and last, week. Huston didn't want to see the picture in its final form. He looked tired – even more tired than he had looked nine months before, at the preview of The Red Badge of Courage in Pasadena, where I had last seen him. The creases between his eyes and at the sides of his mouth looked deeper. His tweed cap seemed too small for him, and so did his suit. Its peg top trousers were the latest thing in England, he told me. 'Dore wrote me a letter,' he said, and took the letter from a pocket and handed it to me.

Dear John:

I don't know if you have seen the finished print of RED BADGE OF COURAGE *but we did have to make some cuts and we did have to bring clarification by the use of narration that helped us enormously and brought the audience reaction from a majority negative response to a big majority positive response. I don't think we sacrificed any of the integrity that you poured into the movie and I hope you like it. The final important thing is that the picture has been accepted by critics as the classic that we thought it would be, and maybe over the long pull we'll get most of the money back.*

If I had to do it all over again I would still let you make it. I hope things are well with you.

My fondest always,

Dore

'I lied to Dore,' he told me, in a mildly conspiratorial tone. 'I called Dore up and said I had seen the picture. I told him I approved of everything he had done.'

Huston planned to spend ten days in New York promoting The African Queen and making various arrangements for his next picture, Moulin Rouge, based on a recent novel, of the same name, about Toulouse-Lautrec. This would be another independent picture.

Schary had agreed to release him from his contractual obligation to make another picture for M-G-M right away, so he was able to go ahead with plans for Moulin Rouge. Huston had a lot to say about The African Queen, and its possibilities of success. He thought it would be a big commercial hit. 'I may yet become the Last Tycoon,' he said. He looked as if he wanted to laugh, but he didn't.

I went with Huston and his wife, who had in the meantime had her second child, to see Reinhardt and his wife, who were staying at the Plaza.

As we got out of the elevator at the Reinhardts' floor, Huston glanced at a small man wearing a derby who was talking to a crumpled old lady in a wheelchair. The small man was talking in a low, hoarse monotone, and at Huston's glance, the man looked over at us sideways, full of mysterious promise. Huston glanced at him again and seemed to lose interest. The small man wearing the derby suddenly lost his promise. There was no Huston scene. Huston led us quickly to the Reinhardts' suite and knocked on the door. Reinhardt opened it.

'Well, Gottfried,' said Huston.

'Hello, John,' Reinhardt said, sounding cordial but ill at ease.

The two men shook hands, then looked uncomfortably at each other. Reinhardt took a white silk handkerchief from his pocket and mopped his brow with it.

'Well!' said Huston to Mrs Reinhardt. 'Well!' The word sounded as small as it was.

Reinhardt put a cigar in his mouth and nervously held a lighter to it.

Mrs Reinhardt and Mrs Huston said hello to each other.

'It's been a long time,' said Reinhardt.

'Yeah,' said Huston.

'Not since the Pasadena preview,' Reinhardt said.

'Yeah,' said Huston.

Mrs Reinhardt gave a shriek of mock laughter.

'Sit down,' Reinhardt said to Huston, and everybody sat down.

'Well, how is everything, Gottfried?' Huston asked.

Reinhardt said that everything was all right. 'Did you see the picture?' he asked.

'No, Gottfried,' said Huston. 'How is the picture, Gottfried?'

'The reviews were wonderful,' Reinhardt began.

'I know, Gottfried,' said Huston. 'I saw the reviews.'

'After you left, we had a lot of trouble –' Reinhardt began.

'I know,' Huston said. 'I got your letter, Gottfried.'

'You read it?' said Reinhardt.

'Of course, Gottfried,' said Huston.

'I fought, but there was nothing I could do,' said Reinhardt. 'You were not here.'

'What are you doing now, Gottfried?' Huston asked. 'You're a director!' He laughed as though it took a great effort to laugh.

Reinhardt said that he had just finished directing a picture and was making plans to start on another.

'That's wonderful, Gottfried,' Huston said.

'What are you doing now?' Reinhardt asked.

Huston said that he was doing some promotion work on *The African Queen* and thought the picture would be a hit. 'I hope it makes a pot of dough,' he said, and added a faint 'Ho! Ho! Ho!'

'You think *The African Queen* will be a commercial success?' Reinhardt asked.

'I hope so, Gottfried,' said Huston. 'You know, there's a strange irony in what happened to *Red Badge*. Even though a lot of people in the business think otherwise, my other pictures did all right at the box office. *The Maltese Falcon* was a very great success. I believed it grossed over four million bucks. Another one was *In This Our Life*. *Across the Pacific* was also very successful, and *Key Largo* was a very great success. *Treasure of Sierra Madre* was a very expensive picture – two million eight, I think it cost – and even though it didn't make an immediate and resounding bang at the box office, it did very well, and by this time it should be showing a profit. *The Asphalt Jungle* made money, and *We Were Strangers*, although it wasn't successful, didn't actually lose money. The only picture I ever made that seems as though it's going to be marked down simply as a box-office failure is *The Red Badge of Courage*. And I thought that was the best picture I ever made.'

There was a heavy silence.

'Hell, let's go to " 21 ",' said Huston.

'Like old times,' Reinhardt said. 'I went to "21" my first evening in America. I adored it. I had dinner at Dinty Moore's. Then I was taken to see Of Thee I sing. Then I went to "21". I adored it. And I adored America.'

'You adored it!' Huston said dimly. 'You adored it, huh, Gottfried?' His tone had a hint of amazement in it.

There was a flicker in Reinhardt's eyes. He took the cigar out of his mouth and shook gently as he laughed.

'Let's go to "21",' Huston said impatiently.

About a month later, after Huston had returned to Europe and Reinhardt to California, Sam Spiegel brought a print of The African Queen from London to New York. United Artists was going to release it. He looked affluent, well-groomed, and at peace. 'I fly to the Coast tonight,' he said. 'Then I fly back to New York. I will be here forty-eight hours, and then I must fly back to London. I must be in a dozen places at once. We are going to have a big hit on our hands. The picture will make a lot of money.'

That week Huston wrote me from the château in Chantilly that he and his family were occupying to say that he was planning to bring a horse over from Ireland and train him on the steeplechase course in Chantilly, and if all went well, he planned to ride the horse himself at some of the race meetings the next year. 'Have you heard that The African Queen is the greatest success England has had in years and years?' Huston wrote. 'Indications are that it will also be very big in America. In England, however, its future is assured. With my percentage, I stand to make a lot of money. . . . I'm going to have it all in twenty-dollar bills with a rubber band around it.'

When The African Queen opened in New York a few weeks later, it was received enthusiastically by both the critics and the public. Among the critics, there were only two dissenters – the reviewer for the Post, who said that the picture had some aspects of a Tarzan movie and that 'Huston has put out two considerably less than perfect pictures in a row', and the reviewer for the Times, who said that the picture had been made to insure popularity, and that 'with this extravagant excursion into realms of adventure and romance of a sort that, to our recollection, Mr Huston has heretofore eschewed, the brilliant director has put himself in a position where he can be charged with compromise'.

A couple of months after that, United Artists announced that *The African Queen* was the biggest hit it had had in five years.

In certain circles, *The Red Badge of Courage* continued to receive tributes of one kind and another. Reinhardt had not succeeded in getting M-G-M to bring out a record album of the score, but the studio did send the original manuscript of the music to Syracuse University, which Stephen Crane attended briefly in 1891. In the Stephen Crane Collection of the University, the score, together with photographs of the cast in costume, is now on file. Lester G. Wells, curator of the university's special collections, saw the movie seven times when it played in Syracuse; then he asked for the original of the score, and M-G-M agreed to lend it to the collection.

The picture was not nominated for any of the Motion Picture Academy awards, but the *Film Daily* included it in its list of the five best-directed pictures of the year. It was named second-best picture of the year by the National Board of Review. (*A Place in the Sun* was first). The Motion Picture Academy nominated Huston for an Oscar for his direction of *The African Queen*, and Bogart was nominated for one for his acting in the picture. Bogart won his Oscar, but the prize for direction went to George Stevens, for *A Place in the Sun*. ('*A Place in the Sun* is only a reasonably good picture,' Stevens said to another director. 'The industry doesn't want good pictures. It wants the norm.') The picture the Academy named the best of the year was Arthur Freed's musical *An American in Paris*. The Irving Thalberg Award, the honour bestowed by the Academy upon the person who is considered to have done most for the movie industry in the past year, was won by Arthur Freed. Darryl Zanuck, who reminded the industry members gathered for the occasion that he had won the Thalberg Award three times, presented it to Freed, describing him as 'a creative producer' and declaring, 'His pictures have been perfect examples of creative art.'

In Paris, Huston was worrying about the business end of pro-ducing *Moulin Rouge*, as well as writing and directing it. 'I am trying to learn all the things Sam Spiegel was born knowing,' he wrote me. 'I find it pretty hard going. As a bona-fide producer, I don't dare admit to being ignorant of what "off the top" means. But I damn well am. I was a couple of days trying to figure out what three and a half per cent of seventy per cent amounted to before giving it up. Now I just try to look wise. I'm afraid it won't be very long before I give that up, too.'

At Metro-Goldwyn-Mayer, it was announced that the studio would be known thenceforward simply as M-G-M, since Goldwyn and Mayer were no longer there. Louis B. Mayer announced that he would produce pictures independently and set about buying film properties; he started off by outbidding Metro for the film rights to the musical *Paint Your Wagon*, for which he paid $225,000. Around that time, Loew's, Inc., paid Mayer $2,750,000 in return for a release from the company's agreement to pay him ten per cent of the net receipts of every picture made between 7 April 1924, and the day he left the company.

Mayer's cream-coloured office at the studio was taken over by Joseph L. Mankiewicz, who had left Twentieth Century-Fox and Darryl Zanuck, because, he said, he was determined to make a drastic change in the conventional pattern most movie makers conformed to. Mankiewicz moved from Fox and Zanuck to M-G-M and Dore Schary, to work on a film as a director and writer.

M-G-M announced that the studio would make forty pictures in the coming year and that eighteen of them would be musicals. Arthur Freed announced that he would produce half a dozen of the musicals himself, including one to be made in France and another in Scotland. Audie Murphy became greatly in demand as a leading man for Western melodramas. John Dierkes was cast as a Western bad man in the movie *Shane*, produced and directed by George Stevens. Royal Dano, whose characterization of the Tattered Man had drawn high praise from everybody who had helped to make *The Red Badge of Courage*, as well as from many others who had seen the early version – in which his death scene was included – did not immediately find any other acting jobs in Hollywood. He returned to his home in New York to do some television work, then appeared in a picture called *Flame of Araby*, then obtained a small part as a Georgia cracker in a Broadway musical called *Three Wishes for Jamie*. When Reinhardt temporarily dropped his activities as a producer and became a full-time director, Albert Band was reassigned from his job as Reinhardt's assistant to a job as assistant to a producer named Armand Deutsch, with whom he set to work on a movie called *The Girl Who Had Everything*. Deutsch was so impressed by Band's abilities that he petitioned Dore Schary for a raise for him, and it was granted.

Reinhardt devoted himself to directing a movie trilogy entitled *The Story of Three Loves*, on which Lee Katz, unit production manager for *The Red Badge of Courage*, was again unit production manager. Reinhardt had finished one part of the trilogy, starring James Mason and Moira Shearer, and he wrote me that Schary and all the other executives at the studio loved it. 'I have to admit it myself; it's really pretty good,' he said. A stray kitten turned up at the Reinhardts' house and was adopted as a playmate for Mocha. It was christened Lee Katz. Mrs Reinhardt was working very hard, too. She was preparing to move. Reinhardt had decided that he might be in Hollywood to stay after all, and this time, instead of renting a house, as he had always done before, he had bought one. The new house had a large garden and a swimming pool, and although he felt a bit more tied down, he told me, it was really terrific, and that was why he had finally, after eighteen years with M-G-M, bought a house.

The total cost of making *The Red Badge of Courage* – Production No. 1512, the fifteen-hundred-and-twelfth picture produced by M-G-M – turned out to be $1,642,117.33. The picture received only slight attention in Nicholas M. Schenck's annual report to the stockholders of Loew's, Inc., for the fiscal year ending 31 August 1951. In this document, the cost of producing and releasing the movie was merely included in the $26,243,848.61 item 'Film Productions Completed – Not Released'. (The report also showed that the net income of Loew's, Inc., for the year was $7,806,571.83, that dividends of $1.50 a share were paid on the 5,142,579 shares of stock outstanding, and that Loew's directors and officers were paid $2,789,079, of which $277,764 was paid to Schenck and

$300,000 to Mayer.) At the annual stockholders' meeting, however, the movie was mentioned by several of the stockholders, as well as by the chairman of the meeting, J. Robert Rubin, a tall, gaunt man with pince-nez and a quiet, gracious manner, who is a vice-president of Loew's and counsel for the firm. (Mr Rubin's compensation for 1951, according to the report, was $224, 439.) The meeting began at ten o'clock on the morning of 29 April 1952, in a projection room on the eighteenth floor of the Loew's State Theatre Building, at 1540 Broadway, at Forty-fifth Street. It was attended by a hundred and fifty stockholders (out of a total of 37,991), who represented three hundred thousand shares of stock. (Four million shares of stock were represented by the management, as holders of proxies for that number.) The first mention of *The Red Badge of Courage* was made by the chairman, during one of his attempts to entertain the stockholders while ballots for the election of a board of directors were being passed out. He took a slip of paper out of his pocket, and, reading from it, informed the stockholders that Esther Williams, who is under contract to M-G-M, had recently been voted one of the year's most popular stars by the magazine *Modern Screen*. Then he took out another slip of paper and read, in a drone, 'Ladies and gentlemen, I'd like to call your attention to the fact that M-G-M pictures have received great honours. Each month, *Coronet* magazine chooses three favourite pictures, to recommend, and during the past twelve months we have had ten of our pictures chosen for recommendation by *Coronet* magazine. I'm sure you'll agree that that is a pretty fine record.' Rubin raised his eyes and, removing his pince-nez, gazed at the stockholders. Their attention seemed to be fixed on their ballots. He cleared his throat, put his pince-nez back on, and read off the names of the ten pictures. *The Red Badge of Courage* was one of them.

A stockholder named Greenstock stood up and asked whether *The Red Badge of Courage* had made money.

'No, *The Red Badge of Courage* did not make any money,' Rubin said.

'Why didn't *The Red Badge of Courage* make any money?' Greenstock asked.

'Well, it was a beautiful picture, but that wasn't enough,' Rubin said. 'It didn't come to a climax, the way a picture is supposed to do.

The picture didn't appeal to the public. Mr Schary was very keen about the picture. It played here in a special house and everything, and the *Times* put it is as one of the best pictures of the year. But the public didn't go for it.' Rubin removed his pince-nez.

'I want to say something,' a stockholder named Mrs Wentig remarked. 'In reference to *The Red Badge of Courage*. I want to say of course, we're interested in dividends, in profits, but it's a tribute to the company that they had the courage to put out a picture that did not make money.'

Rubin gave her a gracious nod. 'It was good for our prestige,' he said.

'It set good standards for the movie industry,' Mrs Wentig said, raising her voice. 'I say do more of it, and I'm glad you made the picture even if it didn't make money. Make more movies like that!'

'Well, thank you,' said Rubin, looking dismayed.

At the conclusion of the meeting, the stockholders were shown *Singin' in the Rain*, a new Arthur Freed musical, and then they descended to the restaurant, in the basement, for the company's annual free lunch. Rubin moved among the stockholders, giving each one a kindly nod. He escorted an elderly, grey-haired lady to a chair and brought her a tongue sandwich. 'It's very good,' he said. 'I could eat one myself. Did you like the meeting?'

'Where is Mr Schenck?' the lady asked. 'Why doesn't he come to the meeting?'

'He leaves this sort of thing to us,' Rubin said. 'You don't want him to neglect important and pressing business matters, do you?'

'Not if he's fixing to increase our dividends,' said the lady.

At a nearby table, Charles C. Moskowitz, vice-president and treasurer of Loew's, Inc. (his compensation was $188,176 for the year), was talking with Eugene W. Leake, chairman of the Retirement Plan Committee of Loew's. Moskowitz is a bald, chunky man with a grey moustache, who wears glasses with heavy tortoise-shell rims, and usually has a white carnation in his lapel. He handed Leake a cigar. 'Smoke a good one, Judge,' he said.

Leake, a white-haired man with a small head and a pink face, put down a half-smoked cigar and lit the good one.

'The meeting went all right, Judge,' said Moskowitz. 'The only thing they're worried about is *The Red Badge of Courage*. They've got worries.'

'Heh-heh-heh,' said Leake.

'Moskowitz!' a stockholder called 'When are we going to hear about the profits from our foreign interests?'

'Forget it, Judge,' Moskowitz said, waving his cigar at the stockholder.

Leake laughed.

'My gosh, I just realized!' Moskowitz said to Leake. 'I haven't seen a picture since yesterday. Can you imagine that, Judge?'

'It's not easy to imagine,' said Leake.

'I try to see every picture that's made. If not at the office, then at home,' Moskowitz said. 'I know every picture that's being made at the studio in Culver City at this very minute. Isn't that right, Judge?'

'That's right,' said Leake.

'I can tell you who is directing every one of our pictures at this very minute, who is producing, and the names of the leading characters,' Moskowitz said. 'Mr Schenck can do the same, only more so. I had Eddie Mannix on the phone last night for an hour. Today, I'll talk to Dore Schary. I know the business inside out. I've worked for Loew's forty years. I started as a bookkeeper. I thought the work was going to be steady, Judge.' He beamed at Leake.

Leake laughed again.

'I worked for Nick Schenck when he was spending days and nights going from theatre to theatre doing everything himself, even being the cashier in the box office – in the days when our theatres had vaudeville,' Moskowitz went on. 'There's not a man in the business who's more respected for his capabilities than Mr Schenck. Put him in a room where *anything* is being talked about and he'll learn it. There's no branch of this business he doesn't know.'

'He keeps tabs on every little thing,' Leake said. 'The minute a picture is released, there he is on the telephone, the reviews in his hand.'

'Brilliant!' said Moskowitz. 'The minute he sees a picture, he knows whether it will go. Brilliant!'

Almost two years before, I had become interested in *The Red Badge of Courage*, and I had been following its progress step by step ever since, to learn what I could about the American motion-picture industry. Now, three thousand miles from Hollywood, in an office building at Forty-fifth and Broadway, I began to feel that I was getting closer than I ever had before to the heart of the matter. Reinhardt's and Huston's struggle to make a great picture, Mayer's opposition, Schary's support, the sideline operations of a dozen vice-presidents, the labour and craftsmanship of the cast and technical crew, the efforts of Huston's aides to help him get his concept of the Stephen Crane novel on film, the long series of artistic problems and compromises, the reactions of the preview audiences – all these seemed to compose themselves into some sort of design, but a few pieces were still missing. I felt that somewhere in the office upstairs I might find them.

The accounting and executive officers of Loew's are on the seventh floor. Moskowitz had two ways he used for getting to his private office – a carpeted corridor leading directly to it, and a roundabout route through a vast, pillared room. After lunch, Moskowitz took Leake and me through the big room. It contained a hundred and twenty-five desks, many of them occupied by clerks or accountants operating machines to tabulate admissions at Loew's theatres and returns on Loew's pictures. To make himself heard, Moskowitz had to raise his voice.

'Looks like we're still in business. Right, Judge?' he said to Leake.

'Heh-heh-heh,' said Leake. 'Looks that way, all right.'

Moskowitz waved his cigar in greeting to the backs of the clerks and accountants, and walked on.

The walls of Moskowitz's outer office covered with photographs of M-G-M stars, all of them autographed. ('To Charles Moskowitz, from a very devoted member of the M-G-M family. My best wishes – Robert Taylor.' 'To Charles Moskowitz – I sincerely hope I shall be able to repay in the future the faith you have in me today. Gratefully, Mario Lanza.') There were photographs of Lionel Barrymore, Walter Pidgeon, Van Johnson, Gene Kelly, Esther Williams and Lassie (this one autographed with a paw print). There was also a photograph of Dore Schary ('For Charlie, with my fond good wishes, Dore').

Moskowitz looked at the pictures proudly and told Leake that he'd be seeing all the stars in a few weeks, at the studio. 'Mr Schenck is going out to see things at first hand,' he said. 'And where Mr Schenck goes, Moskowitz goes close behind.'

Four floors below, I found Howard Dietz, advertising and exploitation head of Loew's, who told me there was no point in throwing good money after bad to promote a picture that was clearly a bust. 'Schenck thinks the picture is doomed to be a box-office failure,' he said. 'As a commerial property, it's no good. The country isn't interested in the picture. It turned it down. I didn't like the picture. Schenck wasn't enthusiastic. But that isn't the point. Anything that makes money we're for.' He smiled wearily, looking as bored as he had looked when he sat in the bar of the Beverly Hills Hotel, a year and a half before, listening to Reinhardt's plea for a good promotion campaign for The Red Badge of Courage. 'The phony talk I've had to listen to about this picture!' he said. '"It's a classic." "Art." Nonsense. A novel is a novel. A poem is a poem. And a movie is a movie. Take the Wordsworth poem "I wandered, lonely as a cloud" and make a movie about it. What can you show visually? "I wandered lonely as a cloud That floats on high o'er vales and hills When all at once I saw a crowd, A host of golden daffodils." We might have a cloud, some vales and hills, and then a batch of daffodils.' He laughed. 'You can't do it. What stops you is the equity that goes with the classic. It's borrowed imagination. You know, I'm not of the school that believes that popular entertainment need be art. And neither is Schenck. He's a showman. That's our business.'

A few doors down, I found Si Seadler, Loew's Eastern advertising manager, in his office working on plans to escort a hundred motion-picture theatre exhibitors from all over the country on a three-day visit to the studio to see all the M-G-M movies awaiting release. (A few days later, the trade papers carried a reprint of a message from Dore Schary to the exhibitors. 'We believe that the sunshine of showmanship can dispel grey clouds of pessimism,' he wrote, in the course of offering a hearty hello on behalf of Mr Nicholas Schenck, the executive staff, and the five thousand employees of M-G-M.) Seadler's telephone kept ringing, and his look of worried amiability increased as he alternated between the phone and giving instructions to a young man whose face reflected Seadler's worry but not his amiability.

'I've got a mob of people all asking whether *Seeing Is Believing* is the official name of the junket and how much it's all gonna cost,' the young man said.

'*Seeing Is Believing* is official, but check with Howard Dietz – it's Howard's idea,' Seadler said. 'The cost is a hundred thousand dollars. Be sure to tell everybody we think it's worth it. It's Howard's idea.'

The telephone rang. 'The minute you called me, I took care of it,' he said. 'You're as big as Charlie. Bigger. Don't worry.' He hung up. 'From the Coast,' he told me, with distaste. 'Everybody fighting with everybody. Human beings in conflict. That's the way it is with creative people. Thank God this is a business office. Any problem or conflict comes up here, Mr Schenck says, "My boy – " and gives us the word.' Seadler waved his hand. 'No more conflict.'

'I like the way he calls everybody "My boy",' said the young man.

'A great executive,' said Seadler.

'Will Mr Schenck get out to the studio in time to play host to the exhibitors?' the young man asked.

Seadler shook his head. 'Dore Schary will do it,' he said. 'Mr Schenck is the president. Dore works for him.'

Seadler told me he had given Schenck his opinion of *The Red Badge of Courage* before it was released, as he had promised Reinhardt he would a year and a half before, when he saw some scenes from the then unfinished film. 'Mr Schenck saw the picture, and he knew right away it wouldn't go over with the public, and I agreed with him,' he said. 'It doesn't pay to be so faithful to a *book*, the way John Huston did it. As a great novel, *The Red Badge of Courage* is a great novel. As a movie, it's too fragmentary. There's no story. The country wasn't interested in the picture, as Howard says. A novel is a novel as Howard says, and a movie is a movie. The picture was beautiful, but it's just a vignette. As soon as Mr Schenck saw the picture, we knew it was a flop. Let's just say it was a flop *d'estime*. I guess that's the way Mr Schenck would put it.'

On the tenth floor, Arthur M. Loew, president of Loew's International Corporation, which is a subsidiary of Loew's, Inc., chatted with me about what he called the pattern of economics of the industry. His office had recently been redecorated, along with all the other offices on the floor, in a style that included streamlined potted plants, African sculpture, desks that were jagged boards attached to walls, and an air-conditioning system that distributed a chemical to prevent people from catching cold. Loew, the son of Marcus Loew, one of the founders of the company, is a wiry, restless man in his early fifties; in addition to supervising the international distribution of pictures owned by Loew's, Inc., he has supervised the production of one movie, The Search, and personally produced another, Teresa, both of which made out very well with movie critics and movie audiences. He started in foreign distribution in 1920, and he is in charge of a hundred and thirty sales offices, in thirty-eight countries. Every day, he checks on the receipts of forty theatres owned and operated by Loew's outside the United States and Canada. (A Supreme Court decision twenty-three months earlier had upheld a lower court's order for the divorcement of motion-picture production from motion-picture exhibition, and Loew's, like other picture corporations, was now working out the separation.) As Loew talked, he played with a button that controlled a sliding cork wall at one end of his office.

'We have a pretty definite knowledge in this office of what the public wants, and we know one thing – pictures that are liked in this country are liked abroad,' Loew said. 'We operate in a pattern of economics brought on by public taste.' He pushed the button, and the cork wall slowly receded. 'The mechanism operating that wall costs only three hundred and seventy-five dollars,' Loew said as the adjoining room came into view. It had a modernistic conference table rimmed by modernistic chairs. 'That's where we confer about foreign sales,' he said.

Internationally, he added, The Red Badge of Courage had not done well at the box office, and, here and there, Loew's was trying to book it as the lower half of a double bill that featured a musical starring Esther Williams, M-G-M's biggest money-making star. At the moment, *The Red Badge of Courage* was playing as the lower half of such a bill in nine theatres in Australia. 'It's a problem picture,' Loew said. 'It gets poor public response. Nothing glamorous always hurts a picture. In England, we put the picture in a theatre in London where it played only on Sunday afternoons. The critics saw it and liked it, so we've put it in a small house for the regular run. But it's not making any money. No point in wasting promotion on a picture that won't go.' Loew pushed the button, and the cork wall slid back into place.

'Nick Schenck was afraid of *The Red Badge of Courage*,' Loew went on. 'In the beginning, when Dore joined the company – I was glad to see him get the job – Schenck gave him free rein. He even let Dore make a few pictures Schenck really didn't want to make. But now Schenck is pulling back on the reins.'

On the sixth floor of the Loew Building, J. Robert Rubin, sitting at his desk, was looking over the papers neatly stacked on it. It was a long, dark desk in a long, businesslike room that had on the walls autographed photographs of half a dozen prominent Republicans, dead and alive. 'I didn't imagine there would be any controversy about a movie at the meeting,' he said to me softly. 'All they usually want to know about is dividends. Well, this is the one day of the year when we like to make the stockholders feel the company is theirs. It's better to have them friendly than unfriendly. My, hasn't *The Red Badge of Courage* created a fuss, though! Mr Mayer was against making it to begin with, but Mr Schary was very keen about it. Funny thing is Mr Schary still likes the picture, even if it didn't make any money.' He gave a thin laugh. 'Can't have much of that sort of thing,' he said. 'We're not in business for our health. We're a business. Just think of our board of directors! There's not only Mr Schenck, Mr Moskowitz, Mr Leake, and myself but Mr George A. Brownell, Mr F. Joseph Holleran, Mr William A. Parker, Mr William F. Rodgers, Mr Joseph R. Vogel, and Mr Henry Rogers Winthrop. We have to make money or we go out of business.'

Rubin, who is a native of Syracuse, and a graduate of the Syracuse University law school, had been in the motion-picture business since 1915. He helped a friend organize a picture company called New York Alco, and when the company failed, after a year, a new company, called Metro Pictures Corporation, was founded in its place, with Louis B. Mayer as one of the owners. Loew's bought out Metro in 1920. In 1918, Rubin and Mayer had founded the Louis B. Mayer Pictures Corporation and made movies for Metro. Irving Thalberg joined them about two years later. Rubin handled many of the legal entanglements involved in the transactions, including the purchase by Metro, in 1924, of the Goldwyn studio, in Culver City, and, that same year, the purchase of the Louis B. Mayer Pictures Corporation by Metro-Goldwyn.

'Mr Mayer, Mr Thalberg, and I made quite a trio,' Rubin said. 'Thalberg was a genius. He had a conception of pictures no one has been able to duplicate. Mr Mayer built up the studio to what we have today. He knew how to build an organization, and how to run it. It was always exciting to work with him. He was dynamic. He would dramatize everything. I used to say, "Louie, you're the best actor on the lot." He'd say, "I only show what I feel." Mr Mayer always liked good pictures. Clean pictures. I don't care too much what kind of pictures we make. When a picture is liked in this office it is liked everywhere. What Mr Schenck is in favour of, we are for. All of us here like the kind of pictures that do well at the box office.'

A dictograph in Rubin's half-open desk drawer clicked.

'You trying to get me?' Rubin said into the machine.

'Come into my office. I want to show you some reviews,' the voice from the drawer said.

'Right away,' said Rubin. 'I'm with Mr Schenck,' he said to his secretary.

As I arrived in Nicholas M. Schenck's office, a little later, he was talking with Howard Dietz about the reviews of the new M-G-M Technicolor movie *Scaramouche*, which had just opened at the Music Hall. 'I would have bet a hundred to one that *Scaramouche* would get the finest notices,' Schenck said. 'I can't understand it. It opens at the

Music Hall, and Mr Tribune knocks it. Three stars in the *News*. I would have given odds it would get four stars.'

'There are no rules in this business,' Dietz said flatly.

'I still think that *Scaramouche* is a very good picture, my boy,' Schenck said seriously, and he raised his right index finger at Dietz in a gesture of kindly warning. 'And I think the audiences will think so, too.'

Schenck spoke decisively, confidently, and with a strong air of knowledgeability about his business. He is a compactly built, energetic man in his late sixties, with greying hair brushed back and parted on the left. He has a quietly direct manner and benevolent air. The day I saw him, he was deeply tanned, and he was wearing a double-breasted grey suit, a white shirt with blue stripes, a small-figured dark-blue necktie, and tortoise-shell glasses. He sat behind a large, highly polished mahogany desk, on which stood framed photographs of his three daughters as children, all with long curls; a carafe and two glasses; an ashtray; a brown leather folder; and four yellow pencils with sharp points. At his feet was a brass spittoon. His office was small and modest. It had a green carpet; a fireplace, on the mantel of which stood a black iron statuette of the M-G-M lion; a couch covered with brown fabric; four worn chairs; and Italian walnut panelling. The panels had been bought from the mansion of Senator William A. Clark, on Fifth Avenue. Schenck had gone to work for Loew's in 1907 and had been in the same office for thirty years. When he shifted from executive vice-president to president of Loew's, after the death of Marcus Loew, in 1927, he refused to leave the office.

Schenck lit a cigarette and cocked his head slightly at Dietz, who took a cigarette, too. 'I like *Scaramouche*,' Schenck said. 'I like entertainment. Clean, wholesome entertainment. Romance and love. I love dramatic, romantic stories. But I can't go only by my own taste. I don't like slapstick. Audiences like slapstick. What are you going to do? The audience is the final judge.'

'I wish I knew who first said that popular entertainment had to be art,' Dietz said blandly.

Schenck shrugged. He had been working hard, he said, studying the budgets of various pictures, considering their casting problems, and seeing, on an average, four films during the week and three over the weekend at his home in Sands Point. 'You have to see other people's pictures as well as your own,' he said. 'Any picture that becomes good or important, I see it. You have to know about everybody's taste. Everybody must work and we all have a job to do.'

'It's no secret around here that you work hard,' Dietz said.

Schenck smiled broadly and, unbuttoning his coat, patted his ribs. 'I weigh a hundred and forty-one in the morning, a hundred and forty-three at night,' he said.

'I don't know whether it's your work or your golf that does it,' Dietz said.

Schenck's smile broadened, and he buttoned his coat. 'You're right, my boy, there are no rules,' he said, raising his right hand again. 'It all comes from the brain. You can't get into the other fellow's brain. You decide what picture will be made. You decide who will be in the cast. You decide what it will cost. The budget means a lot to me. Unfortunately, stories don't grow on trees, so you have to compromise on what you are going to make. You can't take too many chances where you are paying terrific overhead and terrific weekly salaries.'

'There are no rules for choosing what you're going to make,' Dietz said. 'You know what to choose only by growing up in the fabric of the business.'

Schenck said that he did not read the scripts of all the movies M-G-M was planning to make, but he did read an outline of each script or idea for a script. When he read the outline for *The Red Badge of Courage*, he said, he felt that the studio was taking a big chance. At the time, Schary was in New York, and was not feeling well. 'I went right over to Dore's hotel to talk to him,' he said. 'Dore had been having differences with Louie about the picture. They had not been getting on too well before that, even. I found Dore sick, and sicker over the trouble with Louie. Right from the hotel, I called Louie, and had him talk to Dore. I arranged for Dore and Louie to talk it over when Dore got back home. But Louie remained opposed to making the picture, and on other things he wasn't seeing eye to eye with me. Eventually, I had to support Dore.'

Schenck lit another cigarette. 'Dore is young,' he said. 'He has not had his job very long. I felt I must encourage him, or else he would feel stifled. It would have been so easy for me to say no to him. Instead, I said yes. I figured I would write it off to experience. You can buy almost anything, but you can't buy experience.' He smiled in a wise, fatherly manner.

'The Red Badge of Courage was not a whole motion picture,' Dietz said. 'It was a fragment. It wasn't a good picture.'

'Before I saw it, I had heard it was very bad,' Schenck said. 'But it was better than I had been led to expect. I would call it a fairly good picture. Only, it was above the heads of our audiences. For me, it was good entertainment. But not for our audiences. I felt immediately we would have to take a loss on it, and we have. When I saw the picture was not doing any business, we stopped spending money on promoting it.'

'Yes, I decided that,' Dietz said to Schenck. 'You know, I don't always have to go to you about what money I'm going to spend. We tried a concentrated campaign on the picture in a couple of spots and it didn't go.'

'The public didn't take to the picture,' Schenck said. 'The next picture John Huston made – and this time he was making it for his own company – he made a commercial picture, a tremendous hit.'

'Don't forget he made the picture with stars,' said Dietz.

'The best performances I have ever seen them give,' said Schenck.

'Red Badge had no stars and no story,' said Dietz. 'It wasn't any good.'

'They did the best they could with it,' said Schenck. 'Unfortunately, that sort of thing costs money. If you don't spend money, you never learn.' He laughed knowingly. 'After the picture was made Louie didn't want to release it,' he said. 'Louie said that as long as he was head of the studio, the picture would never be released. He refused to release it, but I changed that.'

Schenck puffed quickly on his cigarette. 'How else was I going to teach Dore?' he said. 'I supported Dore. I let him make the picture. I knew that the best way to help him was to let him make a mistake. Now he will know better. A young man has to learn by making mistakes. I don't think he'll want to make a picture like that again.' Schenck picked up one of his yellow pencils and jotted something down on a memo pad. Then he buzzed for his secretary and asked her to get Mr Schary on the telephone at Culver City. After a couple of minutes, he picked up the phone and said, 'Hello, my boy. How are you doing?'